Visual Reference

Microsoft®
Word 97
At a Glance

Jerry Joyce and
Marianne Moon

Microsoft Word 97 At A Glance

Published by **Microsoft Press**
A Division of Microsoft Corporation
One Microsoft Way
Redmond, Washington 98052-6399

Library of Congress Cataloging-in-Publication Data
Joyce, Jerry, 1950–

    Microsoft Word 97 at a glance / Jerry Joyce and Marianne Moon.
      p.   cm.
    Includes index.
    ISBN 1-57231-366-8
    1. Microsoft Word for Windows. 2. Word processing. I. Moon, Marianne. II. Title.
    Z52.5.M523J69   1997
    652.5'5369—dc20   96-36631
                                       CIP

Printed and bound in the United States of America.

    7 8 9 QEQE 10 9 8

Distributed to the book trade in Canada by Macmillan of Canada, a division of Canada Publishing Corporation.

A CIP catalogue record for this book is available from the British Library.

Microsoft Press books are available through booksellers and distributors worldwide. For further information about international editions, contact your local Microsoft Corporation office. Or contact Microsoft Press International directly at fax (206) 936-7329.

Acquisitions Editor: Lucinda Rowley
Project Editor: Marianne Moon
Technical Editor: Michael T. Bunney
Manuscript Editor: Marianne Moon

Contents

Acknowledgments x

1 **About This Book** **1**

No Computerese! 1

A Quick Overview. 2

A Final Word (or Two). 3

2 **Jump Right In** **5**

Microsoft Word at a Glance 6

Creating a Document 8

Working with an Existing Document 10

Editing Text 12

Storing and Reusing Text. 14

So Many Ways to Do It 16

Proofreading a Document 18

Printing a Document 20

3 **Improving the Look of Your Document** **21**

Using Toolbars 22

Word's Most Useful Toolbars 24

Managing Toolbars 26

Adding Character Emphasis 28

Changing Fonts 30

Changing Paragraph Alignment 31

Customizing Paragraphs 32

Indenting Paragraphs 34

Changing the Spacing Between Lines. 36

Creating Tab Stops 37

Copying Paragraph Formats 38

Using Standard Paragraph Formats 39

Creating Lists 40

Converting Paragraphs into a List. 41

Adding Borders to a Paragraph 42

Setting Up the Page. 44

Formatting Unformatted Documents 45

Word's Behind-the-Scenes Magic. 46

Start Word when Windows starts.

See page 8

Bold

Emphasize your words
See page 28

"What do those squiggles mean?"

Ther are alternitives.
There are alternatives.

See page 46

4 **Creating Specialized Documents** **47**

Creating a Letter. 48

Creating a Memo 50

Creating a Fax Cover Sheet. 52

 So Many Ways to View It 54

Creating a Document from Any Template. 56

Creating Your Own Template 58

Customizing a Template 60

Creating a Template from a Document 62

Creating a Sequence of Styles 64

Changing the Design 65

Copying Between Templates 66

Designing for Your Letterhead 67

Creating Your Own Letterhead 68

Creating Mailing Labels 69

Addressing an Envelope 70

Creating Styles from Scratch. 72

5 **Creating a Complex Document** **75**

Putting Information in a Table 76

Anatomy of a Table. 78

Customizing a Table Layout 79

Changing the Size of Columns and Rows 80

Changing the Look of a Table. 82

Changing the Look of Text in a Table 84

Changing the Location of a Table 86

Creating a Large Table 87

Modifying a Large Table 88

Adding Clip Art 90

Adding a Picture 91

Modifying a Picture 92

Alien Objects 94

Inserting Frequently Used Information 96

"Can I make my own templates?"

See page 58

Design for your letterhead
See page 67

Creating Your Own Commands 98
Adding Commands to Your Menus 100
Customizing the Toolbars 102

6 **Creating a Long Document** **105**

Organizing with Styles 106
Keeping Track of Your Styles 108
Controlling Page Breaks 109
Quickly Applying Standardized Formatting. 110
Storing Toolbars 112
Preparing for a Bound Document 113
Creating a Double-Sided Document 114
Creating a Running Head 115
Creating Variable Running Heads 116
Inserting a Word Document 118
Inserting Part of a Word Document 119
Finding Items in a Document 120
Finding Topics in a Long Document 121
Reorganizing a Long Document 122
Finding Text 124
Replacing Text. 126
Replacing a Style. 127
Replacing Text and Formatting 128
Adding Page Numbers. 129
Using Different Layouts in a Document 130
Creating Chapters or Sections. 132
Creating a Table of Contents. 133
Tracking Versions 134
Creating a Summary. 136
Organizing a Multiple-Authors Document 138
Using Multiple Documents as a Single Document. 140

*"What are
styles and how
do I use them?"*

See page 106

Find items in documents
See pages 120–121

Introduction————————1
Methods————————3
    Approved Procedures ----------------3
    Improvised Procedures----------------5
Results————————8
Discussion ————————11

Create a table of contents
See page 133

"How do I insert accented characters?"

See page 144

Figure 1: Transportation issues

Create a caption
See page 153

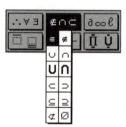

Create an equation
See page 164

7 **Creating a Technical Document** **143**

Inserting Symbols and Special Characters. 144
Inserting Symbols Automatically. 146
Entering Symbols with Keys 147
Creating Footnotes 148
Changing the Look of Footnotes. 149
Editing Footnotes 150
Creating Endnotes. 151
Creating a Table of Figures 152
Creating Captions. 153
Creating Cross-References 154
Numbering Headings 155
Numbering Lines 156
Creating a Numbered Outline. 158
Creating a Chart 159
Summing Table Rows and Columns 160
Calculating a Value 162
Calculating Values Outside a Table 163
Creating an Equation 164
Crunching Data 165
Copying Data from Excel 166
Connecting to Excel Data 167
Adding an Excel Chart 168
Connecting to an Excel Chart. 170
Creating an Organization Chart 171
Opening Files of Different Types. 172
Saving Files in Different Formats 173
Creating an Index 174

Create a form letter
See page 176

Sort the records
See page 196

Highlight text in color
See page 214

8   Creating Merged Documents   **175**

Creating Form Letters 176
Reviewing Mail Merged Documents 178
Addressing Mailing Labels 180
Addressing Envelopes 182
Printing Envelopes Without a Return Address 184
Wandering and Wondering Through Word's Fields 185
Creating Awards 186
Creating a Data Source 188
Editing Data 190
Modifying a Data-Source Document 191
Incorporating Excel Data 192
Incorporating Access Data 193
Selecting Records to Merge 194
Merging Records in Order 196
Merging Conditionally 197
Personalizing Merged Documents 198
E-Mailing Merged Documents 200
Faxing Merged Documents 201

9   Working with Your Workgroup   **203**

Sharing Templates 204
Sending a Document Out for Comments 206
Sending a Document Out for Editing 208
Routing a Document 210
Reviewing a Routed Document 212
Adding Comments to a Document 213
Highlighting Text 214
Tracking Changes to a Document 215
Limiting Access to a Document 216
Reading a Document On Line 217
Summarizing a Document 218

Workgroup
Standard
Document

Send one fax to several
people simultaneously
See page 222

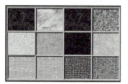

Add a background
to an online document
See page 234

Create drawings with
AutoShapes
See page 250

10 Working On Line   **219**

Using Word in Outlook E-Mail 220

Faxing Several People 222

Creating a Hyperlink to a Document 224

Jumping to Part of a Document 226

Jumping to a Folder 227

Jumping Around in a Word Document 228

Converting Text into Hyperlinks. 230

Making Text Stand Out 232

Creating a Background 234

Recording a Message 235

Adding a Video Clip 236

Adding a Sound Clip. 238

Getting a Document from the Internet. 239

Creating an Online Word Document 240

Jumping to a Web Site 241

Creating a Web Page 242

Converting a Document to a Web Page 244

11 Desktop Publishing   **247**

Wrapping Text Around an Object 248

Creating a Drawing. 250

Positioning Objects on a Page. 252

Aligning Objects. 254

Creating a Callout. 256

Creating a Floating Caption 258

Creating a Dropped Capital Letter 259

Creating a Pull Quote 260

Flowing Text in Columns 261

Creating Margin Notes 262

Creating Side-by-Side Paragraphs 264

Flowing Text Between AutoShapes 265

Flowing Text in Sidebars 266

Turn text into art
See page 268

reccomend	recommend
reccommend	recommend
receieve	receive
recieve	receive
recieved	received
recieving	receiving
recomend	recommend

Word can correct errors
as you type
See page 281

Creating Stylized Text 268

Writing Text Sideways 270

Creating an Inline Heading 271

Adding a Line Border Around a Page 272

Adding an Art Border Around a Page 273

Creating a Watermark 274

Fine-Tuning a Document 276

Adjusting the Spacing Between Characters 278

12 Automating Your Work 279

Controlling Automatic Changes 280

Watching Your Grammar 282

Correcting Your Spelling Dictionary 283

Adding or Creating a Custom Dictionary 284

Changing What Gets Proofed 285

Finding Alternative Wording 286

Keeping Track of Document Information 287

Inserting Document Information 288

Creating an Online Form 290

Using an Online Form 292

Converting a Document into Word 97 Format 293

Adding Components 294

Getting System Information 295

Getting More Help 296

Getting Free Stuff 298

Index 299

Acknowledgments

This book is the result of the combined efforts of people whose work we trust and admire and whose friendship we value highly. Kari Becker and Ken Sanchez, our talented typographers, meticulously laid out the complex design. Michael Bunney, our technical editor, double-checked every procedure and every graphic to verify that things worked as described. Herbert Payton produced the interior graphics and then cheerfully reworked them as the inevitable interface changes occurred. We worked with Susan Bishop on the *Microsoft Publisher Companion,* and we're happy to have her distinctive drawings in our book. We've worked with Alice Copp Smith on other books. She does so much more than proofread: her gentle and humorous chiding teaches us to write better. And our indexer, Kari Bero, seems to inhale the soul of a book and magically exhale an extensive index. Thanks also to Paul Ampadu, Jeanne Lewis, and John Mills.

At Microsoft Press, first and foremost we thank Lucinda Rowley for making it possible for us to write this book. Thanks also to Judith Bloch, Kim Eggleston, Kim Fryer, Mary DeJong, Nancy Jacobs, and Jim Kramer, all of whom provided help and valuable advice along the way.

On the knowledgeable Word 97 Beta Support Team, we thank Mike Maxey and his colleagues Susan Fetter, Chris "C.J." Jones, and Brian Phillips for their diligent work in answering our questions about Word's intricacies.

On the home front, Roberta Moon-Krause and Rick Krause allowed their puppies, Baiser and Pierre, to roam freely on our virtual and literal desktops and to grace some of our pages with their furry little images. Roberta brought us many a wonderful home-cooked meal as we toiled long into the night, and Rick helped with details too numerous to mention. Thanks, kids—you're the greatest.

About This Book

IN THIS SECTION

No Computerese!

A Quick Overview

A Final Word (or Two)

Microsoft Word 97 At A Glance is for anyone who wants to get the most from Microsoft Word 97 with the least amount of time and effort. Whether you write one letter a week or hundreds; whether your documents consist of a few lines of text, or are complex productions with graphics and tables, put together by several authors; whether your documents are printed, shared on a network, e-mailed, faxed, or made into Web pages for the Internet or a company intranet—you'll find this book to be a straightforward, easy-to-read reference tool. With the premise that Word should work for you, not you for it, this book's purpose is to help you get your work done quickly and efficiently so that you can get away from the computer and live your life.

No Computerese!

Let's face it—when there's a task you don't know how to do but you need to get it done in a hurry, or when you're stuck in the middle of a task and can't figure out what to do next, there's nothing more frustrating than having to read page after page of technical background material. You want the information you need—nothing more, nothing less—and you want it now! *And* it should be easy to find and understand. That's what this book is all about. It's written in plain English—no technical jargon and no computerese. No single task in the book takes more than two pages. Just look up a task in the index or the table of contents, turn to the page, and there's the information, laid out step by step and accompanied by illustrations that add visual clarity. You don't get bogged down by the whys and wherefores: just follow the steps, look at the illustrations, and get your work done with a minimum of hassle.

Occasionally you might have to turn to another page if the procedure you're working on has a "See Also" in the left column. That's because there's a lot of overlap among tasks, and we didn't want to keep repeating ourselves. We've also scattered some useful tips here and there, and thrown in a "Try This" once in a while, but by and large we've tried to remain true to the heart and soul of the book, which is that the information you need should be available to you at a glance.

Useful Tasks...

Whether you use Word 97 for work, school, personal correspondence, or some of each, we've tried to pack this book with procedures for everything we could think of that you might want to accomplish, from the simplest tasks to some of the more esoteric ones.

...And the Easiest Way to Do Them

Another thing we've tried to do in *Microsoft Word 97 At A Glance* is to find and describe the easiest way to accomplish a task. Word often provides a multitude of methods to achieve a single end result, which can be daunting or delightful, depending on the way you like to work. If you tend to stick with one favorite and familiar approach, we think the methods described in this book are the way

to go. If you like trying out alternative techniques, go ahead! The intuitiveness of Word invites exploration, and you're likely to discover ways of doing things that you think are easier or that you like better than ours. If you do, that's great! It's exactly what the creators of Word 97 had in mind when they provided so many alternatives.

A Quick Overview

This book isn't meant to be read in any particular order. It's designed so that you can jump in, get the information you need, and then close the book and keep it near your computer until the next time you need to know how to get something done. But that doesn't mean we scattered the information about with wild abandon. If you were to read the book from front to back, you'd find a logical progression from the simple tasks to the more complex ones. Here's a quick overview.

First, because so many computers come with Word 97 preinstalled, we assume that Word is already installed on your machine. If it's not, the Setup Wizard makes installation so simple that you won't need our help anyway. So, unlike many computer books, this one doesn't start out with installation instructions and a list of system requirements. You've already got all that under control.

Sections 2 through 4 of the book cover the basics: starting Word; creating a document, entering, editing, and formatting text; setting up your page layout, and using Word's templates and wizards to create great-looking documents with little effort.

Sections 5 through 8 describe tasks that are a bit more technical but are really useful: working with tables, adding graphics, creating running heads, combining several documents into one, incorporating material from other programs, and even creating junk mail—er—mail-merged documents. If you think these tasks sound complex, rest assured that they're not; Word makes them so easy that you'll sail right through them.

Sections 9 and 10 are all about communicating with your coworkers and reaching out beyond your computer: working together in a workgroup; circulating documents online for comments; sharing documents with others; communicating electronically using e-mail; using *hyperlinks*, or jumps, in your document to access other documents or Web pages; adding special effects such as sound, video, and animated text for online viewing; and expanding your horizons with the Internet and, possibly, a company intranet.

Sections 11 and 12 help you go a little further in using the power of Word: use special techniques to create watermarks, drop caps, pull quotes, margin notes, and drawings; flow text around objects or from place to place; take control of Word to make it do things for you automatically; and connect to the Internet to learn even more about Word.

And What About That Office Assistant?

You'll find that we haven't given you any information about the Office Assistant—that little animated character who hangs around on your Desktop waiting to give you advice and answer your questions. Whether you love or hate the little critter, it can help you get through some tricky procedures. It's so straightforward and intuitive, though, that we figure you'll use it if you like it or shut it down if it drives you crazy. So here's the first tip in the book: right-click the Office Assistant window and customize it. You can set it up to work with you so that you don't find yourself yelling at it if it pops up when you don't want it to.

A Final Word (or Two)

We had three goals in writing this book, and here they are.

◆ Whatever you *want* to do, we want the book to help you get it done.

◆ We want the book to help you discover how to do things you *didn't* know you wanted to do.

◆ And, finally, if we've achieved the first two goals, we'll be well on the way to the third: we want the book to help you *enjoy* doing your work with Word 97. We think that's the best gift we can give you to thank you for buying our book.

We hope you'll have as much fun using *Microsoft Word 97 At A Glance* as we've had writing it. The best way to learn is by *doing*, and that's how we hope you'll use this book.

Jump right in!

2

Jump Right In

IN THIS SECTION

Creating a Document

Working with an Existing Document

Editing Text

Storing and Reusing Text

Proofreading a Document

Printing a Document

You can use Microsoft Word as a smart typewriter or as a multifaceted *thought processor.* Word was designed to be either or both, and it's your choice as to how you want to use its multitude of tools and features. You can stick with the basics, or you can jump right in and go exploring—opening menus and drop-down lists, clicking buttons, turning options on and off to see what happens, and so on. You'll learn a lot about Word and the way it works by simply trying to accomplish a task.

This section covers many of the basic skills that you'll use every day. If you're not familiar with Word, step through these first few tasks and see how easily you can produce professional-looking documents. Once you realize how intuitive Word is, you'll find it easy and rewarding to explore and try things out—in other words, to learn by doing. If you try one of the more advanced tasks and you get stuck in some way, you'll find the answers to most of your questions in other sections of this book, or in Word's Help system. Even if you never try any advanced tasks and never read the rest of this book, you'll have learned the basics, and Word as a smart typewriter will make your life that much easier. But Word really shines as a thought processor. Try it. And read this book!

Microsoft Word at a Glance

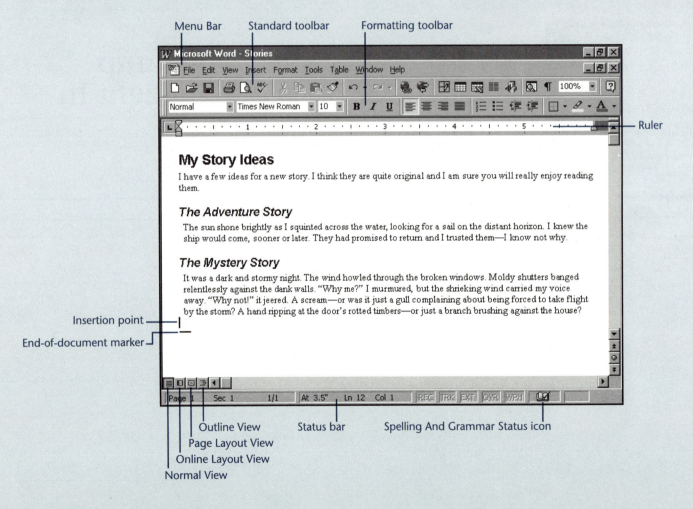

Menu Bar

Standard toolbar

Formatting toolbar

Ruler

My Story Ideas

The Adventure Story

The Mystery Story

Insertion point

End-of-document marker

Outline View

Page Layout View

Online Layout View

Normal View

Status bar

Spelling And Grammar Status icon

2

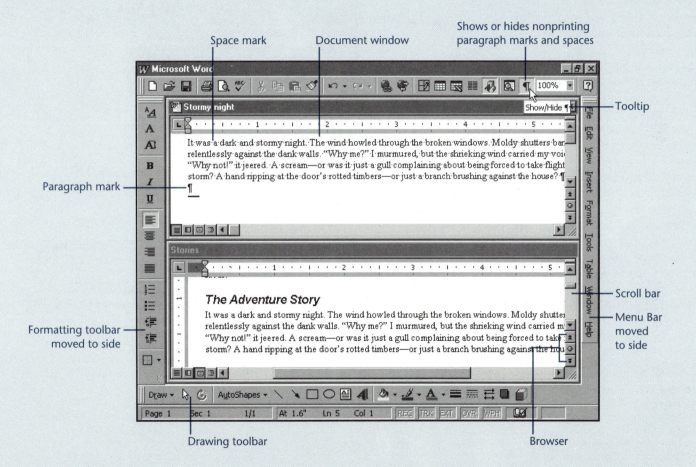

Space mark

Document window

Shows or hides nonprinting
paragraph marks and spaces

Tooltip

Paragraph mark

Formatting toolbar
moved to side

Drawing toolbar

Scroll bar

Menu Bar
moved
to side

Browser

Creating a Document

The way you start Word depends on how it was installed. As with most Windows programs, Word can be started it in several different ways. If Word was installed as part of Office 97, you can start it from the Start menu, from the Office shortcut bar, from the Winword folder, and even from the Run command on the Start menu. Without Office 97, you might have fewer choices but you still have plenty of options. You can try all the different ways until you find the one that you like best, or you can stick with the method we describe here. Word is ready—are you?

Start Word from the Start Menu

1 Click the Start button.

2 Point the mouse pointer to Programs.

3 Choose Microsoft Word.

Enter Text

1 Type your text. It appears on your screen at the left of the blinking insertion point.

2 Continue typing when you reach the end of the line. Word automatically moves—or *wraps*—to the next line.

3 Press Enter only when you want to start a new paragraph.

Press Enter to start a new paragraph.

Word automatically starts a new line.

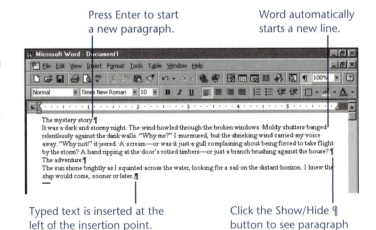

Typed text is inserted at the left of the insertion point.

Click the Show/Hide ¶ button to see paragraph marks and spaces.

Save the Document

1. Click the Save button.

2. If necessary, navigate to the folder in which you want to store the document.

3. Type a name for the document in the File Name box if you don't want the name that Word proposes. Filenames can be up to about 250 characters in length and can include spaces, but you can't use the \ / * ? < > and | characters.

4. Click Save.

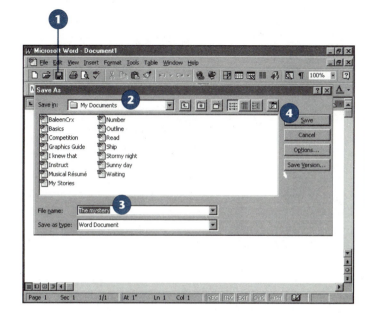

Close the Document

1. Click the Close button.

2. If there are unsaved changes in the document, click Yes if you want to save them.

Closes the document.

Closes all documents and the Word program.

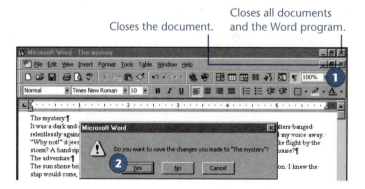

Working with an Existing Document

Unless you always create short documents—letters, memos, and so on—you'll often need to continue working on a document that you started but didn't complete in an earlier session. You simply open the saved document, add more text, and then save and close the document again. And if this cry sounds familiar—"Oh no, I didn't mean to do that!"—you can quickly undo the kinds of mistakes you make when you're working fast and you accidentally delete, replace, or move something.

TIP

Quick Opener. *If the document you want to open is one you used recently, it might be listed at the bottom of the File menu. Click the document's name to open it.*

Open a Document

1 Click the Open button.

2 If necessary, navigate to find the folder that contains the document you want.

3 Select the document.

4 Click Open.

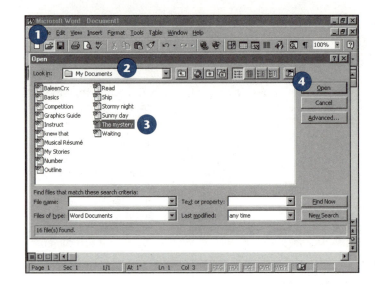

Add Text

1 Click to place the insertion point where you want to add some text.

2 Type the new text. Use the Backspace key to delete incorrectly typed characters.

3 Click the Save button on the Standard toolbar.

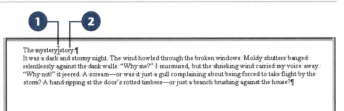

SEE ALSO

"Editing Text" on page 12 for information about selecting, deleting, replacing, and moving text.

TIP

Redo an Undo. *When you've undone one or more mistakes and then decided they weren't mistakes after all, you can restore them with the Redo button. It works exactly like the Undo button—just think of it as the Undo Undo button.*

Undo One Mistake

 1 As soon as you realize the mistake, click the Undo button to restore the document to its original state.

Text was accidentally deleted from here.

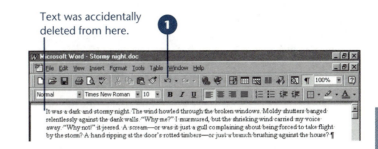

Deleted text is restored.

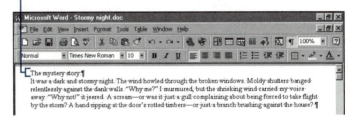

Undo Several Mistakes

When you know you've made several mistakes, and even if those mistakes were a few actions ago, you can

◆ Keep clicking the Undo button until the document has returned to its original state.

◆ Click the down arrow at the right of the Undo button to see a list of actions that you can undo. Wherever you click in the list, that action and all preceding actions will be undone.

Click to see a list of Undo actions. Click at the end of the list to return the document to its original state.

Editing Text

Whether you're creating business letters, financial reports, or the Great American Novel, it's a sure bet that you're going to need to go back into your document and do some editing. Word provides a great variety of ways to edit. To edit existing content, you simply select it and make your changes.

TIP

You're Being Replaced! *If the selected text isn't replaced when you begin typing, the Typing Replaces Selection option has been turned off. To turn it on, choose Options from the Tools menu, click the Edit tab, and put a check mark next to the option.*

SEE ALSO

"So Many Ways to Do It" on page 16 for more information about different ways to select text.

Select Text

1. Click at the beginning of the text to be selected.

2. Drag the mouse over all the text to be selected, and release the mouse button.

The mystery story.¶
It was a dark and stormy night. The wind howled through the broken windows. Moldy shutters banged relentlessly against the dank walls. "Why me?" I murmured, but the shrieking wind carried my voice away. "Why not!" it jeered. A scream—or was it just a gull complaining about being forced to take flight by the storm? A hand ripping at the door's rotted timbers—or just a branch brushing against the house?¶

Delete Text

1. Press the Delete key.

Selected text has been deleted.

The mystery story.¶
It was a dark and stormy night. Moldy shutters banged relentlessly against the dank walls. "Why me?" I murmured, but the shrieking wind carried my voice away. "Why not!" it jeered. A scream—or was it just a gull complaining about being forced to take flight by the storm? A hand ripping at the door's rotted timbers—or just a branch brushing against the house?¶

You can customize the way you edit by changing Word's settings. Choose Options from the Tools menu, click the Edit tab, and turn the options on or off according to your preferences.

It's a Drag. *If you drag the selection to the top or bottom of the window, Word scrolls up or down in the document.*

Quick Escape. *You can cancel a move while dragging text by pressing the Esc key before releasing the mouse button.*

Replace Text

1 Select the text to be replaced.

2 Type the new text.

The mystery story.¶
It was a dark and stormy night. Moldy shutters banged relentlessly against the dank walls. "Why me?" I murmured, but the shrieking wind carried my voice away. "Why not!" it jeered. A scream—or was it just a gull complaining about being forced to take flight by the storm? A hand ripping at the door's rotted timbers—or just a branch brushing against the house?¶

The mystery story.¶
It was a dark and stormy night. Ghostly shadows danced against the dank walls. "Why me?" I murmured, but the shrieking wind carried my voice away. "Why not!" it jeered. A scream—or was it just a gull complaining about being forced to take flight by the storm? A hand ripping at the door's rotted timbers—or just a branch brushing against the house?¶

Move Text

1 Select the text to be moved.

2 Point to the selection and drag the text.

3 Drop it at the new location.

The mystery story.¶
It was a dark and stormy night. Ghostly shadows danced against the dank walls. "Why me?" I murmured, but the shrieking wind carried my voice away. "Why not!" it jeered. A scream—or was it just a gull complaining about being forced to take flight by the storm? A hand ripping at the door's rotted timbers—or just a branch brushing against the house?¶

The mystery story.¶
It was a dark and stormy night. "Why me?" I murmured, but the shrieking wind carried my voice away. "Why not!" it jeered. A scream—or was it just a gull complaining about being forced to take flight by the storm? A hand ripping at the door's rotted timbers—or just a branch brushing against the house? Ghostly shadows danced against the dank walls.¶

2

Storing and Reusing Text

Word uses a feature of Microsoft Windows—the Clipboard—as a temporary holding area for text that you want to move or copy to another part of your document, to another document in the same program, or to a document in another program. You simply park your text on the Clipboard and then, when you're ready, retrieve it and "paste" it into its new location. And once the text is stored on the Clipboard, you can paste it into your document as many times as you want.

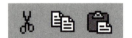

Copy Text

1 Select the text to be copied.

2 Click the Copy button.

3 Click at the location where you want to insert the text.

4 Click the Paste button.

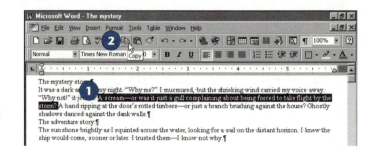

Original text stays where it was.

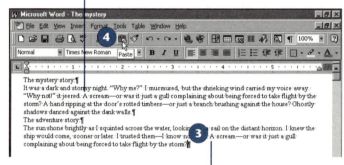

Copied text appears in new location.

Paste Quickly, Paste Often.
Once you've copied or cut text to the Clipboard, it stays there only until you cut or copy something else to the Clipboard or until you quit Windows. To avoid losing your text, find the new location for the text and paste immediately after you cut or copy it.

"So Many Ways to Do It" on page 16 for information about different ways to copy and move text.

Move Text

1. Select the text to be moved.

2. Click the Cut button.

3. Click at the location where you want to insert the text.

4. Click the Paste button.

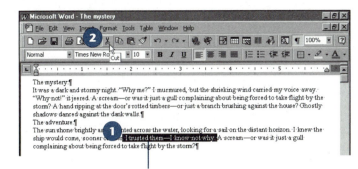

Selected text is cut from here.

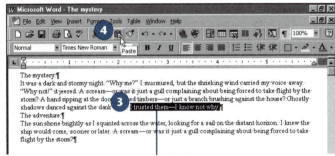

Pasted text appears here.

So Many Ways to Do It

Word offers you a variety of ways to do most things. You might, for example, be able to use a button, a menu item, a key combination, or a mouse-click to accomplish the same thing. Why are there so many choices? Well, one reason is that we all work differently, and, given several choices, we usually do some experimenting, find the way that works best for us and that we're most comfortable with, and then stick with it. Another reason is that certain methods work best in certain situations.

Two procedures that you'll be using frequently—selecting text and moving or copying text—can be accomplished using quite a few different methods, some of which can be difficult if you use them in the wrong situation. The tips we offer here will help you choose which methods to use in which circumstances.

Try these common methods of selecting text. After you've selected the text, your next step might be to move it or copy it. Again, some methods are better than others, depending on the situation.

TEXT-SELECTION METHODS	
To do this	**Use this method**
Select characters in a word	Drag over the characters.
Select a word	Double-click the word.
Select several words	Drag over the words.
Select a sentence	Hold down the Ctrl key and click anywhere in the sentence.
Select a line of text	Move the pointer to the far left of the window and click when you see a right-pointing arrow.
Select a paragraph	Move the pointer to the far left of the window and double-click when you see a right-pointing arrow.
Select a long passage	Click at the beginning of the passage, double-click EXT on the status bar, click at the end of the passage, and double-click EXT on the status bar.
Select the entire document	Choose Select All from the Edit menu.

The main difference between using the Cut and Copy buttons on the Standard toolbar and using the F2 and Shift+F2 keys is that Cut and Copy use the Windows Clipboard. The cut or copied information is stored on the Clipboard, and you can get on with your work until you're ready to retrieve and use the information from the Clipboard. The Clipboard is more than just a holding area, though—it's also a pathway through which you can transfer your cut or copied information to other documents or programs. Unfortunately, the Clipboard stores only one item at a time, so any information that you cut or copy replaces whatever was there before. Here's where the F2 and Shift+F2 keys come in. When you want to move or copy text without replacing the contents of the Clipboard—or if you simply want to ensure that you don't accidentally lose something on the Clipboard— use the F2 or Shift+F2 method.

If this seems like an overwhelming number of ways to accomplish the same tasks, get ready for a shock— there are even more ways. If you really want to explore the full range of different ways to do these tasks, take a stroll through Word's Help and try out some of the other methods.

COPY OR MOVE METHODS	
To do this	Use this method
Move a short distance	Drag the selection and drop it at the new location.
Copy a short distance	Hold down the Ctrl key, drag the selection, drop it at the new location, and release the Ctrl key.
Move a long distance or to a different document or program	Click the Cut button, click at the new location, and click the Paste button.
Copy a long distance or to a different document or program	Click the Copy button, click at the new location, and click the Paste button.
Move a long or short distance, preserving the Clipboard contents	Press the F2 key, click at the new location, and press Enter.
Copy a long or short distance, preserving the Clipboard contents	Press the key combination Shift+F2, click at the new location, and press Enter.

2

Proofreading a Document

After you've completed your document, you'll want to look it over and correct any errors. Word can help you do this in a quick and almost entertaining manner. When you use Word's proofreading tools, you can reduce the likelihood of embarrassing mistakes in your documents.

TIP

You can double-click the Spelling And Grammar Status icon on the status bar to find the next misspelling and open the Spelling shortcut menu.

TIP

If Word offers no suggestions for the misspelled word, retype the word with another spelling and see if that generates any suggestions.

Correct the Spelling

1. Point to a word that's marked as incorrect, and right-click.

2. Click one of the proposed corrections.

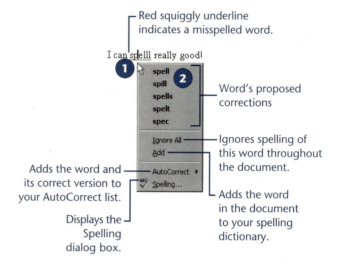

Red squiggly underline indicates a misspelled word.

I can spelll really good!

Word's proposed corrections

Ignores spelling of this word throughout the document.

Adds the word and its correct version to your AutoCorrect list.

Adds the word in the document to your spelling dictionary.

Displays the Spelling dialog box.

Correct the Grammar

1. Point to a grammatical error, and right-click.

2. Click one of the proposed corrections.

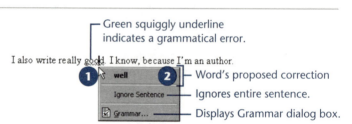

Green squiggly underline indicates a grammatical error.

I also write really good. I know, because I'm an author.

Word's proposed correction

Ignores entire sentence.

Displays Grammar dialog box.

Check the Layout

1. Click the Print Preview button on the Standard toolbar.

2. Click the Multiple Pages button if you want to see a preview of several pages at once.

3. Click the down arrow on the scroll bar to see the next set of pages.

4. Click Close to return to your document and make any necessary edits.

Drag to select the number of pages displayed.

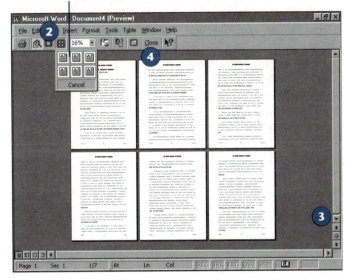

Printing a Document

Although e-mail and Web documents are bringing the paperless office closer to reality, the most common way to distribute your finished document is still to print it. Printing is mostly a job for Windows—Word prepares your document for printing, and then hands it off to Windows.

TIP

Printing Pronto. *If you don't need to change any settings in the Print dialog box, you can quickly print a document by clicking the Print button on the Standard toolbar.*

Print a Document

1. Choose Print from the File menu.

2. Change the settings if necessary.

3. Click OK.

Select printer from list.

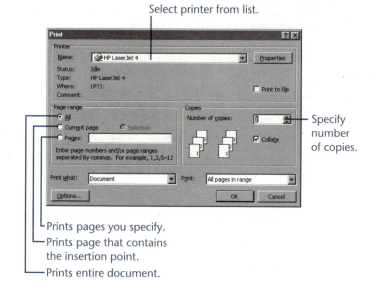

Specify number of copies.

Prints pages you specify.

Prints page that contains the insertion point.

Prints entire document.

3

Improving the Look of Your Document

IN THIS SECTION

Using Toolbars

Changing the Look of Text

Changing the Look of Paragraphs

Changing the Space Between Lines

Creating Tab Stops

Copying Paragraph Formats

Working with Lists

Adding Borders

Setting Margins and Page Orientation

Formatting Unformatted Documents

Different jobs require specialized tools and something to keep them in. In the days when doctors made house calls, they kept their pills and potions in big black bags. Carpenters and electricians keep their tools within easy reach on belts or aprons that they wear as they work. Word, too, has the right tools for the task you're working on, all neatly arranged on *toolbars*. When you're not using a particular toolbar, you can put it away and use the tools from another toolbar. Word's tools are in the form of buttons and lists, and you can use them to accomplish a multitude of tasks.

You can use Word's tools to undo mistakes, change text alignment, create headings, change the style of one paragraph or many, add borders, and create a numbered or bulleted list as you're typing—or convert text you've already typed into either kind of list. Give Word the word, and it does all sorts of helpful things behind the scenes as you're typing: correct transposed letters, add a capital letter to the first word in a sentence if you didn't do it, turn *tuesday* into *Tuesday* and *1st* into *1ˢᵗ*, and tell you when you've misspelled a word or used poor grammar. Word can do all this and more.

It's fun to experiment with different looks for your documents, and it's easy to keep trying new looks until you find the one you like.

Using Toolbars

Word's toolbars are powerful assistants. Each toolbar (and there are *many* of them) contains the most common tools you'll need for a specific task. Word usually displays two toolbars— Standard and Formatting— along with the Menu Bar, but you can change the display of toolbars, and Word will remember which ones you use and will display them each time you start the program.

Display a Toolbar

1 Right-click anywhere in any toolbar or in the Menu Bar.

2 From the shortcut menu that appears, choose the toolbar to be displayed.

Click checked toolbar to hide it.
Click unchecked toolbar to display it.

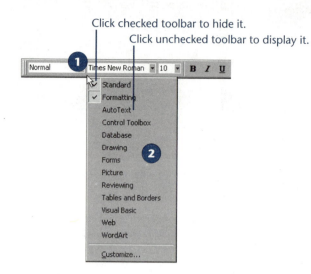

Use a Toolbar Button

1 Point to a toolbar button.

2 If you're not sure whether this is the tool you need, hold the mouse steady until a tooltip (the name of the item you're pointing to) appears.

3 Click the button if the tool is the one you want, or point to another button.

Tooltip identifies the tool.

TIP

To close a drop-down list or a drop-down button without choosing an item, press the Esc key. Press the Esc key a second time to cancel the selection of the list or button.

TIP

Cool Combo. *There is a variant of the drop-down list— it's called a combo box. In this form, the list might not include all the possible choices. If you see what you want in the list, you can choose it; if not, you can type your choice in the box. The Font Size list is an example of a combo box—it doesn't list a 95-point font size, but if you select some text and type 95 in the box, you'll get 95-point type (provided the font you're using supports that size).*

TIP

Whenever a drop-down list or a menu has a little title bar at its top, you can drag the title bar away from its button to change the drop-down list or menu into a stand-alone toolbar.

Use a Drop-Down List

1 Click the down arrow at the right of the list.

2 Click the item you want from the list.

Click to open the list.

Use a Drop-Down Button

1 Click the down arrow at the right of the button.

2 Click the setting you want. The setting is used, and the button changes to that setting.

3 Click the button to use the setting again.

3

Word's Most Useful Toolbars

Word's most useful and most widely used toolbars are the Formatting and the Standard toolbars. In most cases, the picture on the tool's button or the word in the list gives you an idea of what the tool does. If not, just point at the tool you're not sure of and in a second or two you'll see an identifying tooltip.

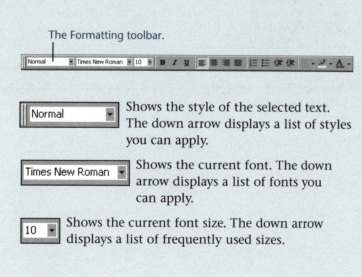

The Formatting toolbar.

Normal — Shows the style of the selected text. The down arrow displays a list of styles you can apply.

Times New Roman — Shows the current font. The down arrow displays a list of fonts you can apply.

10 — Shows the current font size. The down arrow displays a list of frequently used sizes.

B — Turns boldface font emphasis on or off.

I — Turns italic font emphasis on or off.

U — Turns font underlining on or off.

Left-aligns the current paragraph.

Center-aligns the current paragraph.

Right-aligns the current paragraph.

Justifies the current paragraph.

Adds or removes automatic list numbering.

Adds or removes automatic list bullets.

Removes one step of indenting from the current paragraph.

Adds one step of indenting to the current paragraph.

Adds or removes borders. The down arrow displays a menu of different types of borders you can apply.

Turns line highlighting on or off. The down arrow displays a menu of colors you can apply.

A — Changes text color. The down arrow displays a menu of colors you can apply.

The Standard toolbar

Opens a blank document.

Opens an existing document.

Saves the document.

Prints the document using default settings.

Displays the document in Print Preview.

Checks the selection or the document for errors in spelling or grammar.

Copies the selection to the Windows Clipboard and deletes it from the document.

Copies the selection to the Windows Clipboard.

Pastes (inserts) the contents of the Windows Clipboard at the location you specify.

Copies formatting from the selection and applies the formatting to different material.

Undoes the last action. The down arrow displays a series of actions that can be undone.

Redoes the last action that was undone using the Undo button. The down arrow displays a series of actions that can be restored.

Inserts a jump (hyperlink) to another document or to another location.

Displays or hides the Web toolbar.

Displays or hides the Tables And Borders toolbar.

Inserts a Word table. Drag in the drop-down menu to specify the number of rows and columns.

Inserts an Excel worksheet. Drag in the drop-down menu to specify the number of rows and columns.

Changes the number of columns in your text. Drag in the drop-down menu to specify the number of columns.

Displays or hides the Drawing toolbar.

Displays or hides the Document Map.

Displays or hides the nonprinting symbols in your document, including paragraph marks.

100% ▼   Changes the onscreen magnification of your document.

Displays the Office Assistant for on-the-spot help with any document.

3

Managing Toolbars

Pick a task, any task—changing the font, editing pictures, creating a table, setting Internet links—and Word has a toolbar for you. Depending on the way you work and the number of toolbars you use at one time, you might want to resize some toolbars or move them to different parts of the window.

> **TIP**
>
> **Ahoy!** *A toolbar is either "docked" or "floating." A docked toolbar resides at one of the four sides of your Word window, and the document window is sized to provide space for the toolbar. A floating toolbar floats over your text as a little window of its own.*

Move a Docked Toolbar

1. Point to a blank part of the toolbar.

2. Do any of the following to move the toolbar:

   ◆ Drag the toolbar and drop it at any side of the Word window to dock it at that side.

   ◆ Drag the toolbar and drop it in the document area to change it into a floating toolbar.

   ◆ Double-click the toolbar to switch it between docked and floating positions.

Style list

Font list

Font Size list

Standard toolbar dragged from top and dropped in document window

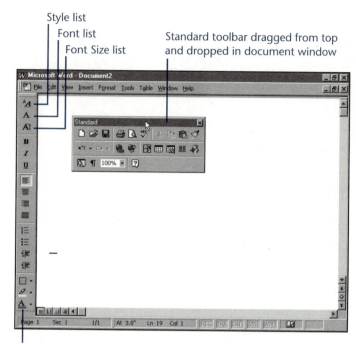

Formatting toolbar dragged from top and dropped on left side

SEE ALSO

"Customizing the Toolbars" on page 102 for information about reorganizing the buttons on toolbars.

"Quickly Applying Standardized Formatting" on page 110 for information about creating your own toolbars.

"Storing Toolbars" on page 112 for information about storing a toolbar out of the way.

TIP

My, How You've Changed!
The look of a toolbar might change when you move its position. When you move the Formatting toolbar from the top of your window to the side, for example, the Style drop-down list box changes into a button that opens the Style dialog box. Use this feature to further customize the window to the way you like to work.

Resize a Floating Toolbar

1 Point to one of the toolbar's borders.

2 Drag the border and drop it to change its dimensions.

Mouse pointer changes to a resizing pointer when positioned over the toolbar's border.

Move a Floating Toolbar

1 Do any of the following to move the toolbar:

◆ Point to the toolbar's title bar, drag the toolbar, and drop it at a new location.

◆ Drag the toolbar to one of the sides of the window to change it into a docked toolbar.

◆ Double-click the toolbar to dock it at its previous docked position.

3

Adding Character Emphasis

Sometimes you'll want to make a word or a phrase stand out by making it bold or italic. With Word, you can apply this formatting when you're typing the text, or later as you edit it. Don't go overboard, though—too many different kinds of emphasis are more distracting than helpful.

TIP

Be Emphatic! *You can click more than one emphasis button to combine the emphases—bold italic, for example, or underlined italic, and yes, even underlined bold italic!*

TIP

Presto Change-o! *Use the toolbar buttons to change one or two characteristics, or when you want to see the immediate effect of each change in your text. Use the Font dialog box to change several characteristics at once.*

Add Emphasis as You Type

1 Type your text as usual.

2 Click an emphasis button.

3 Type your emphasized text.

Click to turn on italic. Click to turn off italic.

2

1 It was dark. The wind *howled* through the window.

3

Add Emphasis as You Edit

1 Select the text you want to emphasize.

2 Click an emphasis button:

◆ *B* indicates Bold—use to add emphasis to headings.

◆ *I* indicates Italic—use to add emphasis to words or phrases in body text.

◆ *U* indicates Underlining—use sparingly, because it sometimes cuts off descenders. It can also be mistaken for a hyperlink in an online document.

1 It was dark. The wind *howled* through the window.

2

TIP

Copycat. *Format Painter
also copies and applies font
and font-size information.*

SEE ALSO

*"Making Text Stand Out"
on page 232 for information
about setting font characteristics in the Font dialog box.*

*"Creating an Inline Heading"
on page 271 for information
about using character styles.*

TIP

Smart Painter. *You don't
need to select a whole phrase,
or even a whole word, when
you're using Format Painter to
copy emphasis; selecting just
one character gives Format
Painter enough information
to do its job.*

Copy the Emphasis

1 Select the text that has
the emphasis you want
to copy.

2 Click the Format Painter
button.

3 Drag the special Format
Painter mouse pointer
over the text you want
to copy the emphasis to,
and then release the
mouse button.

Remove the Emphasis

1 Select the text.

2 Click any of the pressed
emphasis buttons.

2

1 It **was** dark. The wind *howled* through the window.
 It was sunny. The birds chirped from the trees.
3

Pressed buttons show what emphasis is applied
to the selected text.

1 *It was dark.* The wind *howled* through the window.

3

Changing Fonts

The shapes of the characters you type—and, indeed, the look of your entire document—are determined by the font you're using. Fonts (also called *typefaces*) come in a variety of shapes and forms, and some even give you pictures, rather than letters and numbers, as you type. Some fonts come with Windows, some with your printer, and many more with Word. You might also have fonts that came with other programs you've installed, and—if you want or need even more fonts—you can purchase additional fonts or font packages.

SEE ALSO

"Copy the Emphasis" on page 29 for information about copying font information.

Change the Font as You Type

1. Type the text you want in the current font.

2. Choose a different font from the Font drop-down list.

3. Choose a different font size from the Font Size drop-down list.

4. Type some text in the new font and size.

5. Change back to the original font and size.

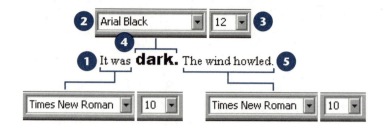

Change the Font as You Edit

1. Select the text you want to change.

2. Choose a different font from the Font drop-down list. (The fonts listed depend on the fonts installed on your computer *and* on the printer you're set up to use.)

3. Choose a different font size from the Font Size drop-down list.

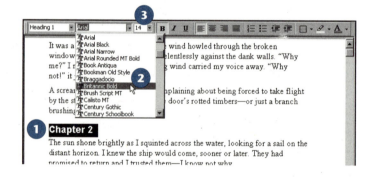

Changing Paragraph Alignment

Paragraph alignment controls how the lines of text in a paragraph are arranged. There are four possible alignments:

Left—start of each line is flush against left margin.

Right—end of each line is flush against right margin.

Centered—all lines are centered between left and right margins.

Justified—all lines are spaced so that start and end of each line are flush against left and right margins.

SEE ALSO

"Creating a Sequence of Styles" on page 64 for information about using styles and "Creating Styles from Scratch" on page 72 for information about creating your own styles.

Choose an Alignment

1 Select the paragraph or paragraphs that you want to have the same alignment.

2 Click an alignment button.

 Left-aligned text with a ragged right edge is the most frequently used alignment because it's the easiest for the eye to follow, especially in long documents.

It·was·a·dark·and·stormy·night.·The·wind·howled·through·the·broken·windows.·Moldy·shutters·banged·relentlessly·against·the·dank·walls.·"Why·me?"·I·murmured,·but·the·shrieking·wind·carried·my·voice·away.·"Why·not!"·it·jeered.·A·scream—or·was·it·just·a·gull·complaining·about·being·forced·to·take·flight·by·the·storm?·A·hand·ripping·at·the·door's·rotted·timbers—or·just·a·branch·brushing·against·the·house?¶

 Centered text is used mostly for short blocks of text, such as invitations, greeting cards, and advertisements.

It·was·a·dark·and·stormy·night.·The·wind·howled·through·the·broken·windows.·Moldy·shutters·banged·relentlessly·against·the·dank·walls.·"Why·me?"·I·murmured,·but·the·shrieking·wind·carried·my·voice·away.·"Why·not!"·it·jeered.·A·scream—or·was·it·just·a·gull·complaining·about·being·forced·to·take·flight·by·the·storm?·A·hand·ripping·at·the·door's·rotted·timbers—or·just·a·branch·brushing·against·the·house?¶

 Right-aligned text has limited uses because it's difficult to read—the left edge is ragged, and the eye struggles to find the beginning of each line. Used mostly in captions that fall on the left side of an illustration.

It·was·a·dark·and·stormy·night.·The·wind·howled·through·the·broken·windows.·Moldy·shutters·banged·relentlessly·against·the·dank·walls.·"Why·me?"·I·murmured,·but·the·shrieking·wind·carried·my·voice·away.·"Why·not!"·it·jeered.·A·scream—or·was·it·just·a·gull·complaining·about·being·forced·to·take·flight·by·the·storm?·A·hand·ripping·at·the·door's·rotted·timbers—or·just·a·branch·brushing·against·the·house?¶

 Justified text is usually used in columnar layouts—in newspapers, for example. Be sure to turn on hyphenation; otherwise, large gaps will occur as words are spread out to fill up each line.

It·was·a·dark·and·stormy·night.·The·wind·howled·through·the·broken·windows.·Moldy·shutters·banged·relentlessly·against·the·dank·walls.·"Why·me?"·I·murmured,·but·the·shrieking·wind·carried·my·voice·away.·"Why·not!"·it·jeered.·A·scream—or·was·it·just·a·gull·complaining·about·being·forced·to·take·flight·by·the·storm?·A·hand·ripping·at·the·door's·rotted·timbers—or·just·a·branch·brushing·against·the·house?¶

3

Customizing Paragraphs

You create a new paragraph every time you press the Enter key, even if you don't add any text, and you apply formatting to the entire paragraph. The formatting information is stored in the paragraph mark—a usually invisible symbol at the end of the paragraph. By displaying paragraph marks, you can ensure that any formatting changes will apply to the entire paragraph. When you can see the paragraph mark, it's also less likely that you'll accidentally delete it and lose its formatting.

SEE ALSO

"Creating Styles from Scratch" on page 72 for information about creating and using styles.

Format as You Type

1. If paragraph marks are not displayed, click the Show/Hide ¶ button.

2. Press Enter to start a new paragraph.

3. Select the paragraph mark.

4. Use the buttons and lists on the toolbars to change the formatting.

5. Press the Home key to unselect (deselect) the paragraph mark.

6. Type your text.

7. Press Enter to start a new paragraph.

8. Press Ctrl+Q to remove any paragraph formatting you don't want to use in the current paragraph.

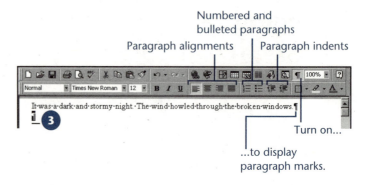

Numbered and bulleted paragraphs

Paragraph alignments

Paragraph indents

Turn on...

...to display paragraph marks.

Format Existing Paragraphs

1. Select the entire paragraph or all the paragraphs that will have the same formatting.

2. Use the buttons and lists on the toolbars to change the formatting.

3. Press the Right arrow key to unselect the paragraphs.

Combine Paragraphs

1. Move the insertion point to the beginning of the paragraph you want to combine with the previous paragraph.

2. Press the Backspace key.

3. Press the Spacebar to add a space.

It was a dark and stormy night. The wind howled through the broken windows. Moldy shutters banged relentlessly against the dank walls. "Why me?" I murmured, but the shrieking wind carried my voice away. "Why not!" it jeered. A scream—or was it just a gull complaining about being forced to take flight by the storm? A hand ripping at the door's rotted timbers—or just a branch brushing against the house? The sun shone brightly as I squinted across the water, looking for a sail on the distant horizon. I knew the ship would come, sooner or later. They had promised to return and I trusted them—I know not why.

Double-click to select entire paragraph. Double-click (without releasing the mouse button) and drag down to select multiple paragraphs.

Deleting the paragraph mark combines the paragraphs and strips the formatting from the first paragraph. The combined paragraph uses the first paragraph's formatting.

It was a dark and stormy night. The wind howled through the broken windows. Moldy shutters banged relentlessly against the dank walls. "Why me?" I murmured, but the shrieking wind carried my voice away. "Why not!" it jeered. A scream—or was it just a gull complaining about being forced to take flight by the storm? A hand ripping at the door's rotted timbers—or just a branch brushing against the house?

3

Indenting Paragraphs

A paragraph is often indented to distinguish it from other paragraphs. There are four types of indent: left, right, first-line, and hanging. The left and right indents are often used together to create a *nested* paragraph for quotations or similar materials. The *first-line indent* is used to distinguish a new paragraph from the previous one. The *hanging indent* indents all the lines of a paragraph except the first one.

TIP

Next Stop. *The Increase Indent and Decrease Indent buttons move the indent to the next or previous tab stop. If you don't want to use the default tab stops for the indent, you can create your own tab stops.*

Indent a Paragraph

1. If the ruler is not displayed, choose Ruler from the View menu.

2. Select the paragraph or paragraphs that you want to indent.

3. Click the Increase Indent button.

4. Click the Increase Indent button to increase the indent or the Decrease Indent button to move back to the previous indent.

Markers on ruler show indents.   Decrease Indent button

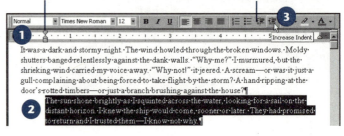

Nest a Paragraph

1. Drag the Left Indent marker and drop it where you want the left indent.

2. Drag the Right Indent marker and drop it where you want the right indent.

Left Indent marker   Right Indent marker

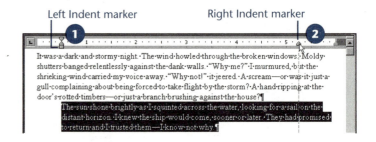

SEE ALSO

"Creating Tab Stops" on page 37 for information about creating and changing tab stops.

TIP

A New Look. *When you change the indent, Word creates a new style, so you can easily apply the same paragraph format to another paragraph. If Word doesn't create a new style, you need to turn on that option on the AutoFormat As You Type tab of the AutoCorrect dialog box.*

SEE ALSO

"Controlling Automatic Changes" on page 280 for information about changing the AutoFormat As You Type settings.

TIP

To Indent or Not To Indent. *You'll notice that in most publications whose paragraphs have first-line indents, the first paragraph under a heading doesn't usually have an indent. That's because its placement indicates clearly that it's a new paragraph.*

Indent the First Line

1. Click in the paragraph that you want to have a first-line indent.

2. Drag the First Line Indent marker and drop it where you want the first-line indent.

First Line Indent marker

First-line indent

Create a Hanging Indent

1. Click in the paragraph that you want to have a hanging indent.

2. Drag the Hanging Indent marker and drop it where you want all lines but the first to align.

Hanging Indent marker

Hanging indent

3

Changing the Spacing Between Lines

The spacing between lines is the same throughout a paragraph. You can increase the spacing between the lines, and you can even add extra space above or below a paragraph.

SEE ALSO

"Creating Styles from Scratch" on page 72 for more information about adding space before or after a paragraph.

TRY THIS

I'll Have a Draft. *Create a draft copy of your document by pressing Ctrl+A to select the entire document, and then press Ctrl+2 to use double spacing. Then save the document using a different filename.*

Adjust Spacing

1. Select the paragraph or paragraphs that will have the same line spacing.

2. Use the key combinations shown at the right to adjust the line spacing.

   ◆ Ctrl+0 (zero) is a toggle that adds or removes a blank line before a paragraph.

   ◆ Ctrl+1, Ctrl+2, and Ctrl+5 each apply a specific amount of line spacing.

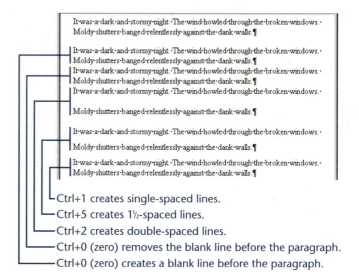

Ctrl+1 creates single-spaced lines.

Ctrl+5 creates 1½-spaced lines.

Ctrl+2 creates double-spaced lines.

Ctrl+0 (zero) removes the blank line before the paragraph.

Ctrl+0 (zero) creates a blank line before the paragraph.

Creating Tab Stops

Tab stops, which are part of a paragraph's formatting, define the distance the insertion point moves each time you press the Tab key. They also affect the location of indents when you use the Indent buttons. If you don't create your own tab stops, Word sets a tab stop every 0.5 inch. Word's tab stops aren't displayed on the ruler. The ones you create yourself are displayed, and there's a different symbol for each kind of tab stop.

SEE ALSO

"Putting Information in a Table" on page 76 for information about creating tables.

Set Tab Stops

1. If the ruler is not displayed, choose Ruler from the View menu.

2. Click in the paragraph or select the paragraphs for which you want to set the tab stops.

3. Click the box at the left end of the ruler to change the type of tab stop. Keep clicking until you see the type of tab stop you want.

4. Click in the bottom half of the ruler where you want the tab stop.

5. Repeat steps 3 and 4 until all tab stops are set.

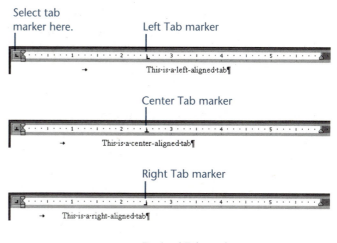

Select tab marker here.

Left Tab marker

This·is·a·left-aligned·tab¶

Center Tab marker

This·is·a·center-aligned·tab¶

Right Tab marker

This·is·a·right-aligned·tab¶

Decimal Tab marker

These·are·decimal-aligned·tabs → 103.456¶
1.0¶
9,999.999999¶

Change Tab Stops

Do either of the following:

- Drag a tab stop and drop it at a new location on the ruler.

- Drag a tab stop and drop it off the ruler to remove it.

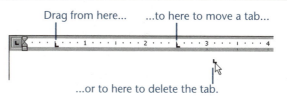

Drag from here...   ...to here to move a tab...

...or to here to delete the tab.

Copying Paragraph Formats

If you've created a paragraph format that you particularly like, you can copy all the formatting to one or more of the other paragraphs in your document.

TIP

If you're going to use a specialized format for several other paragraphs in this document or another, you can have Word save the formatting as a paragraph style, which you can apply to other paragraphs.

SEE ALSO

"Creating Styles from Scratch" on page 72 for information about creating your own styles.

TIP

Word creates new styles for paragraphs that you have formatted in your document, and adds them to the Style list as you create them.

Copy a Format

1. If paragraph marks aren't displayed, click the Show/Hide ¶ button and select the paragraph mark of the paragraph whose format you want to copy.

2. Click the Format Painter button.

3. Drag over the paragraph(s), including paragraph mark(s), to apply the formatting, and then release the button.

Format to be copied from here

Drag over the paragraph to apply formatting.

Copy a Format to Multiple Locations

1. Select the entire paragraph whose format you want to copy, including its paragraph mark.

2. Double-click the Format Painter button.

3. Drag over the paragraph(s) to apply the formatting, and then release the button.

4. Find the next paragraph(s) to be formatted, and repeat step 3.

5. Repeat steps 3 and 4 as desired. Click the Format Painter button to turn it off.

Formatting copied from here...

...can be applied here...   ...and here.

Using Standard Paragraph Formats

Word provides a large selection of predefined paragraph formats, called styles, which you can use to create well-designed documents with consistent formatting. Styles are some of Word's most powerful tools, and to know them is to love them.

TIP

If a style you want to apply has already been used in the document, open the Style list without holding down the Shift key. The list shows the styles that are already in use, and the standard styles: Normal, Headings 1, 2, and 3, and Default Paragraph Font.

SEE ALSO

"Creating Styles from Scratch" on page 72 for information about creating and using styles.

Apply a Heading Style

1. Click in the paragraph you want to format.
2. Open the Style drop-down list box.
3. Select the heading style you want.

Names of styles are shown in their fonts and font sizes.

Click to open list.

Shows style's alignment and font size. ¶ indicates paragraph style.

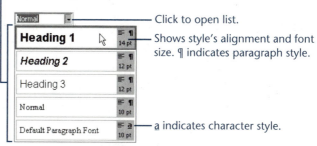

a indicates character style.

Apply a Standard Style

1. Click in the paragraph or select the paragraph(s) you want to format. Make sure that you have the *entire* paragraph selected.
2. Hold down the Shift key and open the Style drop-down list.
3. Select the style you want. (Keep scrolling—it's a long list!)

Shows example of font and size for each style.

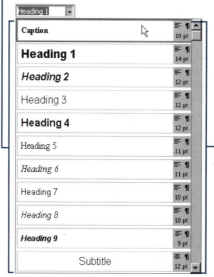

Indicates paragraph alignment and font size.

Creating Lists

Two of the most frequently used and useful types of lists are numbered lists and bulleted lists—and Word practically creates them for you. To create a multi-column list, use Word's table feature.

TIP

Word uses AutoFormat to create numbered and bulleted lists as you type. If the lists aren't being created, you'll need to adjust your AutoFormat As You Type settings.

SEE ALSO

"Controlling Automatic Changes" on page 280 for information about Word's AutoFormat features.

TRY THIS

Different characters create different bullets. Start a list by typing a hyphen or a greater-than (>) sign, add your text, and press Enter.

Create a Numbered List

1 Type the number one (1), a period, a space, and the text of the first list item. Press Enter.

2 Type the rest of the list, pressing Enter at the end of each list item.

3 Press the Backspace key (before typing any more text) to turn off numbering after the last list item.

When you press Enter, Word converts the typed number into automatic numbering and the space into a tab stop.

1 1.→The·first·item·in·the·list¶
2.→The·second·item·in·the·list¶ **2**
3.→The·third·item·in·the·list¶
3 4.→¶

Create a Bulleted List

1 Type an asterisk (*) and a space, and the text of the first list item. Press Enter.

2 Type the rest of the list, pressing Enter at the end of each list item.

3 Press the Backspace key (before typing any more text) to turn off the bullets after the last list item.

When you press Enter, Word converts the asterisk into a bullet and the space into a tab stop.

1 • → The·first·item·in·the·bulleted·list¶
• → The·second·item·in·the·bulleted·list¶ **2**
• → The·third·item·in·the·bulleted·list¶
3 • → ¶

Converting Paragraphs into a List

Sometimes, after you've created a series of paragraphs, you realize that their content would be better expressed and more easily understood as a numbered or bulleted list. You can convert those paragraphs into lists in a matter of seconds. Isn't Word wonderful?

SEE ALSO

"Using Standard Paragraph Formats" on page 39 for information about using styles for special formatting.

"Putting Information in a Table" on page 76 for information about creating lists that have information in columns.

Convert Paragraphs into a Numbered List

1 Select the paragraphs.

2 Click the Numbering button.

Convert Paragraphs into a Bulleted List

1 Select the paragraphs.

2 Click the Bullets button.

Adding Borders to a Paragraph

One way to draw attention to a paragraph is to give it a border of some kind. The type of border you use can define the tone of your message and can help direct your reader's attention to a particular area of your text. A box around a paragraph makes its content stand out from the rest of the text; a bottom border underneath a heading isolates the heading from the following text. Word gives you a variety of quickly applied borders. If you don't like the effect of the one you chose, it's easy to remove it and try another one.

TIP

If you routinely apply a border to one particular type of paragraph, you can include the border as part of the paragraph's style.

Add a Border

1 Click in the paragraph that is to have the border.

2 Open the Borders menu.

3 Click the border you want to apply. The border is applied, and the button name changes to describe that border.

4 Click in a paragraph that is to have the same border.

5 Click the Borders button.

Click to open the Borders menu.

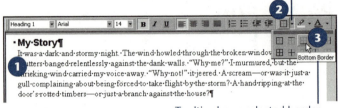

Tooltip shows selected border.

SEE ALSO

"Organizing with Styles" on page 106 for information about defining styles.

"Adding a Line Border Around a Page" on page 272 and "Adding an Art Border Around a Page" on page 273 for information about creating a border for the entire page.

Add Several Different Borders

1 Open the Borders menu.

2 Point at the title bar, drag the Borders menu, and drop it in the document area.

3 Click in a paragraph.

4 Click a border.

5 Repeat steps 3 and 4 until all the borders have been applied.

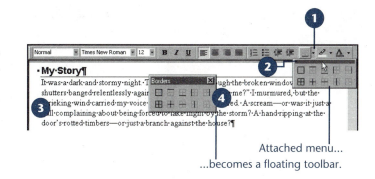

Attached menu...

...becomes a floating toolbar.

Remove a Border

1 Click in the paragraph that has the border you want to remove.

2 Open the Borders menu.

3 Click to turn off the border.

4 Click the Close button.

Turn off a border...

...or turn off all borders at once.

Setting Up the Page

By default, Word creates documents with *portrait* (longer-than-wide) *orientation,* with 1-inch top and bottom margins and 1.25-inch side margins. You can change the orientation to *landscape* (wider-than-long), and can change some or all of the margins, as needed.

TIP

Measure for Measure.
If you have set Word to use units of measure other than inches—centimeters, for example—all settings will be in that unit.

SEE ALSO

"Using Different Layouts in a Document" on page 130 for information about creating different settings for margins and orientation in one document.

The tip on page 253 for information about changing the units of measure.

Change the Margins

1. Choose Page Setup from the File menu.

2. Click the Margins tab if it's not already selected.

3. Change the value for the Top, Bottom, Left, or Right margin.

4. Click OK to close the dialog box.

Preview shows margin settings.

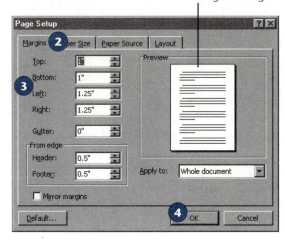

Change the Page Orientation

1. Choose Page Setup from the File menu.

2. Click the Paper Size tab if it's not already selected.

3. Click the Landscape option button.

4. Click OK to close the dialog box.

Preview shows paper orientation.

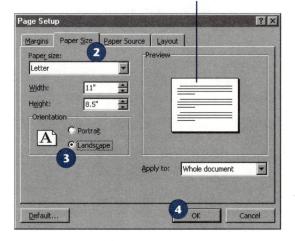

Formatting Unformatted Documents

Electronic mail, text from the Internet, text documents, or Word documents can all look quite unattractive with little or no formatting. Word can apply automatic formatting to these documents for you, freeing you from the drudgery of applying formatting on a paragraph-by-paragraph basis, deleting extra paragraph marks, and so on. The results are usually very professional looking, and all you'll need to do is a quick review to catch anything Word missed. It's a real time-saver.

TIP

Try Again. *If the formatting was not even close to what you wanted, click the Undo button to remove the formatting. Then try it again, but click the Options button and remove some of the formatting options.*

Format the Document

1 Choose AutoFormat from the Format menu.

2 Select the Formatting options.

3 Select a document type.

4 Click OK.

5 Review your document.

AutoFormat converts an unformatted text document...

```
The·Contest¶
¶
We·received·several·different·stories.··Here's·the·first¶
paragraph·of·our·favorite·one.¶
¶
The·sun·shone·brightly·as·I·squinted·across·the·water,··¶
looking·for·a·sail·on·the·distant·horizon.··I·knew·the·¶
ship·would·come,·sooner·or·later.··They·had·promised·to·¶
return·and·I·trusted·them--I·know·not·why.¶
¶
Reviews¶
¶
Dearing·School·of·Fine·Art:·¶
    →    "Greatest·works·I've·read·in·a·long·time!"¶
```

...into a fully formatted Word document.

The·Contest¶

We·received·several·different·stories.·Here's·the·first·paragraph·of·our·favorite·one.¶

The·sun·shone·brightly·as·I·squinted·across·the·water,·looking·for·a·sail·on·the·distant·horizon.·I·knew·the·ship·would·come,·sooner·or·later.·They·had·promised·to·return·and·I·trusted·them—I·know·not·why.¶

Reviews¶

Dearing·School·of·Fine·Art:·¶

    "Greatest·works·I've·read·in·a·long·time!"¶

Word's Behind-the-Scenes Magic

You're typing as fast as you can, trying to meet one of those impossible deadlines. You type *teh* (your usual mistake when you're in a hurry) and, suddenly, it changes to *the*. Then, as if by magic, your straight quotation marks turn into nice curly ones, just like the ones typographers use. And as you type, a red squiggle appears under a misspelled word. A green squiggle appears under a couple of other words. What's going on?

These mysterious and delightful transformations are just a few examples of four features that Word can run behind the scenes while you're working: AutoCorrect, AutoFormat, and Grammar and Spelling checking. As helpful as these features are, you can customize them so that they serve your purposes even better. Later, we'll discuss some ways to do that, along with details of other timesaving features such as AutoText and AutoFormat tables. But right now, let's look at some of the automatic corrections Word can make for you.

Examples of AutoCorrect

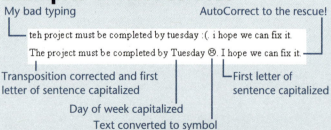

My bad typing — AutoCorrect to the rescue!

teh project must be completed by tuesday :(i hope we can fix it.

The project must be completed by Tuesday ☻. I hope we can fix it.

Transposition corrected and first letter of sentence capitalized

First letter of sentence capitalized

Day of week capitalized

Text converted to symbol

Examples of AutoFormat

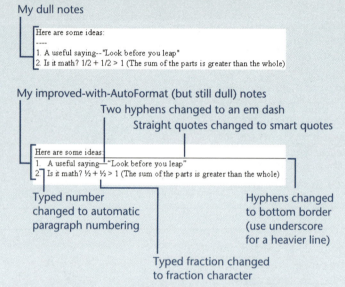

My dull notes

Here are some ideas:
----
1. A useful saying--"Look before you leap"
2. Is it math? 1/2 + 1/2 > 1 (The sum of the parts is greater than the whole)

My improved-with-AutoFormat (but still dull) notes

Two hyphens changed to an em dash

Straight quotes changed to smart quotes

Here are some ideas:
1.   A useful saying—"Look before you leap"
2.   Is it math? ½ + ½ > 1 (The sum of the parts is greater than the whole)

Typed number changed to automatic paragraph numbering

Hyphens changed to bottom border (use underscore for a heavier line)

Typed fraction changed to fraction character

Examples of Grammar Checker

My poor grammar

This is not never a question.?

This is never a question. — My corrected grammar

Examples of Spelling Checker

My poor spelling

Ther are alternatives to most situations.

There are alternatives to most situations. — My corrected spelling

Creating Specialized Documents

IN THIS SECTION

Creating a Letter

Creating a Memo

Creating a Fax Cover Sheet

Creating a Document from Any Template

Creating Your Own Template

Creating a Sequence of Styles; Copying Styles Between Templates

Creating a Template from a Document

Working with Letterhead Stationery

Addressing Mailing Labels and Envelopes

Creating Styles from Scratch

When you don't have the time or the inclination to design your own business documents, you can still produce professional-looking, well-designed letters, memos, faxes, and other types of documents, using either of two powerful tools that Word provides: *wizards* and *templates*. Each provides a variety of design elements, allowing you to concentrate on adding the content. Which one you choose to use depends largely on the desired end result and on how little or how much involvement you want in the design.

A template has the basic elements predesigned and in place: styles that define the formatting, layouts whose placeholders you replace with your own content, information such as date and page number that updates itself automatically, and, in some cases, nifty macros that do special work for you. Use a template as the basis for a document that you create repeatedly, or when you want to add information without making design changes. You can modify a template to tailor it precisely to your needs.

A wizard asks you a series of questions and, based on your responses, designs a document and completes part of it for you. Use a wizard when you want a hand in the design, when you want each new document to be unique, or when you want Word to give you some help in completing the document.

Creating a Letter

The easiest and quickest way to create a letter is to use the Letter Wizard. You make a few choices and fill in a few blanks, and you have everything you need in the letter except your message.

Start the Letter

1 Start a new document.

2 Choose Letter Wizard from the Tools menu.

3 Complete the items on each tab of the wizard.

4 Click OK.

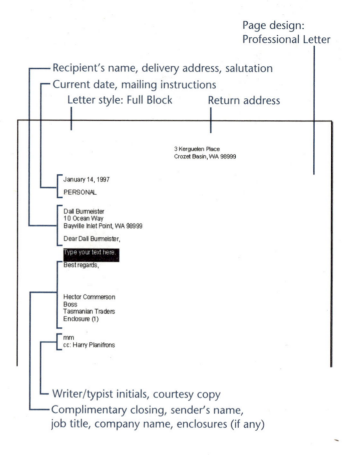

Page design: Professional Letter

Recipient's name, delivery address, salutation

Current date, mailing instructions

Letter style: Full Block   Return address

3 Kerguelen Place
Crozet Basin, WA 98999

January 14, 1997

PERSONAL

Dall Burmeister
10 Ocean Way
Bayville Inlet Point, WA 98999

Dear Dall Burmeister,

Type your text here.

Best regards,

Hector Commerson
Boss
Tasmanian Traders
Enclosure (1)

mm
cc: Harry Planifrons

Writer/typist initials, courtesy copy

Complimentary closing, sender's name, job title, company name, enclosures (if any)

Complete the Letter

1 Replace the placeholder text with your own words.

2 Review any items that were completed by the wizard, and edit as desired.

3 Save the letter.

Right-click item completed by the wizard to see alternative choices.

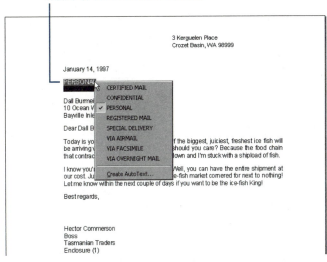

4

Creating a Memo

A well-designed, professional-looking memo can create a good impression and can help convey your message. With the design already created for you, you can concentrate on the content. Word's Memo Wizard lets you customize every memo you create. The wizard remembers your last settings, too, so to create your next memo, you only need to make a few changes.

Start the Memo

1 Choose New from the File menu.

2 Click the Memos tab. The tabs that are available depend on which groups of templates you installed.

3 Double-click the Memo Wizard. If the Memo Wizard isn't on the Memos tab, rerun Word's installation and include the Memo Wizard in the installation.

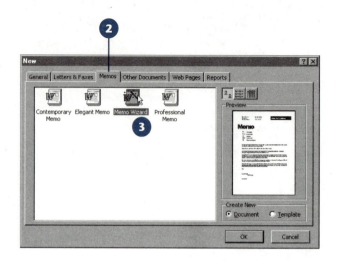

TIP

If your memo is longer than one page, you can use the wizard to set up running heads.

TIP

If you want to make several changes to the items inserted by the wizard, rerun the wizard from the Tools menu and make your changes. The changes in the wizard will be made in your document.

SEE ALSO

"Creating a Letter" on page 48 for information about modifying the fields completed by the wizard.

"Creating a Running Head" on page 115 for information about creating a running head.

"Adding Components" on page 294 for information about installing Word components.

Complete the Memo

1 Work your way through the wizard, choosing settings and clicking Next to move to the next screen of choices. When you've made all your settings, click Finish.

2 Type your content to complete the memo.

Memo style: Professional

Title text   Current date, recipients' names, courtesy copy, sender's name, subject, priority

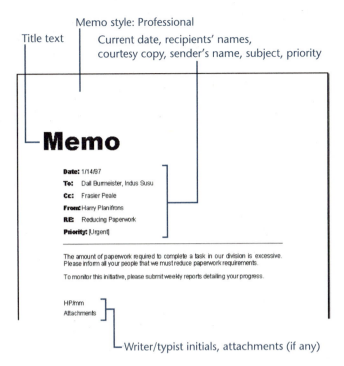

Memo

Date: 1/14/97
To: Dall Burmeister, Indus Susu
Cc: Frasier Peale
From: Harry Planifrons
RE: Reducing Paperwork
Priority: [Urgent]

The amount of paperwork required to complete a task in our division is excessive. Please inform all your people that we must reduce paperwork requirements.

To monitor this initiative, please submit weekly reports detailing your progress.

HP/mm
Attachments

Writer/typist initials, attachments (if any)

4

Creating a Fax Cover Sheet

Word gives you several options for sending faxes, depending on your faxing method. If you use a fax machine, it's a good idea to create a printed fax cover sheet to identify recipient, sender, and so on. You can use one of Word's three fax templates to create a fax cover sheet with the look you like. You can also use Word's Fax Wizard if you send your faxes through a computer rather than using a fax machine.

Start the Fax

1. Choose New from the File menu.

2. Click the Letters & Faxes tab.

3. Double-click one of the fax templates.

Contemporary Fax

Elegant Fax

Professional Fax

SEE ALSO

"Creating Your Own Template" on page 58 for information about storing frequently used information in a template.

"Faxing Several People" on page 222 for information about sending faxes directly from Word using the Fax Wizard, and creating cover sheets for multiple recipients.

Add Your Information

1 Complete the cover sheet by replacing the placeholder information and adding any notes.

2 Print and send the document.

Type your return address, phone number, and fax number.

Replace with your company's name.

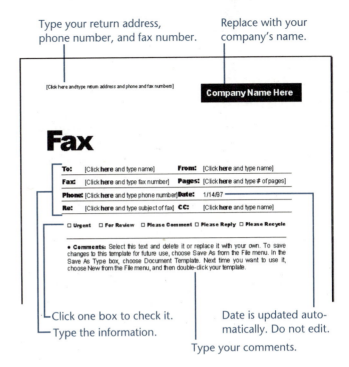

Click one box to check it.

Type the information.

Date is updated automatically. Do not edit.

Type your comments.

4

So Many Ways to View It

Normal View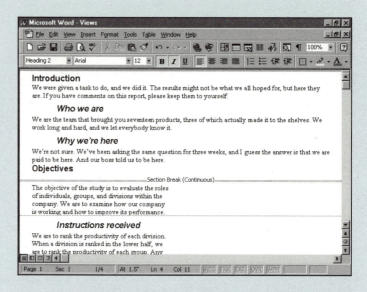

Word gives you several ways to view your document as you work on it, and you'll find that your efficiency increases and your work becomes easier when you use the correct view for the task at hand. You can use the View menu or the four view buttons at the bottom left of the window to switch between views.

The standard working view, Normal view, is designed for speed of entry and editing. It's based on the commercial publishing technique of creating galleys: you place the text and other elements in one long, continuous column that flows from one page to the next, and deal with placement after you've ironed out any content problems.

Page Layout View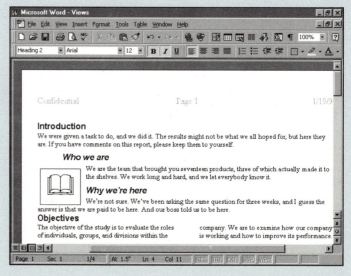

When you're concerned about the look of your document—placement of pictures, arrangement of columns, and so on—switch to Page Layout view to see an accurate onscreen representation of the page. You can use the Zoom Control drop-down list on the Standard toolbar to change the magnification of the page and how much of it you can see and work with on the screen.

Outline View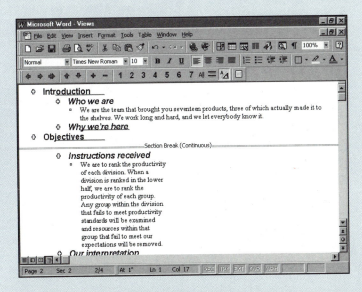

If you use an outline to create your work, you know how valuable it is for organizing information. Outline view displays your document as an outline, with the paragraph formatting defining the levels of the outline. By default, Word's standard heading styles have corresponding outline levels—Heading 1 is level one, Heading 2 is level two, and so on—and other paragraph styles, such as Normal, are treated as regular text. You can use Outline view to organize your topics before you start writing, or you can use it to reorganize an existing document.

Online Layout View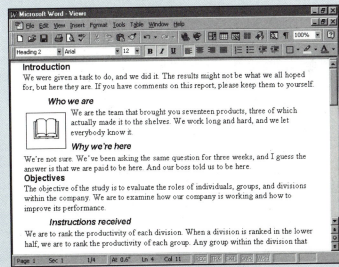

This view is exclusively for *reading* documents on line. Although all the elements are in place as they are in Page Layout view, the font size, line length, and page length all change to improve the onscreen readability of the document. Online Layout view is "tree-saver view"—use it when you want to read, but not print, an online document.

There's More...

Although these four views are the ones you'll probably use most frequently, there are other views and options: Print Preview, Full Screen view, Document Map, draft font, picture placeholders, and more. We'll discuss them in the tasks where their use is the most relevant.

4

Creating a Document from Any Template

A template provides the basis for a document: the layout and styles, and even the toolbars and AutoText. Word provides you with a variety of templates, and you can purchase or download additional templates, use templates created by the company you work for, or create your own templates.

TIP

If you use the same template frequently but you modify some of the elements each time you create a particular document, turn the modified document into a template so that you don't have to make the same changes every time.

SEE ALSO

"Sharing Templates" on page 204 for information about using workgroup templates.

Start a New Document

1. Choose New from the File menu.

2. Click the tab that contains the template. The tabs that are available depend on which groups of templates you installed.

3. Double-click the template.

Click a view button to change the way the templates are listed.

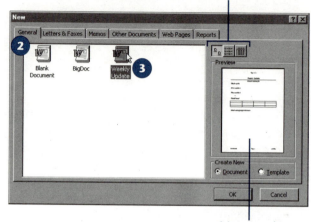

Most templates display a preview.

Word has a built-in macro virus-protection feature that will alert you if there are macros, custom menus or toolbars, or shortcuts in the template or document you're using. If you feel certain that your templates or documents will never be in danger of becoming infected with a virus, you can turn off this feature—but do so at your own risk. Word template viruses are becoming increasingly common. Choose Options from the Tools menu, and turn off the Macro Virus Protection check box on the General tab.

SEE ALSO

"Creating Your Own Template" on page 58 for information about creating your own template.

"Getting More Help" on page 296 for information about connecting to the Microsoft Office Web site, where you can download additional templates.

Complete the Document

1 Edit the document to complete it.

2 Save and distribute the completed document.

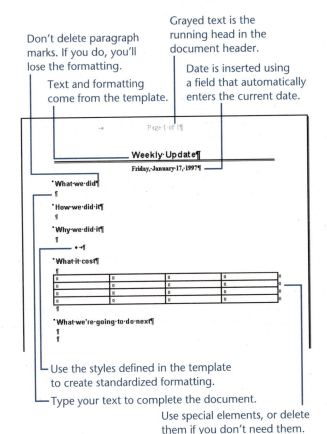

Don't delete paragraph marks. If you do, you'll lose the formatting.

Grayed text is the running head in the document header.

Text and formatting come from the template.

Date is inserted using a field that automatically enters the current date.

Use the styles defined in the template to create standardized formatting.

Type your text to complete the document.

Use special elements, or delete them if you don't need them.

4

Creating Your Own Template

When you use any of Word's templates, or any generic template with lots of placeholders, you can save yourself the time and effort of making changes each time you create a document by customizing the template and then saving it as your own template. And if you save a preview of your template, Word will display its picture when you select the template in the New dialog box.

SEE ALSO

"Creating a Document from Any Template" on page 56 for information about starting a document based on a template.

Create a Sample Document

1 Start a new document based on the template that you want to replicate most closely.

2 Modify the document:

◆ Replace the placeholder text with any text that will be common to all documents based on your new template.

◆ Add any new text or other page elements.

◆ Redefine or create your own paragraph and character styles.

Leave placeholders for text that will be different in every document.

Add your own text.

Replace placeholders with text that will be the same in every document.

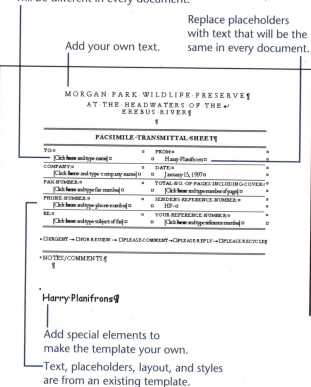

Add special elements to make the template your own.

Text, placeholders, layout, and styles are from an existing template.

Save the Preview Picture

1 Choose Properties from the File menu, and click the Summary tab.

2 Turn on the Save Preview Picture check box.

3 Click OK.

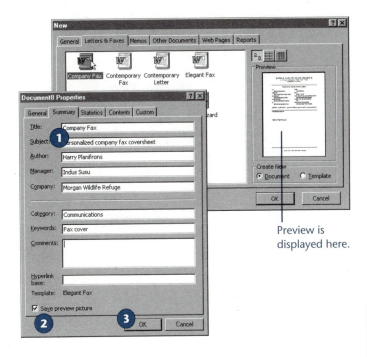

Preview is displayed here.

Create the Template

1 Click the Save button on the Standard toolbar.

2 Select Document Template.

3 Open the appropriate folder.

4 Type a new name for the template.

5 Click Save, and close the template.

The folder you store the template in determines which tab the template appears on in the New dialog box.

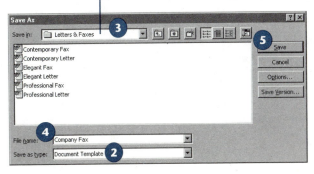

Customizing a Template

Although a template is not dynamic in the same way that a wizard is dynamic, neither is a template a completely static tool. If your needs change or if you want to tweak a design, you can make substantial changes to a template. To do this, you open the existing template for editing, and make your changes.

TIP

Most paragraph styles are based on the Normal style, so when you make any changes to the Normal style, the changes also take place in these other styles.

SEE ALSO

"Creating Styles from Scratch" on page 72 for information about using styles in your documents.

Open the Template

1. Choose Open from the File menu.

2. Select Document Templates.

3. Navigate to the Templates folder to locate the template. Open a subfolder to locate the template, if necessary.

4. Double-click to open the template.

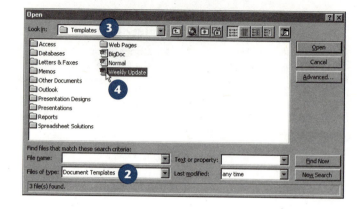

TIP

If you installed Word as part of Office 97 and you used the default folders, the Templates folder is in the Microsoft Office folder, which is in the Program Files folder. If you can't find the Templates folder, choose Options from the Tools menu, and click the File Locations tab. The path to the Templates folder is listed in the User Templates entry. If you can't see the whole path, double-click the User Templates entry to display the Modify Location dialog box. Note the path, and click Cancel.

TRY THIS

In Normal view, choose Options from the Tools menu, enter 0.7" in the Style Area Width box on the View tab, and click OK. You'll see the name of each paragraph style next to the paragraph.

Modify the Template

1 Make changes to the content, formatting, and layout.

2 Save and close the template.

Change text that will be the same in every document.

Use AutoText entries in running heads to insert fields that will update automatically.

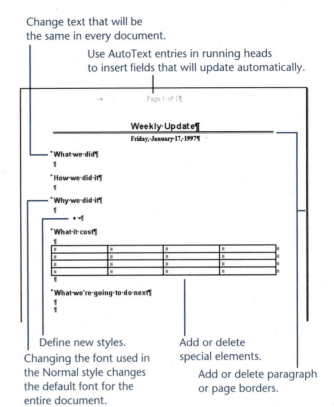

Define new styles.
Changing the font used in the Normal style changes the default font for the entire document.

Add or delete special elements.

Add or delete paragraph or page borders.

4

Creating a Template from a Document

You can easily convert an existing document into a template, and use that template to create documents with the same basic layout and design. And if some or all of the same content is repeated in all documents of this type, you can include the content in the template so that you don't have to type it every time you create the document.

TIP

If your template folders aren't displayed when you select Document Template, the path to your templates is probably incorrect. Choose Options from the tools menu, and set the correct path to the User Templates on the File Locations tab.

Convert a Document into a Template

1 Open the document that you want to use as the basis for your template.

2 Choose Save As from the File menu.

3 Select Document Template. Word immediately switches you to the default Templates folder.

4 Double-click a folder to save your template in that folder and to have the template appear on the corresponding tab of the Open dialog box, or stay in the default Templates folder to have your template appear on the General tab.

5 Type a new name for the template.

6 Click Save.

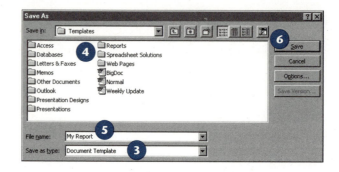

Finding a Field. *To see the names and codes for all the fields in your document, press Alt+F9. Press Alt+F9 again to hide the field codes.*

"Creating Styles from Scratch" on page 72 for information about using styles in your document.

"Inserting Frequently Used Information" on page 96 for information about Word's AutoText feature.

Customize the Content

1 Turn on the Show/Hide ¶ button on the Standard toolbar if it's not already turned on.

2 Edit the document so that it contains only the material you want to appear in all the documents you'll create from this template.

3 Click the Save button on the Standard toolbar.

Delete text that won't appear in every document.

Use a date that updates automatically.

Use AutoText in running heads to insert information that updates automatically.

Leave paragraph marks as placeholders.

→ Page 1 of 12¶

Report·to·the·Manager¶
Friday,·January·17,·1997¶

Introduction¶
We·are·given·a·task·to·do·,·and·we·did·it.·The·results·might·not·be·what·we·all·hoped·for,·but·here·they·are.·If·you·have·comments·on·this·report,·please·keep·them·to·yourself.¶

Who·we·are¶
We·are·the·team·that·brought·you·seventeen·products,·three·of·which·actually·made·it·to·the·shelves·.·We·work·long·and·hard,·and·we·let·everybody·know·it.¶

Why·we're·here¶
We're·not·sure.·We've·been·asking·the·same·question·for·three·weeks,·and·I·guess·the·answer·is·that·we·are·paid·to·be·here.·And·our·boss·told·us·to·be·here.¶

What·we·do¶
Sometimes·we·work·hard.·Other·times·we·sit·around·and·eat·pizza.·Whatever·looks·like·fun·we·do,·whatever·looks·boring·we·assign·to·others.¶

Objectives¶
The·objective·of·the·study·is·to·evaluate·the·roles·of·individuals,·groups,·and·divisions·within·the·company.·We·are·to·examine·how·our·company·is·working·and·how·to·improve·its·performance.¶

Instructions·received¶
We·are·to·rank·the·productivity·of·each·division.·When·a·division·is·ranked·in·the·lower·half,·we·are·to·rank·the·productivity·of·each·group.·Any·group·within·the·division·that·fails·to·meet·productivity·standards·will·be·examined,·and·resources·within·that·group·that·fail·to·meet·our·expectations·will·be·removed.¶

This text appears in every document.

→ Page 1 of 1¶

Report·to·the·Manager¶
Friday,·January·17,·1997¶

Introduction¶
¶

Who·we·are¶
¶

Why·we're·here¶
¶

What·we·do¶
¶

Placeholder paragraph marks contain formatting for inserted text.

Paragraphs are formatted based on the style definitions saved in the template.

4

Creating a Sequence of Styles

A design often dictates that one style is always followed by another specific style. You can set up the first style so that after you complete the first paragraph and press Enter, the next paragraph you create uses the style specified as the following style. If you then specify another style to follow the second style, Word will be doing most of the work of choosing styles for you. If you've specified a sequence that doesn't quite work, you can always change some of the paragraph styles yourself.

Select the First Style

1. Choose Style from the Format menu.

2. Select the style to be changed.

3. Click Modify.

Preview of selected style

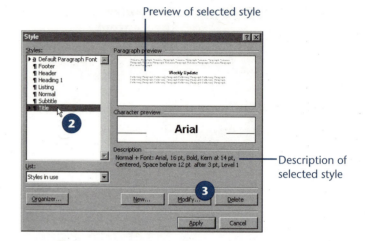

Description of selected style

Specify a Sequence

1. Select a following-paragraph style.

2. Turn on the Add To Template option to save the changed style in the document template (rather than in the active document only).

3. Click OK.

4. Click Close to close the Style dialog box.

Changing the Design

After you've created a document based on an existing template, you might decide that you prefer the design of another template style. You can easily change the look of your document by switching between templates.

Switch Templates

1 Choose Style Gallery from the Format menu.

2 Click Document if it's not already selected.

3 Select the template you want to switch to.

4 Decide whether you like the way your document will look if you apply the new template, or try other templates.

5 Click OK to accept the change.

Preview of document using the current template (Professional Memo)

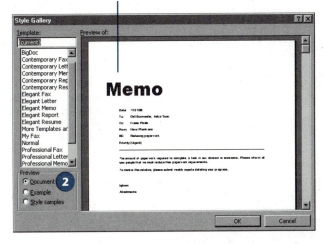

Preview of same document using a different template (Elegant Memo)

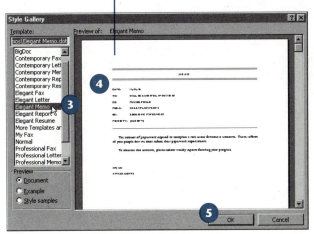

4

Copying Between Templates

If you have a template that contains styles, custom toolbars, macros, or AutoText, and you'd like to use those elements in another template, you can copy them quickly and easily using the Organizer.

TIP

You can select several items at one time in the list you're copying from by holding down the Ctrl key and clicking each item.

SEE ALSO

"Customizing a Template" on page 60 for information about using the Open dialog box to open a template.

Start the Organizer

1 Start a document based on the template into which you want to copy items from another template.

2 Choose Templates And Add-Ins from the Tools menu to display the Templates And Add-Ins dialog box.

3 Click the Organizer button.

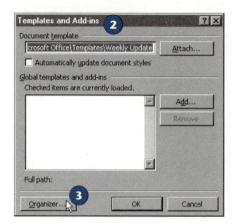

Select and Copy Items

1 Select the template into which you'll insert the copied items.

2 Click the Close File button.

3 Click the Open File button, and open the template you want to copy from.

4 Select the items to be copied.

5 Click Copy.

6 Click a different tab, and copy any other items.

7 Click Close when you've finished.

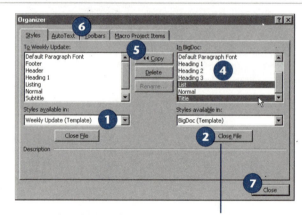

The Close File button becomes the Open File button after you close the template.

Designing for Your Letterhead

If you use letterhead stationery, you can modify your letter template to allow space for the letterhead. If your printer allows it, you can tell Word to print the first page of your letter on letterhead, and subsequent pages on standard paper.

TIP

If you're using the Letter Wizard, you can have the wizard automatically leave room for the letterhead.

If the letterhead is on the side rather than at the top of the page, you can insert a text box into your template to accommodate the letterhead's position.

SEE ALSO

"Creating a Letter" on page 48 for information about using the Letter Wizard, and "Writing Text Sideways" on page 270 for information about rotated text in text boxes.

Leave Space for a Letterhead

1. Open the template if it's not already open.

2. On a sheet of letterhead, measure the distance from the top of the page to the top of the first paragraph.

3. Subtract the height of the top margin.

4. Select the first paragraph, choose Paragraph from the Format menu, enter the resulting distance in the Space Before box, and click OK.

5. Save the template.

Specify Paper Options

1. Choose Page Setup from the File menu, and click the Paper Source tab.

2. Select the source for your letterhead paper.

3. Select the source for your standard paper.

4. Click OK.

5. Save and close the template.

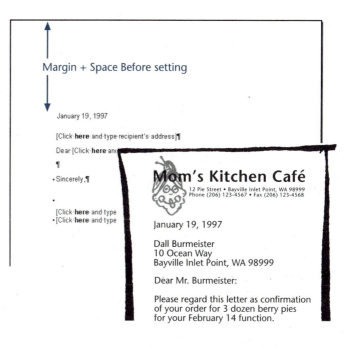

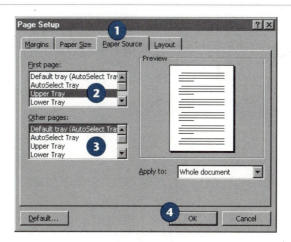

Creating Your Own Letterhead

Instead of using preprinted letterhead stationery, you can create a letterhead in your template, and the letterhead will be printed whenever you use that template. By placing the letterhead in the first-page header, you eliminate the need to worry about margins, positioning of the first paragraph of the letter, and so on.

Create a First-Page Header

1. Open the template if it's not already open.

2. Choose Page Setup from the File menu, and click the Layout tab.

3. Turn on the Different First Page option.

4. Click OK.

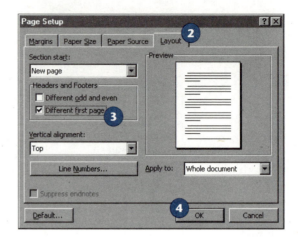

Create a Letterhead

1. Choose Header And Footer from the View menu.

2. Create your letterhead, using paragraph and font formatting.

3. Click the Close button on the Header And Footer toolbar.

4. Save and close the template.

Use a distinctive font.

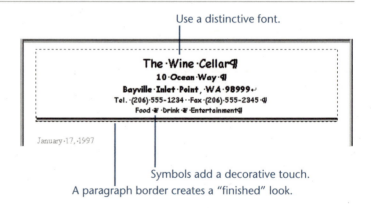

Symbols add a decorative touch.

A paragraph border creates a "finished" look.

Creating Mailing Labels

If you use stick-on mailing labels that you print from your computer, you can easily set up Word so that you can print on just about any size label. You can also choose to print a whole sheet of labels with the same address on each label, or print a single label on a sheet.

SEE ALSO

"Addressing Mailing Labels" on page 180 for information about creating labels using Word's Mail Merge feature.

TRY THIS

Set up to print a full page of labels. Click the New Document button, and save the document with the labels. Whenever you need a page of labels for that address, just print the document.

Add the Address

1. In your document, select the entire inside address.

2. Choose Envelopes And Labels from the Tools menu, and click the Labels tab.

Click to use another address from your address book.

Turn on to use the address from the user information you supplied to Word.

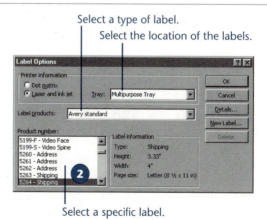

Preview of current label

Click to print only one label. Specify the label by its row and column numbers.

Click to print the same address on an entire sheet of labels.

Turn on to include bar code if address includes ZIP code and label is large enough for a bar code.

Select a Label

1. If you're not set up for the label you want to use, click the Options button.

2. Select a label, and click OK.

3. Click Print to print your labels, or click New Document to create a document laid out to print the labels later.

Select a type of label.

Select the location of the labels.

Select a specific label.

4

Addressing an Envelope

When you've taken the time and trouble to create a professional-looking letter or other document, you don't want to ruin the good impression with a hand-written envelope! Word makes it easy for you to create crisp, businesslike printed envelopes. You can easily include your return address, and, in the United States, you can even add a postal bar code.

TIP

To change your user information, choose Options from the Tools menu, click the User Information tab, and change the information.

SEE ALSO

"Addressing Envelopes" on page 182 for information about creating envelopes using Word's Mail Merge feature.

Add the Address

1. In your document, select the entire delivery address.

2. Choose Envelopes And Labels from the Tools menu, and click the Envelopes tab.

Delivery address from your letter

Adds address and envelope layout to the beginning of the current document.

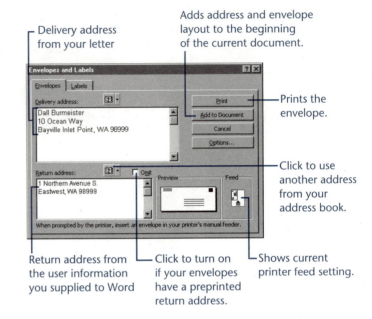

Prints the envelope.

Click to use another address from your address book.

Return address from the user information you supplied to Word

Click to turn on if your envelopes have a preprinted return address.

Shows current printer feed setting.

Change the Setup

1 Click the Options button, and click the Envelope Options tab.

2 Change the settings as desired.

3 Click OK.

Turn on to include bar code based on ZIP code.

Select an envelope size, or click Custom Size to define a nonstandard size.

Customize the delivery and return-address fonts and locations.

Prints FIM-A code (available only if Delivery Point Barcode check box is turned on).

Change the Printer Settings

1 Click the Print button in the Envelopes And Labels dialog box to test-print an envelope.

2 If the envelope doesn't print correctly, open the Envelopes And Labels dialog box again, click the Options button, click the Printing Options tab, and change the settings to correct the problem.

Click a picture to change envelope's orientation.

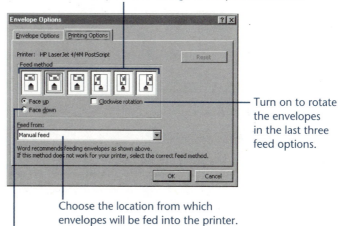

Turn on to rotate the envelopes in the last three feed options.

Choose the location from which envelopes will be fed into the printer.

Click if address was printed on the wrong side of the envelope.

4

Creating Styles from Scratch

Whether you are creating a new template, modifying an existing one, or including a special element in a document, you can create a style and define all its elements in a few quick steps.

SEE ALSO

"Making Text Stand Out" on page 232 for information about setting text effects for characters, adding animation, and changing text color.

"Creating an Inline Heading" on page 271 for information about creating character styles.

TIP

When you save the document or the template, the style is saved in the template.

Create a Style

1. Choose Style from the Format menu, and click the New button in the Style dialog box.

2. Name the style and select a style type.

3. Select a style whose properties you want to start with, and select a style to follow it.

4. Turn on the Add To Template option to add the style to the current template, or turn the option off to add the style to the current document only.

5. Click Format, and choose Font.

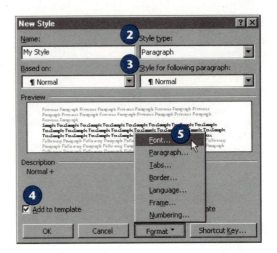

Set Up the Font

1. Select a font, style, and size.

2. If you want any underlining, select its style.

3. Select a font color.

4. Turn on the options for any special effects.

5. Click OK.

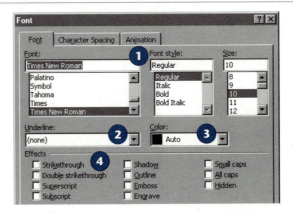

SEE ALSO

"Creating a Sequence of Styles" on page 64 for information about specifying following styles.

"Copying Between Templates" on page 66 for information about transferring styles between templates and documents.

"Organizing With Styles" on page 106 for information about modifying existing styles.

"Keeping Track of Your Styles" on page 108 for information about printing descriptions of your styles.

"Controlling Page Breaks" on page 109 for information about setting a paragraph's line- and page-breaking options.

"Numbering Headings" on page 155 for information about setting numbering formatting.

"Creating Margin Notes" on page 262 for information about using a style's frame settings.

"Fine-Tuning a Document" on page 276 for information about controlling paragraph text flow over pages.

"Changing What Gets Proofed" on page 285 for information about setting proofreading criteria.

Set Up the Paragraph

1. Click the Format button in the New Style dialog box, and choose Paragraph.

2. Select a paragraph alignment.

3. Select an outline level if the paragraph is a heading.

4. Specify any indentation.

5. Specify any first-line paragraph indent or outdent (hanging indent).

6. Specify how much space you want before or after the paragraph.

7. Select the line spacing.

8. Click OK.

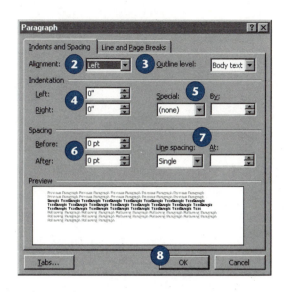

Complete the Style

1. Click the Format button, and apply any other formatting to the style. Click OK to close the New Style dialog box.

2. Click the Close button to close the Style dialog box.

4

Creating a Complex Document

IN THIS SECTION

Creating and Customizing Tables

Creating and Modifying Large Tables

Adding Clip Art to Documents

Modifying Pictures

Inserting Frequently Used Information

Creating Your Own Commands

Adding Commands to Your Menus

Customizing Toolbars

A complex document is one that contains more than just text. In the not-too-distant past, creating a complex document was an expensive and time-consuming proposition. You'd collect all the separate pieces—your typed text, photographs, illustrations, tables, and so on—and take them to a typographer. Type shops were the only businesses that could afford the equipment that was able to combine text, pictures, and other elements. Now, using the power of Word, you can create complex documents with very little effort. You can organize information in tables and then customize the tables in countless ways. You can combine pictures with text, and you can modify the pictures by changing their size, turning them into watermarks behind your text, cropping out the parts you don't want, and so on.

You can also make Word work harder so that you don't have to. You can create a shortcut so that Word will insert a long word or an entire phrase when you type only four characters. You can record a series of steps that you have repeat to accomplish a frequently executed task, make that recording into a single command, and watch Word execute the steps for you.

In this section, you'll see that creating a complex document is a lot less complex than it used to be!

Putting Information in a Table

Tables are a superb way to organize almost any kind of information, and Word makes it so easy. You can actually draw your table with a little onscreen pencil. Then you put your content in the cells, adding more rows and columns if you need to, or changing their sizes to make everything fit. Your table can contain numbers, words, pictures and hyperlinks. You can add borders, colors, and other special effects to create a very professional look.

	Fruit	Vegetable
Option 1	Apple	Potato
Option 2	Orange	Corn
Option 3	Pear	Eggplant

TIP

You can remove a boundary you've just drawn by clicking the Undo button on the Standard toolbar.

Create a Table

1 Click the Tables And Borders button to display the Tables And Borders toolbar.

2 Click the Draw Table button if it's not already turned on.

3 Drag the pencil pointer to create the outline of the table, and release the mouse button.

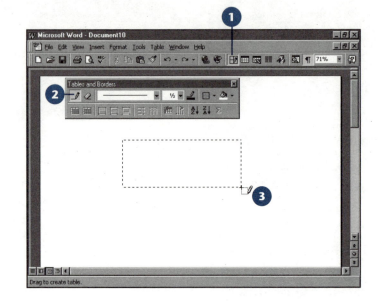

Add Columns and Rows

1 Drag the pencil pointer from the top table boundary to the bottom table boundary, and release the mouse button to create a column.

2 Drag the pencil pointer from the left or right table boundary to the opposite table boundary, and release the mouse button to create a row.

Draw vertical lines to create all the columns you need.

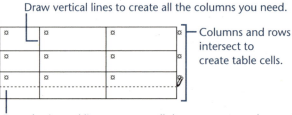

Columns and rows intersect to create table cells.

Draw horizontal lines to create all the rows you need.

TIP

Control Your Tab! *To insert a tab inside a table cell, press Ctrl+Tab.*

TRY THIS

If the table is going to have several rows, all with the same dimensions, create only the first couple of rows. You can add new rows automatically by pressing the Tab key when you're in the last (bottom right) cell of the table.

SEE ALSO

"Changing the Size of Columns and Rows" on page 80 for information about adjusting the size of table cells.

"Changing the Look of a Table" on page 82 for information about adjusting the appearance of table cells.

Add Content

1. Click the Draw Table button to turn it off.

2. Click in the first cell and insert your content.

3. Press the Tab key to move to the next cell, and add your content. Press Enter only to start a new paragraph inside a table cell. Continue using the Tab key to complete your table.

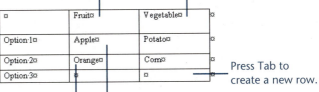

Press Tab to move to the next cell.

Press Tab to move to the first cell in the next row.

Press Tab to create a new row.

Press the Up or Down arrow key to move to the previous or next row.

Press Shift+Tab to move to the previous cell.

Format a Table

1. Click anywhere inside the table.

2. Click the Table AutoFormat button on the Tables And Borders toolbar to display the Table AutoFormat dialog box.

3. Select a format, or select (None) to remove all formatting.

4. Turn formatting options on or off, as desired.

5. Click OK.

Preview the selected format.

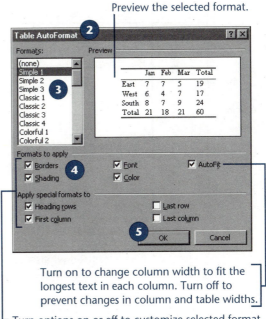

Turn on to change column width to fit the longest text in each column. Turn off to prevent changes in column and table widths.

Turn options on or off to customize selected format.

Anatomy of a Table

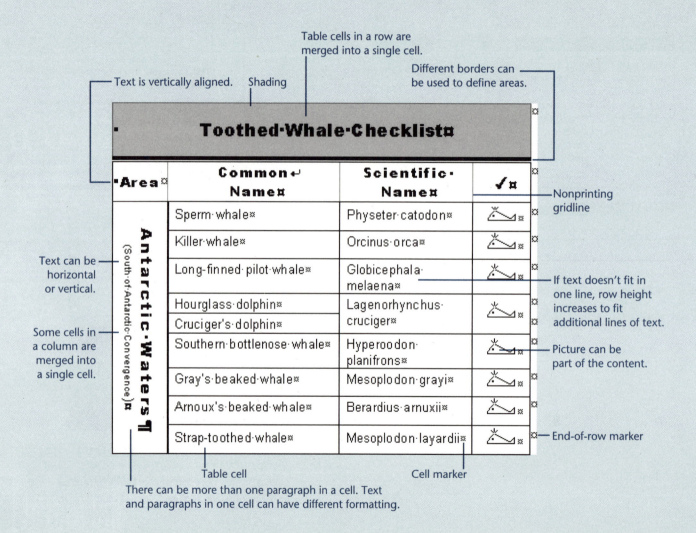

Table cells in a row are merged into a single cell.

Text is vertically aligned.

Shading

Different borders can be used to define areas.

Toothed·Whale·Checklist¤

·Area¤

Common↵
Name¤

Scientific·
Name¤

✓¤

Nonprinting gridline

Text can be horizontal or vertical.

Some cells in a column are merged into a single cell.

Antarctic·Waters¶
(South·of·Antarctic·Convergence)¤

Sperm·whale※

Killer·whale※

Long-finned·pilot·whale※

Hourglass·dolphin※

Cruciger's·dolphin※

Southern·bottlenose·whale※

Gray's·beaked·whale※

Arnoux's·beaked·whale※

Strap-toothed·whale※

Physeter·catodon※

Orcinus·orca※

Globicephala·melaena※

Lagenorhynchus·cruciger※

Hyperoodon·planifrons※

Mesoplodon·grayi※

Berardius·arnuxii※

Mesoplodon·layardii※

If text doesn't fit in one line, row height increases to fit additional lines of text.

Picture can be part of the content.

End-of-row marker

Table cell

Cell marker

There can be more than one paragraph in a cell. Text and paragraphs in one cell can have different formatting.

Customizing a Table Layout

A Word table can be more than just a grid of equally sized rows and columns. If you want a table heading to span several columns, you can simply draw new cell boundaries and erase old ones. You can combine two cells into one larger one, or split one cell into two smaller ones.

Menu Options		Week 3
	Fruit	Vegetable
Option 1	A: Apple	Corn
	B: Banana	
Option 2	Orange	Potato
Option 3	Pear	Eggplant

TIP

Cell Division? *Create all your columns and rows, and make any adjustments to them before you combine or split individual cells. When cells are combined, your computer understands Word's logic for identifying adjacent cells, but to us mortals the logic can be convoluted and confusing.*

Divide One Cell into Two

1 Display the Tables And Borders toolbar if it's not already displayed.

2 Click the Draw Table button.

3 Drag from one cell boundary to the opposite boundary and release the mouse button. Add as many cell boundaries as needed.

4 Click the Draw Table button to turn it off.

Combine Two Cells into One

1 Click the Eraser button.

2 Drag from one cell boundary to the opposite boundary and release the mouse button. Delete as many cell boundaries as needed.

3 Click the Eraser button to turn it off.

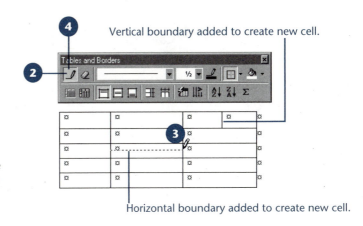

Vertical boundary added to create new cell.

Horizontal boundary added to create new cell.

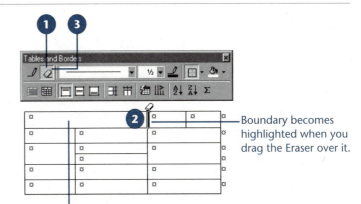

Boundary becomes highlighted when you drag the Eraser over it.

Boundary removed to merge cells.

5

Changing the Size of Columns and Rows

You can change the width of any columns and the height of any rows. If, when you drew your table, you wanted your rows and columns to be of equal dimensions but they turned out to be different sizes, a click of a button will even them up for you. You can also manually adjust the dimensions of rows and columns, or even of individual cells.

No.	Name	Job Title
1.	Rick	Problem-solver
2.	Roberta	Monarch of her domain
3.	Pierre	Irrigator, cultivator
4.	Baiser	Vintner

TIP

If the row height isn't tall enough to fit all your text (including all paragraph formatting), the row height adjusts automatically.

Standardize Column Width

1. Select the columns that are to be the same width.

2. Click the Distribute Columns Evenly button.

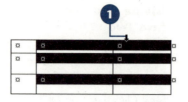

Columns are now the same width.

Standardize Row Height

1. Select the rows that are to be the same height.

2. Click the Distribute Rows Evenly button.

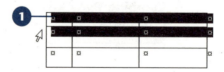

Rows are now the same height.

TIP

If some cells are selected when you resize a row or column, only the selected cells are affected. To resize several rows or columns, make sure that all the cells in the rows or columns are selected; to resize all cells in a column or row, make sure you have the insertion point in the table, not in a selection.

TIP

You can adjust the column width but you can't adjust the row height with the mouse when you're in Normal view.

SEE ALSO

"Putting Information in a Table" on page 76 for information about automatically formatting tables, and "Modifying a Large Table" on page 88 for information about using different techniques to modify a large table.

Adjust Column Width

1. Click anywhere in the table so that no cells are selected.

2. Move the mouse pointer over the right boundary of a column until the mouse pointer changes into a resizing pointer.

3. Drag the boundary to the left to decrease the column width or to the right to increase the column width.

Boundary is moved to new location, changing the width of both columns.

Adjust Row Height

1. Move the mouse pointer over the bottom boundary of a row until the mouse pointer changes into a resizing pointer.

2. Drag the boundary up to decrease the row height or down to increase the row height. Use the measurements on the vertical ruler to make precise adjustments.

Boundary is moved to new location, changing the height of the top row only.

Changing the Look of a Table

Although the easiest and quickest way to give your table a distinctive, professionally designed look is to use the Table AutoFormat feature, you can also create your own custom design by adding borders and shading. You can place a border around the entire table, of course, but you can also add borders to individual cell boundaries, or to groups of cells, to emphasize and delineate their contents. The borders can be formatted to your design and will print with the document. You can also add shading to cells for extra emphasis.

	Unit 1	Unit 2	Unit 3
Part 1102	$13.50	$17.75	$19.90
Part 1103	$16.50	$16.65	$22.10
Part 1104	$18.32	$20.12	$25.21
Part 1105	$20.07	$21.01	$32.50

Add a Border

1 Switch to Page Layout view if you're not already in it, and display the Tables And Borders toolbar if it's not already visible.

2 Select the cells that are to have the same type of border.

3 Select a line style.

4 Select a line weight.

5 Select a line color.

6 Select a border style.

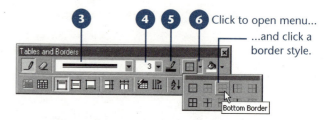

Click to open menu...

...and click a border style.

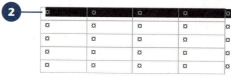

Add an Individual Cell Border

1. Select a new line style, weight, and color for the border.

2. Click the Draw Table button.

3. With the pencil pointer, draw along the cell boundary to add the border.

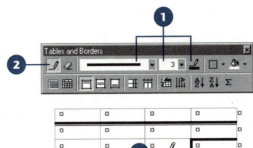

Boundary becomes highlighted when you draw along it with the Draw Table Pointer.

Add Shading

1. Select the cells that are to have the same type of shading.

2. Select the shading.

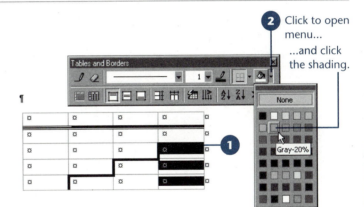

Click to open menu...

...and click the shading.

Changing the Look of Text in a Table

As you create and modify a table, you might want to adjust the look of the text. For example, you might want your table headings to be bigger and bolder than the text in the individual cells. You might want to change the alignment of the headings, or of the text in the cells. You might even want text to run vertically instead of horizontally. Here's how.

Change the Look

Do any of the following:

♦ Select the cells that are to have the same format and apply the formatting.

♦ Apply formatting to the paragraph or paragraphs within a cell.

♦ Apply formatting to text within a paragraph in a cell.

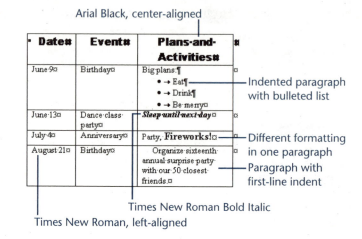

Arial Black, center-aligned

Indented paragraph with bulleted list

Different formatting in one paragraph

Paragraph with first-line indent

Times New Roman Bold Italic

Times New Roman, left-aligned

Turn Your Head. *When you change the direction of the text, all your formatting is rotated too. Several of the buttons on the Formatting and the Tables And Borders toolbars rotate to reflect the text rotation, but line spacing and other para- graph formatting can still be confusing. If you're disoriented, rest your head on your right shoulder to look at text that runs from top to bottom, or on your left shoulder for text that runs from bottom to top. Now it should almost make sense!*

To change the alignment of ver- tical text, use the alignment buttons on the Formatting toolbar.

"Customizing Paragraphs" on page 32 for information about applying paragraph and text formatting.

"Set the Alignment" on page 86 for information about setting the alignment of the table on the page.

Set the Vertical Alignment

1 Display the Tables And Borders toolbar if it's not already visible.

2 Select the cells to be changed.

3 Click an alignment button.

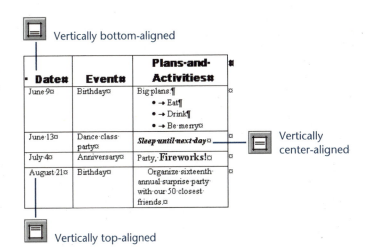

Vertically bottom-aligned

Vertically center-aligned

Vertically top-aligned

Set the Text Direction

1 Select the cells to be changed.

2 Click the Change Text Direction button. (You might have to click the button two or three times to get the text direction you want.)

3 Adjust the height of the rows if necessary, and change the text alignment as desired.

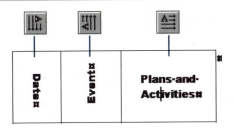

5

Changing the Location of a Table

When you draw a table, you can position it anywhere in your document. When you create a table using the Insert Table command, though, the table's left edge will align with the left margin of your document or, in a multicolumn document, with a column's left boundary. You can change the table's alignment as desired, or you can indent the table from the left edge.

It was a dark and stormy night. The wind howled through the broken windows.

The sun shone brightly as I squinted across the water, looking for a sail on the distant horizon.

SEE ALSO

"Creating a Large Table" on the facing page for information about creating a table using the Insert Table command.

Set the Alignment

1. Click anywhere in the table so that no cells are selected.

2. Choose Cell Height And Width from the Table menu.

3. Click the Row tab if it's not already selected.

4. Select an alignment.

5. Click OK.

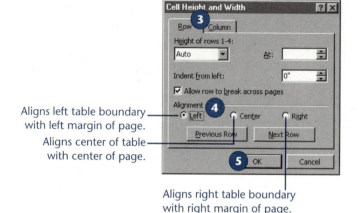

Aligns left table boundary with left margin of page.

Aligns center of table with center of page.

Aligns right table boundary with right margin of page.

Indent the Table

1. Choose Cell Height And Width from the Table menu.

2. Select the left-alignment option.

3. Enter a distance for the left indent.

4. Click OK.

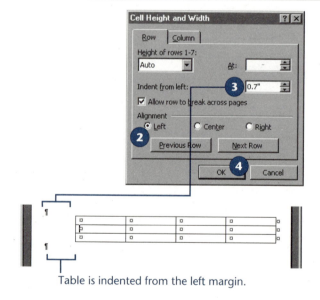

Table is indented from the left margin.

Creating a Large Table

Although it's fun to use the Draw Table pencil, when you need to create a really large table you undoubtedly don't want to draw dozens—or even hundreds—of rows and columns. You don't have to. If you know the dimensions of the table, you can use the Insert Table command to instantly create a table with the correct number of rows and columns. If the table is so long that it spans pages, you can have the table headings repeat at the top of the table on each page.

TIP

All Change! *If you want to set all the cells to the same column width, row height, or alignment, choose Select Table from the Table menu to apply the change to all cells before you choose the Cell Height And Width command.*

Create a Table

1. Choose Insert Table from the Table menu.

2. Specify the dimensions of the table.

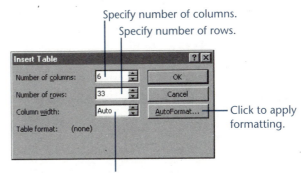

Specify number of columns.

Specify number of rows.

Click to apply formatting.

Specify width of all columns, or keep Auto setting to have column widths automatically calculated so that table fits exactly between left and right margins.

Specify Headings

1. Select the entire first row.

2. Choose Headings from the Table menu.

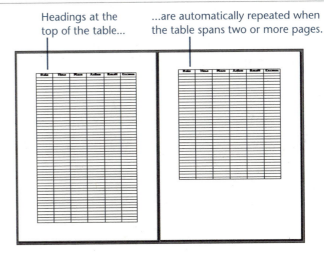

Headings at the top of the table...

...are automatically repeated when the table spans two or more pages.

5

Modifying a Large Table

Word gives you a variety of ways to modify your tables. You'll find that some techniques work best for small tables, while others are geared to larger tables. When you're working on a large table, you probably want changes to happen quickly and automatically. It takes just a few clicks to add or delete rows or columns and to have new rows and columns take the same formatting as adjacent rows and columns.

Add Rows

1. Select the same number of rows as you want to insert above the first selected row.

2. Click the Insert Rows button on the Standard toolbar.

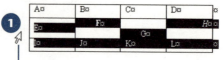

2 Insert Table button becomes Insert Rows button when rows are selected.

1 Click to select a row, or drag to select multiple rows.

Add Columns

1. Select the same number of columns as you want to insert at the left of the selection. (However, if you want to add a column to the right of the *rightmost* column, see "Add a Column to the Right Side of a Table" on the facing page.)

2. Click the Insert Columns button on the Standard toolbar.

2 Insert Table button becomes Insert Columns button when columns are selected.

Column selection arrow appears when the mouse pointer is moved over the top boundary of the table. Click to select a column, or drag to select multiple columns.

SEE ALSO

"Putting Information in a Table" on page 76 for information about adding a row to the bottom of a table.

"Format a Table" on page 77 for information about using AutoFormat.

"Changing the Look of Text in a Table" on page 84 and "Changing the Location of a Table" on page 86 for information about changing a table's alignment.

Add a Column to the Right Side of a Table

1. Turn on the Show/Hide ¶ button if it's not already turned on.

2. Select all the end-of-row markers.

3. Click the Insert Columns button on the Standard toolbar.

Use column selection arrow to select all the end-of-row markers.

Delete Rows

1. Select the rows to be deleted, and right-click.

2. Choose Delete Rows from the shortcut menu.

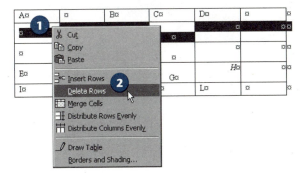

Delete Columns

1. Select the columns to be deleted, and right-click.

2. Choose Delete Columns from the shortcut menu.

5

Adding Clip Art

The Clip Gallery contains a variety of clip-art pictures that you can include in your Word documents. When you add a piece of clip art, it becomes part of the document. If you decide that you don't like it, you can replace it or delete it.

TIP

Art Installation. *If you don't see the Clip Gallery listed, you can install it by rerunning your installation.*

TIP

Art Lite? *Clip art is set to float over the text layer. To place clip art on the text layer, choose Picture from the Format menu, and turn off the Float Over Text option on the Position tab.*

SEE ALSO

"Modifying a Picture" on page 92 for information about modifying clip-art images.

Add Clip Art

1 Click in your document where you want to place the clip art.

2 Point to Picture on the Insert menu and choose Clip Art from the submenu.

3 Click the Clip Art tab if it's not already selected.

4 Locate the clip art you want to use.

5 Click Insert.

Click the clip art you want.

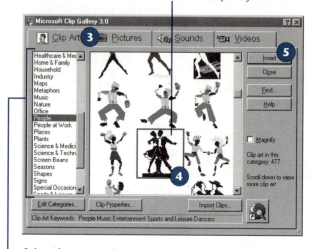

Select the appropriate category, or select All Categories to scroll through the entire collection.

Replace Clip Art

1 Double-click the clip art.

2 Select another piece of clip art, and click Insert. The newly selected clip art replaces the previous clip art.

Double-click to display the Clip Gallery.

Delete Clip Art

1 Click the clip art.

2 Press the Delete key.

Adding a Picture

You can add different types of pictures—photographs and drawings, as well as clip art—provided the pictures are stored as files and you have the proper file converters for the formats. Word comes with a variety of converters, and many graphics programs supply their own converters.

TIP

To see a list of file formats that you can use, open the Files Of Type drop-down list in the Insert Picture dialog box. Only the converters that have been installed are shown.

SEE ALSO

"Wrapping Text Around an Object" on page 248 for information about wrapping text around a picture.

"Creating a Floating Caption" on page 258 and "Creating a Watermark" on page 274 for information about layering graphics and text.

Insert a Picture

1 Click in your document where you want to insert the picture.

2 Point to Picture on the Insert menu, and choose From File from the submenu.

3 Select a picture from the Insert Picture dialog box.

4 Click Insert. If you see only the outline of a picture instead of the whole picture, choose Options from the Tools menu and turn off the Picture Placeholder option on the View tab.

Navigate through your folders to locate the picture.

Click to change view of file information.

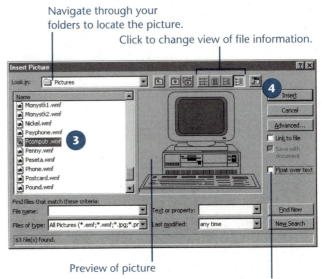

Preview of picture

Turn on to layer graphics and text, or turn off to place the picture on the same layer as the text.

Modifying a Picture

It's a rare occurrence when an inserted picture fits your document perfectly, so you'll often need to modify an image by resizing it or cropping it. Depending on how you'll be printing the image, you might need to make other changes so that the picture will look its best when printed. Word has a toolbar to help you with all these modifications, and it pops up whenever you select a picture.

> **TIP**
>
> *When you make changes to a picture, the changes are made in Word, not in the original picture file.*

> **TIP**
>
> *If you click the Close button on the Picture toolbar, the toolbar won't pop up when you select a picture. To display the Picture toolbar, right-click any toolbar and choose Picture from the shortcut menu.*

Resize a Picture

1. Click the picture.

2. Place the mouse pointer over a sizing handle, drag the picture's boundary, and drop it when the picture is the correct size.

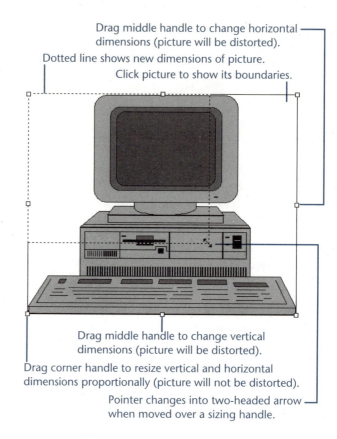

Drag middle handle to change horizontal dimensions (picture will be distorted).

Dotted line shows new dimensions of picture.

Click picture to show its boundaries.

Drag middle handle to change vertical dimensions (picture will be distorted).

Drag corner handle to resize vertical and horizontal dimensions proportionally (picture will not be distorted).

Pointer changes into two-headed arrow when moved over a sizing handle.

Crop a Picture

1 Click the picture if it's
not already selected.

2 Click the Crop button
on the Picture toolbar.

3 Place the mouse pointer
over a sizing handle,
drag the picture's
boundary, and drop it
when the picture is the
correct size.

4 Click the Crop button
to turn it off.

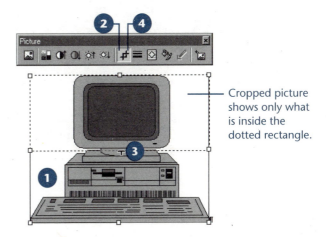

Cropped picture
shows only what
is inside the
dotted rectangle.

Change the Image

1 Click the picture if it's
not already selected.

2 Click the Image Control
button on the Picture
toolbar.

3 Click the type of image
you want.

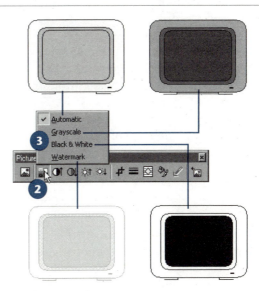

5

Alien Objects

Several accessory programs come with Word, and others are already installed on your computer, thanks to Windows. These accessory programs are designed specifically to create and insert special content—graphs and mathematical equations, for example. Because such content is *alien* to Word—that is, Word doesn't have the ability to work directly with graphs, complex equations, and whatever else these programs insert—it resides as a separate object that is contained in Word. By categorizing this type of content as an object, Word doesn't need to know much about it: Word simply reserves the space for the object and lets the accessory program take care of creating and editing it.

However, Word isn't limited to objects from these accessory programs. Word can contain objects from other major programs such as Microsoft Excel and PowerPoint, and it can even contain objects from Word. And not only can you create an object by using any of these programs in Word, you can also add an object that was previously created—that is, you can use a document file as the source of an object.

This might sound scary, but it's not. Word has made it easy to work with any of these programs and their objects. You can run many of the programs with a click of a toolbar button or from a simple menu command. When one of these programs is running, you're still working in Word, but the accessory program's tools have been added to Word. You'll see changes to the menus, and maybe an extra toolbar or two. When you've finished with the accessory program, Word comes back as its old self, and you have some new content in your document.

If you've ever added a piece of clip art to a document, you've already created an object from a file—it's just that Word did most of the work for you. So if Word does so much of the work for you, why do you need to know about objects? For one thing, Word often refers to them—you "insert objects," "format objects," "edit objects." And, despite the benefits of using objects—and there are many—you can also run into some problems. If your document is used on another computer, for example, an inserted object can be displayed but can't be edited unless that computer has the same program as (or a program similar to) the one that created the object. That means, for instance, that you can read the data in an Excel worksheet object, but if you want to edit the data, Excel must be installed on your computer.

So work with objects with a little care and the knowledge that they're from other programs, and you'll find the added power to achieve exactly the results you want. We'll be working with objects throughout the rest of this book because it's often the best, fastest, and easiest way to get things done.

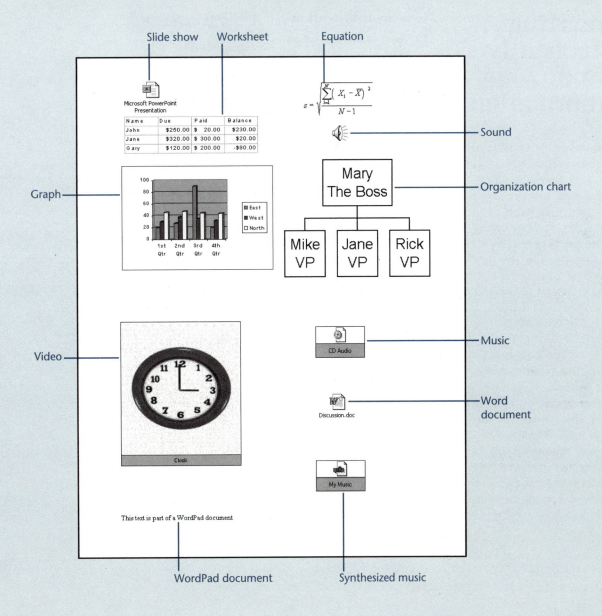

Slide show   Worksheet   Equation

Sound

Organization chart

Graph

Music

Video

Word document

WordPad document   Synthesized music

5

Inserting Frequently Used Information

If you type the same words or phrases repeatedly, you can save yourself a lot of time (especially if you use long scientific terms or difficult names) by saving those words or phrases as AutoText. You give the AutoText a short name—a nickname of sorts—and when you type the nickname, or just the first few letters of it, Word is ready to insert the long word or phrase into your document. The information can be anything that you can put in a document—text, pictures, even fields. Word comes already equipped with numerous AutoText entries for some of the most common types of information.

Store the Information

1. Select all the information to be included in the entry.

2. Point to AutoText on the Insert menu, and choose New from the submenu.

3. Accept the suggested name or type a new name for the entry, and click OK. (The name must contain at least four characters for the AutoComplete feature to work.)

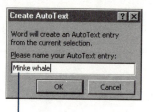

Enter the name you'll type to retrieve the information.

Insert Frequently Used Information

1. Start typing the AutoText name.

2. When the AutoComplete tip appears with the AutoText entry, press Enter.

3. If the AutoComplete tip doesn't appear, turn on the AutoComplete option on the AutoText tab of the AutoCorrect dialog box and repeat steps 1 and 2.

...displays the AutoComplete tip with the beginning of the AutoText entry.

minke whale (Balaenoptera acut...

This is a report on the mink

Typing part of the name...

Type sund *and press Enter to insert the AutoComplete suggestion,* Sunday. *Word has a long list of built-in AutoText entries that frequently show up as AutoComplete entries.*

The AutoText list is very dynamic...it lists different entries depending on which template you're using, what you're working on, and where you're working on it. If you see the AutoText entry listed on the first submenu, you're set up to insert AutoText entries from a specific template. To see all the entries, choose AutoText from the submenu, select Normal from the Look In list, and click OK.

"Copying Between Templates" on page 66 for information about copying AutoText entries into specific templates.

"Creating a Running Head" on page 115 for information about inserting AutoText into headers and footers.

Insert Less Frequently Used Information

1 Point to AutoText on the Insert menu.

2 Point to Normal on the submenu.

3 Choose the AutoText name from the submenu.

Click to delete an AutoText entry or to change which open template is used.

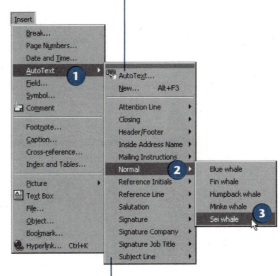

Most AutoText entries are either built-in or are created as you complete a wizard.

Creating Your Own Commands

As a document becomes longer and more complex, you often find yourself executing a specific series of actions over and over again. This can be very tedious and time-consuming. If you record each step of that series of actions, thus creating a macro, you can then run the whole series as if it were a single command. However—and this is important—macros have difficulty figuring out where the mouse is in text, so your mouse actions are limited to choosing commands and clicking buttons. Use only keyboard actions for selecting text and moving the insertion point.

SEE ALSO

"Adding Commands to Your Menus" on page 100 for information about assigning a macro to a menu.

Set Up a Macro

1 Click in the document where you want to execute the first of the repetitive actions.

2 Point to Macro on the Tools menu, and choose Record New Macro from the submenu.

3 Type a name for the macro. The macro name must begin with a letter; it can be up to 80 characters long but can't contain any spaces or symbols.

4 Select where the macro will be stored:

♦ In the Normal.dot template so that it's available to all documents

♦ In the current document so that it's available only in this document

♦ In the template the document is based on so that it's available to all documents based on that template

5 Type a description so that you'll know what the macro does.

6 Click OK.

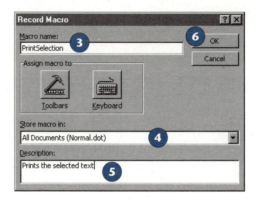

Record Your Actions

Execute whatever actions you want to record as a macro. The illustration at the right is just one example. To replay the macro, point to Macro on the Tools menu, choose Macro from the submenu, and double-click the macro you want to run.

1 Work with text.

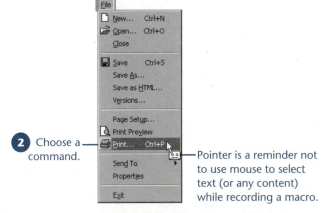

2 Choose a command.

Pointer is a reminder not to use mouse to select text (or any content) while recording a macro.

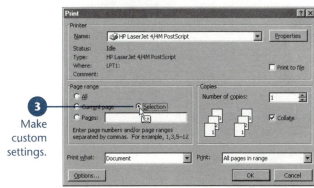

3 Make custom settings.

5 Click to stop recording after you've recorded all actions.

4 Click to pause recording before you take any actions that are not part of the macro. Click again to resume recording.

5

Adding Commands to Your Menus

Word displays the most common commands on its menus, but you can put additional commands on any menu to simplify your work. Also, if you create your own commands by recording macros, you can place the macros, with appropriate descriptive names, on a menu.

Add a Command

1 Choose Customize from the Tools menu, and click the Commands tab.

2 Select a category to find the command.

3 Drag the command up to the menu you want it on, wait for the menu to open, and drop the button where you want it to appear.

4 Click the menu name to close the menu.

Drag from here...

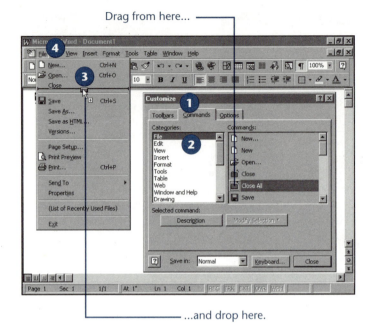

...and drop here.

SEE ALSO

"Creating Your Own Commands" on page 98 for information about creating a macro.

"Customizing the Toolbars" on page 102 and "Quickly Applying Standardized Formatting" on page 110 for information about assigning an item to a toolbar or key combination.

TIP

Although you can't use spaces in a macro name when you create the macro, you can use spaces in the name you give the macro when you place it on a menu.

Add a Macro

1 Select Macros in the Categories list.

2 Select the macro to be added.

3 Drag the macro to the menu you want it on, wait for the menu to open, and drop the button where you want it to appear.

Rename a Menu Item

1 Right-click the command or the macro name in the menu where you placed it.

2 Change the text in the Name box.

3 Click outside the menu to close it.

4 Click Close to close the Customize dialog box.

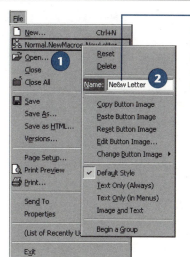

Use spaces to separate words, and add an ampersand (&) before the letter you want to use as the access key (the underlined letter in a command).

5

Customizing the Toolbars

As you work with different types of materials, you might find yourself wishing that some of Word's toolbars could be arranged more conveniently for your purposes. Well, guess what... they can! You can change the placement of tools on a toolbar, move tools from one toolbar to another, and add new tools to a toolbar.

Specify What's Changed

1. Choose Customize from the Tools menu, and click the Toolbars tab.

2. Check the boxes for any toolbars you'll be using.

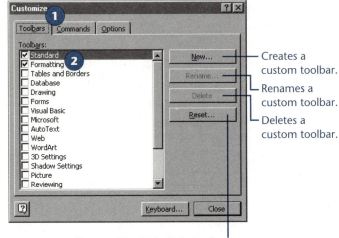

Creates a custom toolbar.

Renames a custom toolbar.

Deletes a custom toolbar.

Restores Word's built-in toolbars to their original settings.

Add a New Item

1. Click the Commands tab.

2. Select the category that contains the item to be added.

3. Click the command, drag it, and drop it on the toolbar.

Drag from here...   ...and drop button here.

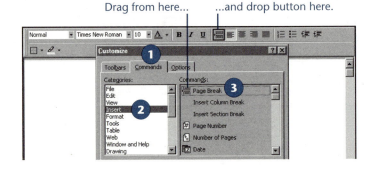

Move a Button or a List Box

1 Point to a button or a list box that you want to move.

2 Drag it and drop it at the new location on the same toolbar or on a different one.

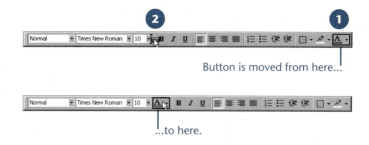

Button is moved from here...

...to here.

Modify a Button

1 Right-click the button.

2 Use the menu to change the button.

3 Click Close in the Customize dialog box.

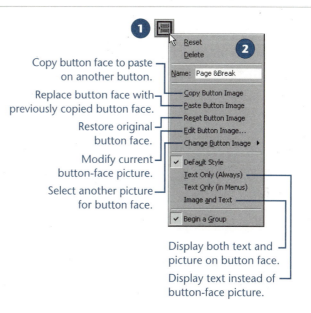

Copy button face to paste on another button.

Replace button face with previously copied button face.

Restore original button face.

Modify current button-face picture.

Select another picture for button face.

Display both text and picture on button face.

Display text instead of button-face picture.

5

Creating a Long Document

IN THIS SECTION

Working with Styles and Toolbars

Creating a Double-Sided Document

Working with Running Heads

Inserting All or Part of a Word Document

Reorganizing a Long Document

Using Different Layouts

Creating Chapters or Sections

Tracking Versions

Creating a Summary

Working with Master Documents and Subdocuments

What's the difference between creating a long document and creating a short document? Well, a long document can give you a bigger headache, for one thing! If your long document is simply pages and pages of text with absolutely nothing else—no headings, no graphics, no sections—the only difference between it and a short document might be that you'd add page numbers. Many long documents, however, contain elements such as tables, graphics, several levels of headings, footnotes, and so on. In addition, a long document is often made up of several smaller documents, or *subdocuments*, which might be written by several authors.

A long document involves a lot of planning, many revisions, and careful tracking of versions. Unexpected things happen: for example, the marketing department changes the name of the product you're writing about. The original name appears in about a zillion places in a report that you're presenting at a big meeting in the morning. It'll take all night to make those changes. Don't panic! You won't have to work until the wee small hours, because Word can make those changes for you in just a few minutes.

Use Word's powerful tools to help you manage and produce a long document, and your long-document headaches will be long gone!

Organizing with Styles

Paragraph styles do more than quickly apply formatting to paragraphs: they also assign an *outline level* to each paragraph in a document. Word uses these levels to understand how you're organizing the document—which paragraphs are headings, which are sub-headings, and which are text. You can use Word's defined outline hierarchy, or you can create your own structure by defining the outline levels for your styles.

SEE ALSO

"Copying Between Templates" on page 66 for information about transferring styles between templates and documents.

"Creating Styles from Scratch" on page 72 for information about creating styles.

Create a Heading Hierarchy

1 Switch to Normal View if you're not already in it.

2 Choose Options from the Tools menu, and click the View tab.

3 Specify 0.7" in the Style Area Width box.

4 Turn on the Wrap To Window option.

5 Click OK.

6 Scroll through the document, adjusting style assignments:

- Apply appropriate heading styles to heading paragraphs.

- Apply appropriate body-text styles to body-text paragraphs.

- Apply appropriate special styles (captions, for example) to special paragraphs.

Styles are listed next to their paragraphs.

Drag left or right to resize the style area.

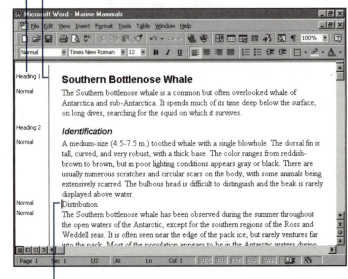

Apply an appropriate heading style to create a hierarchy.

Define a Style as a Heading

1 Select a paragraph containing the style to be defined as a heading.

2 Choose Paragraph from the Format menu.

3 Select an outline level.

4 Click OK.

5 Click the style name to select it, and press Enter.

6 Click OK in the Modify Style dialog box to update the style.

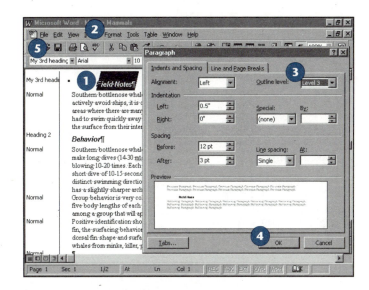

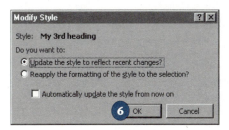

Keeping Track of Your Styles

If you have difficulty remembering all the styles in your document and exactly what their formatting is, you can print a list of the styles and their descriptions. You can also print a list of the shortcut keys that you assigned to the styles.

Print a List of Styles

1 Choose Print from the File menu to display the Print dialog box.

2 In the Print What list, select Styles.

3 Click OK.

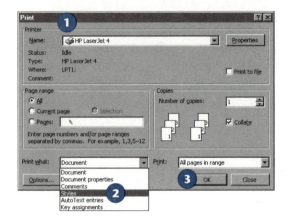

Body Text

    Normal + Space after 6 pt

Body Text 2

    Normal + Line spacing double, Space after 6 pt

Caption

    Style for Next Paragraph: Normal

    Normal + Bold, Space before 6 pt after 6 pt

Default Paragraph Font

    The font of the underlying paragraph style +

Print a List of Shortcut Keys

1 Choose Print from the File menu.

2 In the Print What list, select Key Assignments.

3 Click OK.

Key Assignments for Document Template:
C:\Program Files\Microsoft Office\Templates\BigDoc.dot

    Alt+Ctrl+Shift+T   Title Style

Global Key Assignments

    Alt+Ctrl+Shift+L   List   Style

Controlling Page Breaks

In a multipage document, the design often dictates where one page ends and the next one starts. You can let Word control the page breaks automatically, or you can specify where you want the pages to break.

SEE ALSO

"Creating Chapters or Sections" on page 132 for information about starting text on the next odd-numbered page.

"Fine-Tuning a Document" on page 276 for information about refining line breaks and page breaks.

Modify a Style

1. Select a paragraph containing the style to be modified.

2. Choose Paragraph from the Format menu.

3. Click the Line And Page Breaks tab.

4. Choose the pagination options you want.

5. Click OK.

6. Click the Style name in the Style box on the Formatting toolbar to select it, and press Enter.

7. Click OK in the Modify Style dialog box to update the style.

Prevents paragraph from breaking across pages.

Prevents single line of paragraph by itself at top or bottom of page.

Creates a page break before paragraph.

Keeps paragraph on same page as next paragraph.

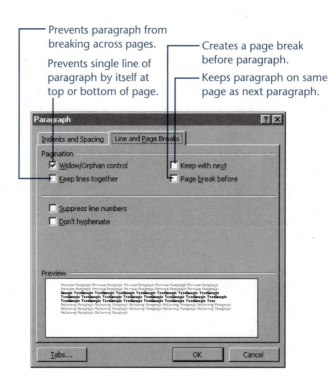

Insert Page Breaks

1. Click in the document where you want the page break to occur.

2. Press Ctrl+Enter.

Page break is inserted at the insertion point.

In areas where there are many Southern bottlenose whales, or when a Southern bottlenose whale had to swim quickly away to avoid a ship, there may be discarded squid mantles floating on the surface from their interrupted meal. ¶

————————Page Break————————

Positive identification should be based on the size, color, presence of scars, the thick dorsal fin, the surfacing behavior, and, if observed closely, the bulbous head and short beak. The dorsal fin shape and surfacing behavior are the best ways to distinguish Southern bottlenose whales from minke, killer, pilot, and Amoux's beaked whales. ¶

6

Quickly Applying Standardized Formatting

Paragraph styles are useful in any document, but they're a necessity in a long document, where each type of paragraph must be formatted consistently throughout the document. Styles are real time-savers, too: just choose a style, and all the formatting is applied at once. You can save even more time and effort by assigning frequently used styles to a custom toolbar, and assigning shortcut keys to less frequently used styles.

Create a Toolbar

1. Choose Customize from the Tools menu.

2. Click the Toolbars tab.

3. Click the New button.

4. Type a name for the toolbar.

5. Select where you want to save the toolbar.

6. Click OK.

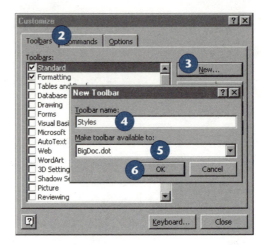

Add a Style

1. Click the Commands tab.

2. Select Styles.

3. Click a style you want to add to the toolbar.

4. Drag the style and drop it on the toolbar.

TIP

Save a new toolbar in Normal.dot to make it available to all documents; save it in the document template (if there is one) to make it available to documents based on that template; or save it in the document to make it available only in the current document.

TIP

Don't use a key combination that's already been assigned unless you want to delete that assignment and assign the key combination to your own use.

SEE ALSO

"Keeping Track of Your Styles" on page 108 for information about printing a listing of your shortcut-key assignments.

Label the Button

1 Click the Modify Selection button.

2 Type the button caption, and press Enter.

3 Keep adding styles and labeling buttons until you've assigned all the styles you want to the toolbar.

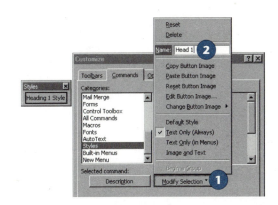

Assign Shortcut Keys

1 In the Customize dialog box, click the Keyboard button.

2 Specify where you want the shortcut saved.

3 Select Styles.

4 Select the style that will have the shortcut keys.

5 Click in the Press New Shortcut Key box, and press the key combination.

6 Click Assign. Continue assigning shortcut keys to other styles.

7 Click Close when you've finished.

8 Click Close to close the Customize dialog box.

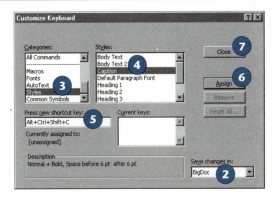

Storing Toolbars

Custom toolbars are great timesaving tools, but if you create and display several of them along with some of Word's own toolbars, your work area keeps shrinking. You can organize the toolbars, both Word's and your own, by stacking some of them in a single row.

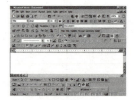

SEE ALSO

"Using Toolbars" on page 22 for information about displaying and hiding toolbars.

Stack the Toolbars

1 Drag a toolbar on top of a docked toolbar.

2 Drag other toolbars on top of the same toolbar.

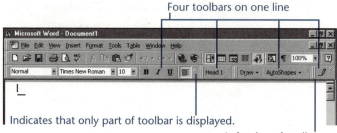

Four toolbars on one line

Indicates that only part of toolbar is displayed.

Left edge of toolbar

Access Stacked Toolbars

1 Double-click the left edge of the toolbar.

2 Use the floating toolbar.

3 Double-click the title bar to return the toolbar to its stacked position.

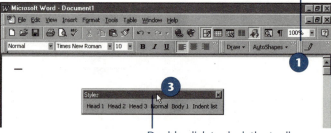

Double-click to float the toolbar.

Double-click to dock the toolbar.

Preparing for a Bound Document

Whichever method you use to bind your long document, whether you place it in a three-ring binder or have it professionally bound, you'll need to allow a large enough *gutter* to accommodate the binding. Word will add this gutter for you and, if you are going to print on both sides of the paper, will add the extra space to the appropriate side of the page.

SEE ALSO

"Setting Up the Page" on page 44 for information about setting margins.

"Creating a Double-Sided Document" on page 114 for information about working with double-sided documents.

Add a Gutter

1 Choose Page Setup from the File menu.

2 Click the Margins tab.

3 Set the gutter value equal to the room required for the binding.

4 Click OK.

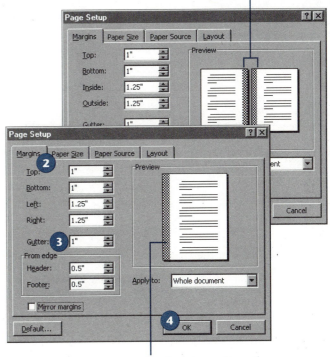

Gutter is always on the inside edge of a double-sided document.

Preview shows size and location of the gutter.

Creating a Double-Sided Document

When you're printing a long document, you can give it a professional look (and help conserve a few trees) by formatting it to print on both sides of the paper. When set up for double-sided printing, Word differentiates between the front (odd-numbered, or *recto*) side of a page and the back (even-numbered, or *verso*) side. You can then print the document on a duplex printer; or you can print it single-sided and then photocopy it to be double-sided; or you can print the front sides, reload the paper, and print the back sides.

> **TIP**
>
> **Double Trouble.** *Some printers, especially color printers, are not suited for double-sided printing. Check your printer manual before you try double-sided printing, or you could create a big bad mess. You could even damage your printer.*

Set Up a Double-Sided Page

1. Choose Page Setup from the File menu.

2. Click the Margins tab.

3. Turn on the Mirror Margins check box.

4. Set the margins for the inside and outside of the page instead of for the left and right sides.

5. Add a gutter setting if you're going to bind the document.

6. Click OK.

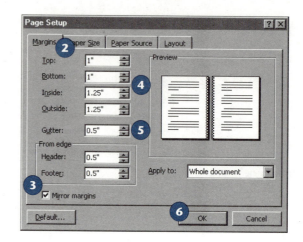

Print Both Sides on a Single-Sided Printer

1. Choose Print from the File menu.

2. Select Odd Pages.

3. Click OK.

4. Remove the printed front sides and restack the paper in the printer so that the back of the first page is printed first.

5. Choose Print from the File menu.

6. Select Even Pages, and click OK.

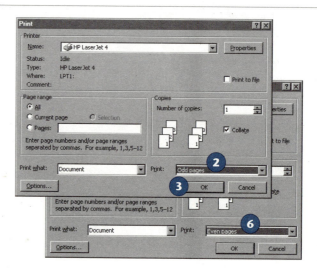

Creating a Running Head

A running head is little message or identifier that appears at the top or bottom of a page, above or below the normal text area. All you need to do is create a running head once, and Word will automatically place it on the page. For the sake of consistency, we're using the term "running head" for the heading itself, and the terms "header" and "footer" to describe the running head's position on the page. Note that you can see the headers and footers on your page only in Page Layout view or in Print Preview.

TIP

The running head exists on a different layer from that of your main document text. You can't edit your document text while you're working on the running head, or vice versa.

Create a Header

1. Choose Header And Footer from the View menu.

2. Type the running head in the "header" position.

3. Use any of the toolbar buttons or AutoText entries to insert information.

4. If you don't want to add a footer, click Close.

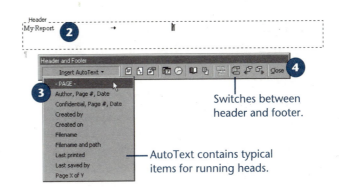

Switches between header and footer.

AutoText contains typical items for running heads.

Create a Footer

1. Click the Switch Between Header And Footer button.

2. Type the running head in the "footer" position.

3. Use any of the toolbar buttons or AutoText entries to insert information.

4. Click Close.

6

Creating Variable Running Heads

Look through this book and you'll see that the odd- and even-numbered pages have alternating running heads in the footer. This is a fairly standard design, especially for double-sided documents, and you can set it up quite easily in Word.

TIP

There must be a minimum of three pages in your document before you can insert first-, odd-, and even-numbered page running heads. If your document doesn't have three pages, press Ctrl+Enter twice to create two extra pages. You can delete these manual page breaks later.

SEE ALSO

"Creating a Running Head" on page 115 for information about creating a running head.

Specify Different Headers and Footers

1 Choose Page Setup from the File menu.

2 Click the Layout tab.

3 Turn on the option for different odd and even running heads.

4 Turn on the option for a different or blank first-page running head.

5 Click OK.

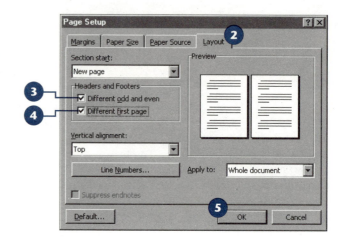

Create a First-Page Running Head

1 Press Ctrl+Home to move to the beginning of the document.

2 Choose Header And Footer from the View menu.

3 Enter the header information.

4 Click the Switch Between Header And Footer button.

5 Enter the footer information.

Label tells you which header you're working on.

Use any formatting you want.

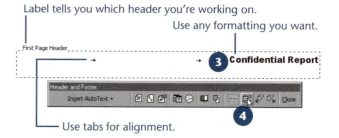

Use tabs for alignment.

Show Next button

Use unique information for the first page, or leave header and footer blank for no running heads on first page.

Create an Even-Page Running Head

1 Click the Show Next button.

2 Enter the footer information.

3 Click the Switch Between Header And Footer button.

4 Enter the header information.

Create an Odd-Page Running Head

1 Click the Show Next button.

2 Enter the header information.

3 Click the Switch Between Header And Footer button.

4 Enter the footer information.

5 Click the Close button on the Header And Footer toolbar.

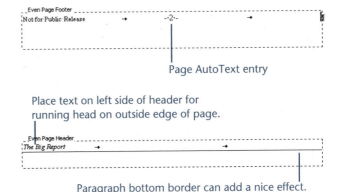

Page AutoText entry

Place text on left side of header for running head on outside edge of page.

Paragraph bottom border can add a nice effect.

Place text on right side of header for running head on outside edge of page.

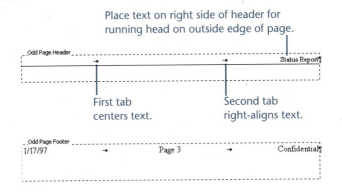

First tab centers text.

Second tab right-aligns text.

6

Inserting a Word Document

Sometimes parts of a large document are created as separate documents: chapters of a book, for example, or sections of a report. You can insert the contents of a separate document into the main document. When you do, the styles in the inserted document are copied into your main document, and the formatting and the running heads are set by the main document. You can also link to the inserted document so that any changes made to it will appear in the main document.

Insert a Word Document

1. Click in the main document where you want the inserted document to appear.

2. Choose File from the Insert menu to display the Insert File dialog box.

3. Select the type of document, if necessary. You can insert a document of any of the types shown in the Files Of Type list box.

4. Locate and select the document to be inserted.

5. Turn on the Link To File check box if you want to keep the main document linked to the inserted (source) document.

6. Click OK.

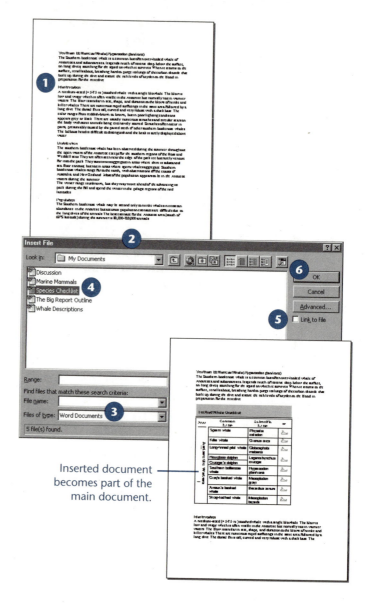

Inserted document becomes part of the main document.

Inserting Part of a Word Document

You can insert part of another document into your main document, and if the content of the part you added changes in the "source" document, the changes will be updated in your main document. Updates usually occur as soon as you open the main document, or when you're working in the main document and the linked information changes in the source document.

SEE ALSO

"Storing and Reusing Text" on page 14 for information about selecting and copying text.

"Using Multiple Documents as a Single Document" on page 140 for information about creating a document from several other documents.

Insert Part of a Document

1. Open the document containing the content to be included.

2. Select and copy the content.

3. Switch to your main document, and click where you want the content to appear.

4. Choose Paste Special from the Edit menu to open the Paste Special dialog box. Verify that the Formatted Text (RTF) option is selected.

5. Click the Paste Link option.

6. Click OK.

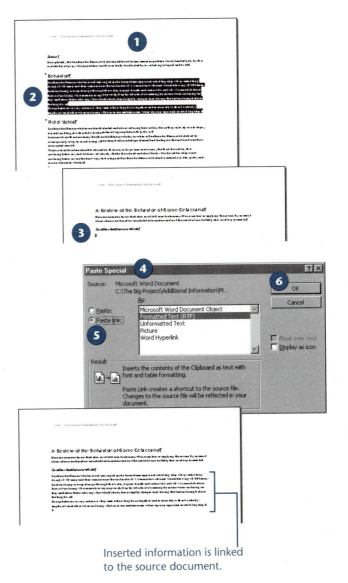

Inserted information is linked to the source document.

Finding Items in a Document

When you're reviewing a document, you often do so in stages: you might check the tables, for example, and then the graphics, and so on. You can browse through your document, jumping to the next occurrence of a specific kind of item, with the help of a tiny button that does a big job. Use the table at the right to achieve the results you want.

SEE ALSO

"Finding Topics in a Long Document" on the facing page for information about using the Document Map to find topics.

Browse by Item

1 Click the Select Browse Object button.

2 Click the type of item you're looking for.

3 Click the appropriate button to go to the next or previous occurrence of the item.

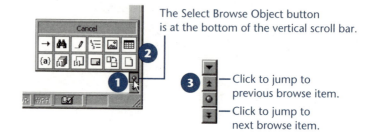

The Select Browse Object button is at the bottom of the vertical scroll bar.

Click to jump to previous browse item.

Click to jump to next browse item.

THE SELECT BROWSE OBJECT BUTTON	
Use this button	**To do this**
→	Select the type of item to jump to.
🔍	Find a specific item.
✎	Browse by edit.
☰	Browse by heading.
🖼	Browse by graphic.
▦	Browse by table.
{a}	Browse by field.
📑	Browse by endnote.
📄	Browse by footnote.
💬	Browse by comment.
🔀	Browse by section.
📄	Browse by page.

Finding Topics in a Long Document

The longer a document gets, the more difficult it can be to find a specific topic. This is when you'll really appreciate Word's Document Map. With the Document Map displayed, you can see an outline view of your document, and, with a click or two, you can jump to the appropriate topic. The outline structure is based on the heading levels assigned to the styles you used.

SEE ALSO

"Organizing with Styles" on page 106 for information about structuring your document.

TIP

Drag the border between the Document Map and the text area to see more or less of the Document Map.

Navigate with the Document Map

1 Switch to the view you want to use.

2 Click the Document Map button.

3 Browse through the Document Map to find the topic you want to review:

◆ Point to a topic to see its full text.

◆ Expand the list of headings to see more topics.

◆ Collapse the list of headings to hide topics you don't need to see.

4 Click the topic.

5 Click the Document Map button to hide the Document Map.

Click a minus sign to collapse the headings directly below it.

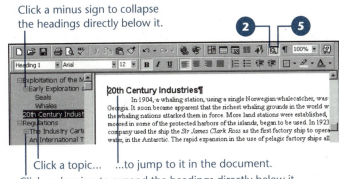

Click a topic... ...to jump to it in the document.

Click a plus sign to expand the headings directly below it.

6

Reorganizing a Long Document

Outline view provides a powerful way for you to view the structure of your document and to rearrange the order of presentation of topics in the document. The outline structure assumes that you have used specific styles to organize your document into a hierarchy of topics and subtopics.

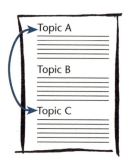

View a Document's Outline

1 Switch to Outline view.

2 Click in a heading, and use the tools on the Outlining toolbar to expand or collapse the outline, to promote or demote heading levels, or to move topics.

Promotes or demotes level.

Moves topic.

Expands or collapses topics.

Specifies lowest heading level displayed.

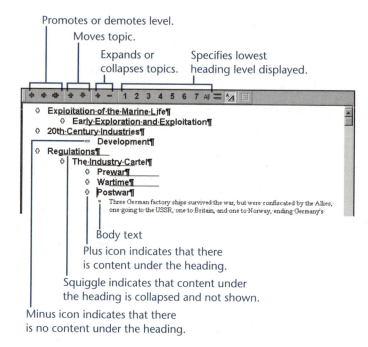

Body text

Plus icon indicates that there is content under the heading.

Squiggle indicates that content under the heading is collapsed and not shown.

Minus icon indicates that there is no content under the heading.

Move a Topic

1 Place the pointer over a plus or minus sign.

2 Drag the topic up or down.

3 Drop the topic at a new location.

Shows where topic will be moved to.

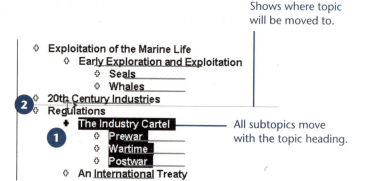

All subtopics move with the topic heading.

Change a Topic's Level

1. Place the pointer over a plus or minus sign.

2. Drag the topic to change its level:

   ◆ Drag it to the left to promote its level.

   ◆ Drag it to the right to demote its level.

   ◆ Drag it to the far right to demote it to body text.

3. Drop the topic at its new level.

Shows level topic is changed to.

+ **Exploitation of the Marine Life**
+ **Early Exploration and Exploitation**
   + Seals
   + Whales
+ **20th Century Industries**
   + **The Industry Cartel**
      + Prewar
      + Wartime
      + Postwar
+ **Regulations**
   + An International Treaty

All subheads are promoted or demoted with the topic heading.

6

Finding Text

If you're not sure where to find some text in your document, Word can locate it for you. You can broaden the search so that Word finds similar words, or you can narrow the search to a designated part of the document or to text that uses specific formatting.

TIP

*"Wildcard" characters are used to represent other characters. The two most common wildcards are ? and *. The ? wildcard specifies any single character, and the * wildcard indicates any number of characters. For a complete list of wildcards, turn on the Use Wildcards check box, and click the Special button.*

SEE ALSO

"Replacing Text" on page 126, "Replacing a Style" on page 127, and "Replacing Text and Formatting" on page 128 for information about finding and replacing special characters and formatting.

Search for Text

1 Specify what is to be searched:

   ◆ Select some text to limit the search to the selection.

   ◆ Click in the document so that there is no selection if you want to search the entire document.

2 Choose Find from the Edit menu.

3 Type the text you want to find.

4 Click Find Next.

Broaden the Search

1 Click the More button (if it's displayed).

2 Select the appropriate option for the results shown in the table at the right.

3 Click Find Next.

OPTIONS TO BROADEN A SEARCH

Option	Effect
Use Wildcards check box	Uses certain characters as wildcard characters.
Sounds Like check box	Finds words that sound the same but are spelled differently.
Find All Word Forms check box	Finds all words that are forms of the word in the Find What box.
All (from the Search list)	Searches the entire document.

In your document, type the text To be or not to be is asked too often. *Choose Find from the Edit menu. In the Find What box, type* o?t *and turn on the Use Wildcards check box. Click Find Next until the entire selection has been searched. Then change the Find What text to* o*t *and repeat the search. Then use* to *as the search text, turn on the Sounds Like option, and search the document. Finally, use* is *as the search text, turn on the Find All Word Forms option, and search the document. Note the different results.*

Narrow the Search

1 Use any combination of these methods:

 ◆ Select text to limit the search to the selection.

 ◆ Be as specific as possible in the text you type in the Find What box.

 ◆ Choose the appropriate option for the results shown in the table at the right.

 ◆ Click Format and specify the format of the text.

2 Click Find Next. Repeat the search if necessary.

3 Click Close.

OPTIONS TO NARROW A SEARCH

Option	Effect
Match Case check box	Finds only text that exactly matches the capitalization of the text in the Find What box.
Find Whole Words Only	Finds text only if the matching text consists of whole words, not parts of words.
Down (from the Search list)	Searches only from the location of the insertion point to the end of the document.
Up (from the Search list)	Searches only from the location of the insertion point to the beginning of the document.

6

Replacing Text

When a word or phrase needs to be replaced with a different word or phrase in several places in your document, Word can replace it for you. This is a great way to use Word's speed and power to make quick work of those tedious document-wide changes.

SEE ALSO

"Finding Text" on page 124 for information about broadening or narrowing a search.

Replace Text

1 Specify what is to be searched:

- ◆ Select text to limit the search to the selection.

- ◆ Click in the document so that there is no selection if you want to search the entire document.

2 Choose Replace from the Edit menu.

3 Click in the Find What box and type the text to be found.

4 Press Tab to move to the Replace With box, and type the replacement text.

5 Click Replace All.

Finds text without replacing it.

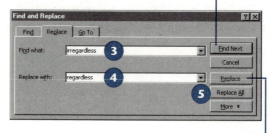

Replaces found text and finds next instance of text.

Replacing a Style

If you discover that you've used the wrong style for a specific purpose or, conversely, that you've used different styles for the same purpose, you can use Word's search-and-replace feature to switch styles.

Replace a Style

Choose Replace from the Edit menu, and specify the style to be found and the replacement style.

1 Delete previous search text, if any.

5 Verify that correct style is selected.

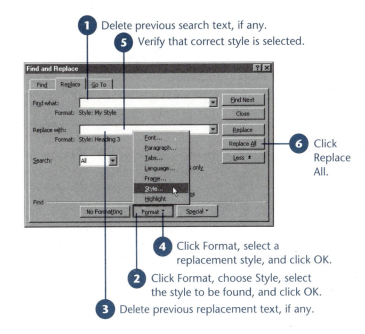

6 Click Replace All.

4 Click Format, select a replacement style, and click OK.

2 Click Format, choose Style, select the style to be found, and click OK.

3 Delete previous replacement text, if any.

6

Replacing Text and Formatting

Let's say that the word *computer* is lowercased in your headings and you realize that it should have an initial capital letter. You don't want to replace every instance of the word throughout the entire document, because it's perfectly correct in the body text. When you need to replace an often-used word, but only in instances where it has a specific style or format, you can use Word's Find command. Simply specify the search text and formatting and the replacement text and formatting, and Word will produce precise and powerful modifications.

Replace Text and Formatting

Choose Replace from the Edit menu, and specify the style to be found and the replacement style.

1 Enter the text to be found.

5 Verify that text and formatting are correct.

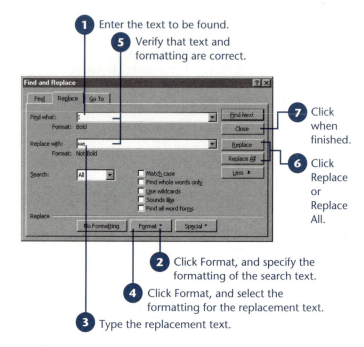

7 Click when finished.

6 Click Replace or Replace All.

2 Click Format, and specify the formatting of the search text.

4 Click Format, and select the formatting for the replacement text.

3 Type the replacement text.

Adding Page Numbers

If you've ever dropped a stack of unnumbered pages, you'll want to add page numbers to any document that's more than a couple of pages long! Page numbers are essential, too, in a book such as this one, in which there's a great deal of cross-referencing. Word will automatically number the pages for you.

TIP

If you're creating a double-sided document, choose Inside or Outside for the page-number alignment.

SEE ALSO

"Creating a Running Head" on page 115 for information about adding page numbers to a custom header or footer.

Place the Page Number

1 Choose Page Numbers from the Insert menu.

2 Select a location.

3 Select an alignment.

4 Click Format if you want to change the numbering format or the starting page number.

5 Click OK when finished.

Preview shows placement of number.

Turn off if you don't want number on first page.

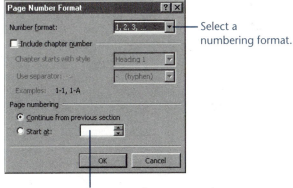

Select a numbering format.

Enter a starting page number.

Using Different Layouts in a Document

In a long document, different parts of the document sometimes require different layouts. By taking your existing content and dividing the document into sections, you can set up each section in its own way.

SEE ALSO

"Flowing Text in Columns" on page 261 for information about using a multiple-column layout.

TIP

When you create a section for selected text, you're actually creating two new sections: one section for the selected text and another one for the text that follows the selection.

Change the Page Orientation

1. Select the part of the document whose page orientation you want to change.

2. Choose Page Setup from the File menu.

3. Click the Paper Size tab.

4. Select the orientation you want.

5. Select Selected Text.

6. Click OK.

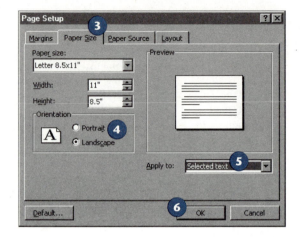

Portrait...   ...Landscape...   ...and Portrait orientation, all in one document

Open or create a document with a few pages of text. Somewhere in the middle of the document, insert a table that has 10 columns and 10 rows. Select the table, and change the page orientation to Landscape. In the landscape-oriented section of your document, reduce the left and right margins to 0.5". Now resize the table so that it stretches between the left and right margins.

If you try to change the margins in a section that follows a section in which the page orientation was changed, you won't be able to choose the Continuous option. If you want a Continuous break, create the new section with a Next Page or Odd Page section break. Then, after you've clicked OK, click in the new section, choose Page Setup again, and change the Section Start to Continuous.

Change the Margins

1. Select the part of the document whose margins you want to change.

2. Choose Page Setup from the File menu.

3. Click the Margins tab.

4. Set the new margins.

5. Select Selected Text.

6. Click the Layout tab.

7. Select the point where the changed section starts.

8. Click OK.

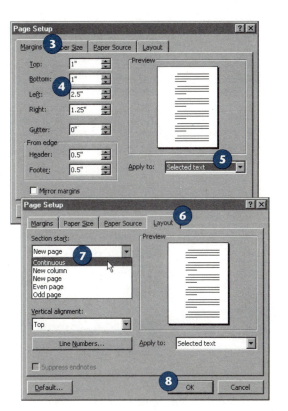

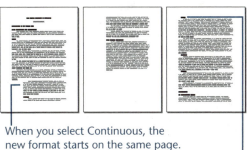

When you select Continuous, the new format starts on the same page.

By default, the following section starts on the next page.

6

Creating Chapters or Sections

A long document is often divided into chapters or sections, each of which should begin on an odd-numbered (right-hand) page. Word will start your chapters or sections on odd-numbered pages and will create running heads to your specifications.

SEE ALSO

"Creating a Running Head" on page 115 and "Creating Variable Running Heads" on page 116 for information about creating running heads.

TIP

Turn on the Show/Hide ¶ button on the Standard toolbar if the section break isn't visible.

If the document is set for different running heads on the first page, or on odd and even pages, make any changes to running heads after turning off the Same As Previous button.

Start a New Chapter or Section

1 Place the insertion point at the beginning of a new chapter or section.

2 Choose Break from the Insert menu.

3 Select the Odd Page option.

4 Click OK.

Change the Running Heads

1 Choose Header And Footer from the View menu.

2 Click the Same As Previous button to turn it off.

3 Make changes to the running head.

4 Switch to the footer.

5 Click the Same As Previous button to turn it off.

6 Make changes to the running head.

7 Click Close.

The section break is inserted in front of the insertion point.

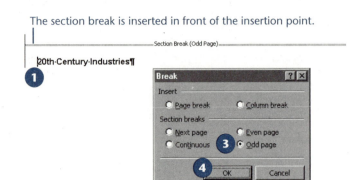

Label tells you the header is the same as the previous header.

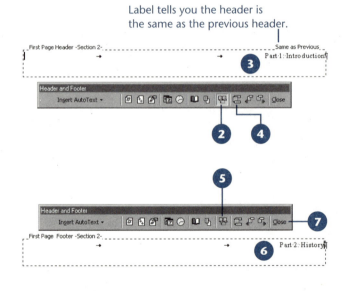

Creating a Table of Contents

Provided your document is organized by styles, it's a snap to have Word create a well-organized table of contents for you.

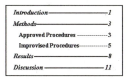

TIP

When you're creating a table of contents, keep in mind that Word doesn't search text boxes, so any text you've put in a text box won't appear in the table of contents. You can decide not to put items in text boxes if you want them to appear in the table of contents or you can add text-box entries manually after you've compiled the final table of contents.

TIP

You can assign the same table-of-contents (TOC) level to different styles.

Choose a Layout

1. Choose Indexes And Tables from the Insert menu.

2. Click the Table Of Contents tab.

3. Select a format.

4. Choose the options to be included.

Includes current page number for each entry.

Displays sample table of contents based on format and options selected.

Automatically right-aligns page numbers against right margin.

Specify Styles

1. Click the Options button.

2. Enter the level number for the styles you want to use.

3. Change the level number for a style you want to use at a different level.

4. Delete the number from styles you don't want to use.

5. Click OK.

6. Look at the preview again, and adjust the settings if necessary.

7. Click OK.

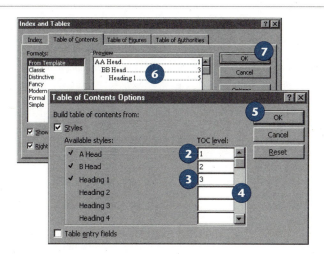

6

Tracking Versions

During the creation of a long document, the text might be changed a dozen times. If you want to refer to a previous edition, you can save versions. When you print the document, you can include information that will clarify which version you're printing.

TRY THIS

Start a document, and add and save some text. Save a version of the document, make some changes, and save another version. Open the first version and compare the documents.

Save a Version

1. Choose Versions from the File menu.

2. Turn on the option to save a version whenever the document is closed.

3. Click Save Now.

4. Enter your comments.

5. Click OK.

6. If the Save As dialog box appears, type a name for the file, and click Save.

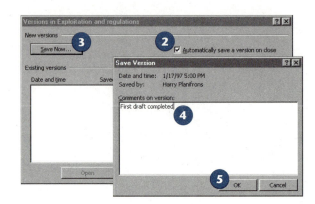

Review a Previous Version

1. Choose Versions from the File menu.

2. Click the version you want to review.

3. Click the View Comments button if the entire comment isn't shown.

4. Click Open.

5. Close the document when you've finished reviewing it, or save it with a different name to use this version.

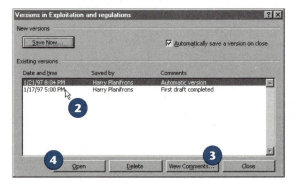

Print Version Information

1 Choose Header And Footer from the View menu.

2 Switch to the footer.

3 Click the Insert AutoText button.

4 Click the items you want to be printed in the document.

5 Format the paragraph in a small font, if necessary.

6 Click Close.

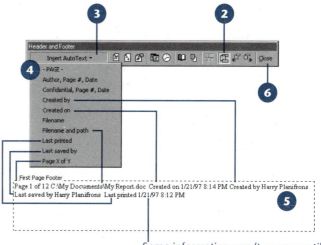

Some information won't appear until you save and print the document.

Creating a Summary

Hard to believe, but some people might not take the time to savor every word of your document! To make sure they don't miss the important parts, you can create a summary of the completed document that contains all the pertinent information. You can use the summary as a starting point, but you'll need to review and tailor it as desired.

SEE ALSO

"Summarizing a Document" on page 218 for information about creating a summary of an online document.

Create a Summary

1. Choose AutoSummarize from the Tools menu. Wait patiently while Word summarizes the document.

2. Select the type of summary you want. For most standard printed documents, you'll want to select the option that creates the summary at the top of the document.

3. Select the length you want the summary to be.

4. Click OK.

Select for online documents.

Select to place a summary before the main text.

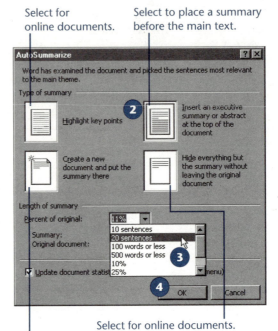

Select for online documents.

Select to circulate the summary separately from the document.

Compare the Summary with the Text

1 Drag the split bar down and drop it to create two windows.

- ◆ Read the summary in one pane.

- ◆ Scroll through the text in the other pane and compare it with the summary.

- ◆ Copy any important missing information from the text and paste it into the summary.

- ◆ Delete any unimportant information from the summary.

- ◆ Change the formatting of the summary as desired.

2 Double-click the split bar to close the pane.

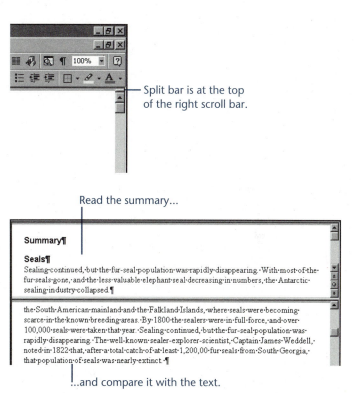

Split bar is at the top of the right scroll bar.

Read the summary...

Summary¶

Seals¶
Sealing·continued,·but·the·fur-seal·population·was·rapidly·disappearing.·With·most·of·the·fur-seals·gone,·and·the·less·valuable·elephant-seal·decreasing·in·numbers,·the·Antarctic·sealing·industry·collapsed.¶

the·South·American·mainland·and·the·Falkland·Islands,·where·seals·were·becoming·scarce·in·the·known·breeding·areas.·By·1800·the·sealers·were·in·full·force,·and·over·100,000·seals·were·taken·that·year.·Sealing·continued,·but·the·fur-seal·population·was·rapidly·disappearing.·The·well-known·sealer-explorer-scientist,·Captain·James·Weddell,·noted·in·1822·that,·after·a·total·catch·of·at·least·1,200,00·fur·seals·from·South·Georgia,·that·population·of·seals·was·nearly·extinct.·¶

...and compare it with the text.

6

Organizing a Multiple-Authors Document

A single long document often comprises several smaller documents: each section of a report, for example, might be created by a different person. In this situation, there's a strong possibility of inconsistency in writing or formatting, and of repetition of content. To organize the individual sections and to ensure that they cover the required material without being redundant, you can create an outline, divide the parts of the document into separate but connected *subdocuments*, and review the completed documents as one. The main document in which the subdocuments are contained is called the *master document.*

Create an Outline

1. Start a new document, using the appropriate template.

2. Switch to Outline view.

3. Create the outline, using the appropriate heading styles.

4. Save the outline in the folder where you want all the related documents to be saved.

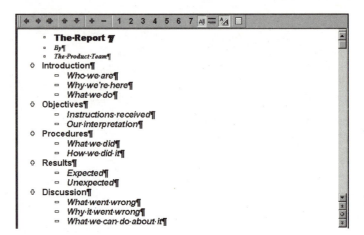

Divide the Document into Subdocuments

1. Click the Master Document View button.

2. Select the part of the outline to be completed by one author.

3. Click the Create Subdocument button.

4. Repeat steps 2 and 3 until all the parts of the outline have been made into subdocuments.

5. Click the Save button on the Standard toolbar.

6. Close the document.

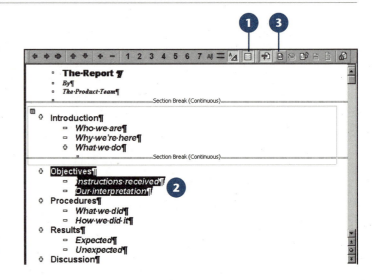

SEE ALSO

*"Organizing with Styles"
on page 106 for information
about organizing a document
with styles.*

*"Reorganizing a Long Docu-
ment" on page 122 for information about using Outline
view to organize a document.*

*"Using Multiple Documents
as a Single Document" on
page 140 for information about
creating a master document
from existing documents.*

TIP

*To share subdocuments over a
network, share the folder they
are contained in so that the
current document is always in
the correct folder. To distribute
the documents by disk, e-mail,
or some other connection, use
the Windows Briefcase to keep
the document in your folder
current. See your Windows
documentation for information
about sharing folders and
using the Briefcase.*

*To use a name for the subdocu-
ment other than the one Word
assigns, open the subdocument,
save it using the name you
want, and close the subdocument before saving the master
document for the first time.*

Distribute the Subdocuments

1. Open the folder that contains the master document.

2. Distribute the subdocuments created from the master document to the appropriate authors.

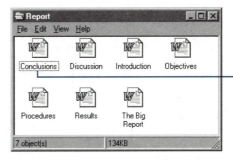

Word automatically names the subdocuments.

Compile the Completed Document

1. Make sure the most recent version of each subdocument is in the original folder, using its original subdocument name.

2. Open the master document.

3. Review the document:

   ◆ Click a hyperlink to open an individual subdocument.

   ◆ Click the Expand Subdocuments button to review the content of all the subdocuments.

Hyperlink to subdocument   Click to show the content of all the subdocuments.

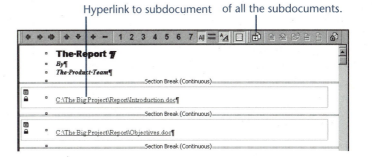

Click to show hyperlinks to subdocuments.

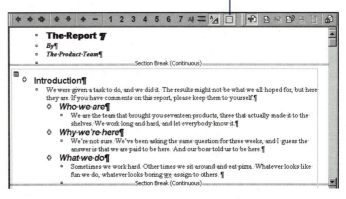

Using Multiple Documents as a Single Document

When several documents are part of the same project, you can combine them by making them into *subdocuments* of a *master document*. You can then work on the entire project as if it were a single document: create a table of contents, use the same template and styles, and copy information from one subdocument into another. But several authors can still work on the subdocuments individually. All changes are coordinated, so whether you edit documents separately or as part of the master document, all the changes are saved. You can assemble the master document periodically, check the page count, and so on, and then return to working on the individual documents.

Create a Master Document

1 Start a new document, using the template that will be used for the entire document.

2 Add text and any other items to the master document.

3 Save the document.

4 Choose Master Document from the View menu.

Master Document View turns on the Outlining toolbar...

...and the Master Document toolbar.

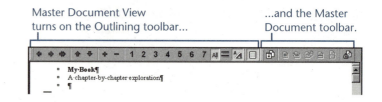

Add Subdocuments

1 Click the Insert Subdocument button, and open the subdocument.

2 Click OK if Word informs you that the subdocument has a different template.

3 Move to the paragraph following the inserted subdocument if the insertion point is not already there, and repeat steps 1 and 2 until all the subdocuments have been added.

Subdocument in master document

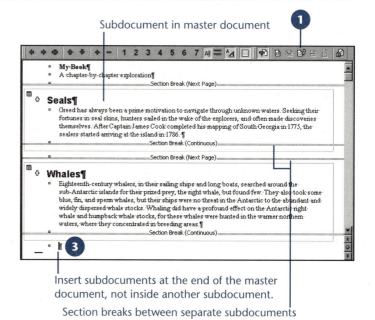

Insert subdocuments at the end of the master document, not inside another subdocument.

Section breaks between separate subdocuments

Edit the Document

1. Use the outline tools to hide or display material.

2. Use standard editing techniques to change the content of the subdocuments.

3. Save the master document. Any changes to the subdocuments will be saved in their own files.

Work on a Single Subdocument

1. Click the Collapse Subdocuments button if the text of the subdocuments is displayed.

2. Click the hyperlink to the subdocument.

3. Do your editing.

4. Save and close the subdocument when you've finished.

Insert document-wide information, such as a table of contents or an index, outside all subdocuments.

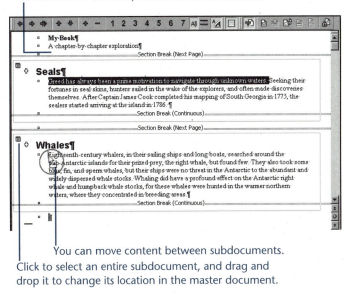

You can move content between subdocuments. Click to select an entire subdocument, and drag and drop it to change its location in the master document.

The Collapse Subdocuments button becomes the Expand Subdocuments button when the subdocuments are collapsed.

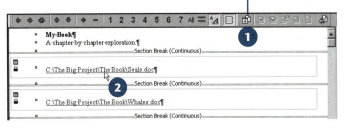

6

7

Creating a Technical Document

IN THIS SECTION

Inserting Symbols and Special Characters

Creating Footnotes and Endnotes

Creating Tables of Figures, Captions, and Cross-References

Numbering Headings and Lines; Creating a Numbered Outline

Creating a Chart; Summing Table Rows and Columns

Creating an Equation

Working with Excel Data and Charts

Creating an Organization Chart

Opening Files of Different Types

Creating an Index

Elsewhere in this book we've talked about complex documents and long documents. A technical document can integrate some or all of the elements of complex documents and long documents, while still having its own set of requirements. Conversely, some elements of a technical document might often be incorporated into a nontechnical document. In reality, there are few elements that are unique to any one type of document, and you can use the techniques we describe to achieve the results you want regardless of the heading under which you find them.

So what *is* a technical document? It could be a doctoral dissertation, a high-school paper, a scientific report, your company's quarterly financial statement, or an annual report to stockholders. It could be an ongoing analysis of a medical experiment, the written specifications for an architectural design, a grade-school teacher's compilation of test scores, or a comparison of various sets of data. What all these examples have in common is that they must present a lot of sometimes complicated information in a format that is inviting rather than daunting, that is organized for ease of reference rather than confusion, and that conveys the information with simplicity and clarity so that it can be understood by a receptive and interested audience.

Inserting Symbols and Special Characters

With at least 101 keyboard keys at your fingertips, you'd think that every character you could possibly need would be there. But what about the accented characters in other languages? And how do you insert trademark and copyright symbols? You'd need a keyboard with thousands of keys! As you can see in the illustrations at the right, Word gives you a huge assortment of symbols and special characters, and several ways to insert them into your documents.

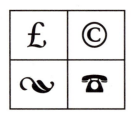

Insert a Text Symbol

1 Click where you want to place the symbol.

2 If you want the symbol to be in a different font from the current one, select the font.

3 Choose Symbol from the Insert menu, and click the Symbols tab.

4 Select (Normal Text) from the Font list.

5 Select the symbol's category.

6 Click the symbol you want to use.

7 Click Insert.

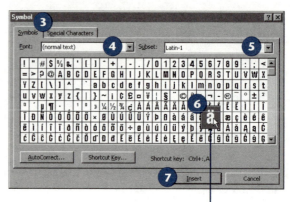

Click the character to see its enlarged view.

Insert Other Symbols

1 Move the Symbol dialog box out of the way, click your document to activate it, and then click where you want to place another symbol.

2 Move the Symbol dialog box back again.

3 Select a font.

4 Click the symbol you want to use.

5 Click Insert.

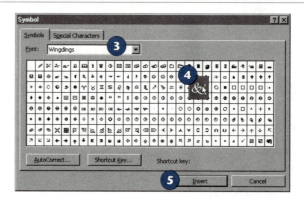

SEE ALSO

"Inserting Symbols Auto-matically" on page 146 for information about the symbols that Word can insert automatically.

TRY THIS

Create Your Own Secret Code. *Type some text, select it, and then choose Symbol from the font list. To make the text readable again, select it, and choose a standard character font such as Times New Roman. This code might not keep your messages secret from prying eyes, but it can be fun.*

TIP

All Boxed Up. *Word now supports Unicode fonts, which is why there's such a huge number of characters available. Unicode is a new standard for fonts, and is currently being adopted by font makers and programmers. If you see empty boxes on your screen instead of the symbols you chose, the font you're using might not support Unicode. To be safe, use the fonts that came with Word.*

Insert Special Characters

1 Click your document to activate it, and then click where you want to place the special character.

2 Click the Special Characters tab.

3 Double-click the character you want to insert.

4 Click Close after you've inserted all your symbols and special characters.

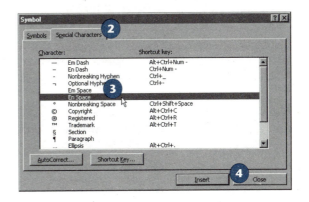

Inserting Symbols Automatically

Word has a list of symbols that it inserts automatically when you type the characters that represent the symbol. If a symbol you want to use isn't in the list, you can add it and assign normal characters to represent it.

TIP

If the last character of the Replace text is a letter or a number, you'll need to type a space after it in your text before Word replaces the characters with a symbol. In all other cases, the text is replaced immediately.

TIP

Choose the Replace text very carefully, or you might get symbols when you're not expecting them. It's a good idea to enclose the Replace text in seldom-used characters, such as square brackets ([ ]) or angle brackets (< >)—also called less-than and greater-than signs.

Insert a Listed Symbol

1. Choose AutoCorrect from the Tools menu.

2. Examine the list of symbols.

3. Verify that the Replace Text As You Type option is turned on.

4. Click OK.

5. Type the text for the symbol.

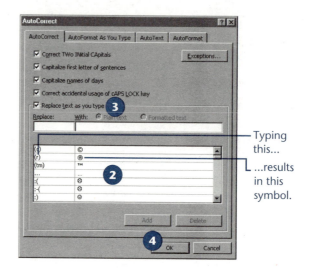

Typing this...

...results in this symbol.

Add a Symbol

1. Choose Symbol from the Insert menu, and click the Symbols tab.

2. Select a font.

3. Click a symbol.

4. Click AutoCorrect.

5. Type the characters the symbol will replace.

6. Click Add.

7. Click OK.

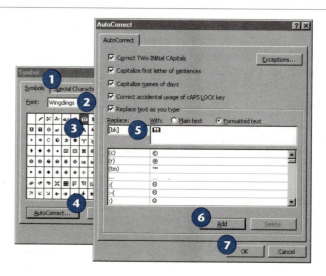

Entering Symbols with Keys

You can assign a key combination to a frequently used symbol so that all you have to do to insert the symbol is press the keys.

SEE ALSO

"Keeping Track of Your Styles" on page 108 for information about printing a list of key combinations.

Assign the Keys

1. Choose Symbol from the Insert menu.

2. Click the Symbols tab, select a font, and click the symbol you want to use.

3. Click the Shortcut Key button.

4. Select where you want to save the key combination.

5. Click in the Press New Shortcut Key box, and press the key combination.

6. Click Assign.

7. Click Close.

8. Click Close.

Insert the Symbol

1. Click where you want to place the symbol.

2. Press the key combination.

Using a key combination places the symbol where you want it.

Enclosed is a money order for the amount of £135 to guarantee our room reservation. We will arrive on

Creating Footnotes

Word makes it so easy to add footnotes to a document! Word can mark the footnoted material for you with an automatic series of numbers or symbols, or you can insert your own choice of symbols. When you leave it to Word to insert the footnote number or mark, it updates the mark if you add or delete footnotes. Word also figures out how much space is required at the bottom of the page for the footnote, and if a footnote is too long for the page, Word automatically continues it on the next page.

```
1, 2, 3, ...
a, b, c, ...
A, B, C, ...
i, ii, iii, ...
I, II, III, ...
*, †, ‡, §, ...
```

Insert a Footnote Mark

1 In Normal view, click where you want to place the footnote mark.

2 Choose Footnote from the Insert menu.

3 Select Footnote.

4 Select AutoNumber, or choose a symbol.

5 Click OK.

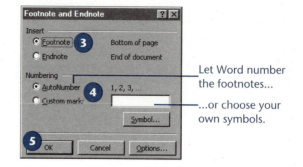

Let Word number the footnotes...

...or choose your own symbols.

It·was·a·dark·and·stormy·night.

Footnote mark is added to text.

Enter Footnote Text

1 Type the footnote text.

2 Click Close.

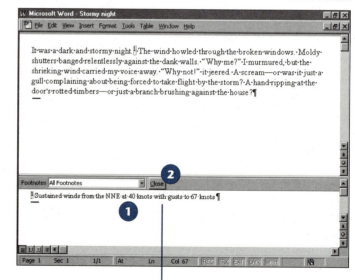

In Normal view, Word opens a special area for the footnote text.

Changing the Look of Footnotes

Word places your footnotes using the most commonly accepted settings: consecutive numbering throughout the document, footnotes at the bottom of each page, a short line, or rule, to separate footnotes from text, and a long line to separate from the text a footnote that was continued from the previous page. If you want, you can change these settings to create your own look.

TIP

If you want to use the default separator after you've deleted it, click the Reset button.

TIP

Increase the Zoom Control to 200% if you need to see the footnote marks more clearly.

Change the Look

1. Choose Footnote from the Insert menu.

2. Click the Options button.

3. Select the options.

4. Click OK.

5. Click Close to close the Footnote And Endnote dialog box.

6. Change the Footnote Reference text style to change the footnote mark. Change the Footnote Text paragraph style to change the text of the footnote.

Change the Separator

1. Verify that you're in Normal view.

2. Choose Footnotes from the View menu.

3. Select the item you want to change.

4. Delete the current separator.

5. Create a new separator.

6. Click Close.

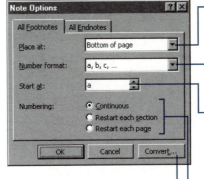

Footnote text can appear at the bottom of page or directly below the text it refers to.

Use a number, letter, or symbol scheme for footnote marks.

Select a number, letter, or symbol for first footnote mark.

Converts all footnotes to endnotes.

Use continuous numbering throughout document, or restart numbering at the beginning of each section or page.

Select to change the separator between the text and footnotes, the separator between the text and footnotes continued from the previous page, or the notice that the footnote is continued on the next page.

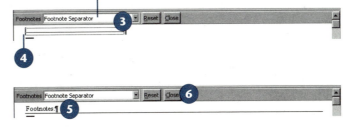

7

Editing Footnotes

Footnotes, like most text, usually need some review and editing. You'll really like the way the footnote pops up in your text so that you can read it in context.

TIP

If the footnote text doesn't appear, choose Options from the Tools menu, and on the View tab, turn on the Screen Tips check box.

TIP

To delete a footnote, drag the mouse over the footnote mark to select it. Press the Delete key, and the footnote mark and the footnote text are gone!

TIP

If you forget which buttons or tools are which, just hold the mouse pointer over any of them to see an identifying tooltip.

Review the Footnotes

1. Click the Select Browse Object button on the vertical scroll bar, and click Browse By Footnote.

2. Use the Previous Footnote or Next Footnote arrow to locate the footnote marks.

3. Point to the word preceding the footnote mark, and read the footnote.

It·was·a·dark·and·stormy·night. The·wind·howled·through·the·broken·windows.·Moldy·

Probably Larus delawarensis ssly·against·the·dank·walls.·"Why·me?"·I·murmured,·but·the·
my·voice·away.·"Why·not!"·it·jeered.·A·scream—or·was·it·just·a·
gull complaining·about·being·forced·to·take·flight·by·the·storm?·A·hand·ripping·at·the·
door's·rotted·timbers—or·just·a·branch·brushing·against·the·house?¶

Placing the mouse pointer here...   ...displays the footnote text here.

Edit a Footnote

1. Double-click the footnote mark.

2. Edit the footnote text.

3. Click Close.

Double-click here...

It·was·a·dark·and·stormy·night. The·wind·howled·through·the·broken·windows.·Moldy·
shutters·banged·relentlessly·against·the·dank·walls.·"Why·me?"·I·murmured,·but·the·
shrieking·wind·carried·my·voice·away.·"Why·not!"·it·jeered.·A·scream—or·was·it·just·a·
gull complaining·about·being·forced·to·take·flight·by·the·storm?·A·hand·ripping·at·the·
door's·rotted·timbers—or·just·a·branch·brushing·against·the·house?¶

Footnotes All Footnotes   Close

Sustained·winds·from·the·NNE·at·40·knots·with·gusts·to·67·knots·¶
Probably *Larus·delawarensis*¶
Cercocarpus·ledifolius¶

...to move to here.

Move a Footnote

1. Select the footnote mark.

2. Drag it and drop it at a new location.

It·was·a·dark·and·stormy·night. The·wind·howled·

Creating Endnotes

An endnote is just like a footnote, except that all the notes are listed together at the end of the document instead of a few notes being listed at the foot of each page. If the document has more than one section, you can also control where in the document the endnotes print—you might want them grouped at the end of each section.

TIP

Endnotes and footnotes are identical in purpose and content. They differ only in their location in a document and in the fact that endnotes don't need separators. You use the same techniques for creating, modifying, and editing endnotes as you do for footnotes.

TIP

By default, Word uses different numbering schemes for footnotes and for endnotes.

Insert an Endnote

1. In Normal view, click where you want to place the endnote mark.

2. Choose Footnote from the Insert menu.

3. Select Endnote.

4. Select AutoNumber, or choose a symbol.

5. Click OK.

6. Type the endnote text.

7. Click Close.

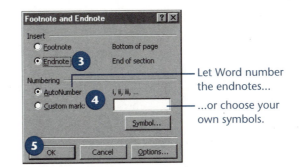

Let Word number the endnotes...

...or choose your own symbols.

Control Where Endnotes Appear

1. Choose Footnote from the Insert menu.

2. Click the Options button.

3. Select a location for the endnote.

4. Click OK.

5. Click Close in the Footnote And Endnote dialog box.

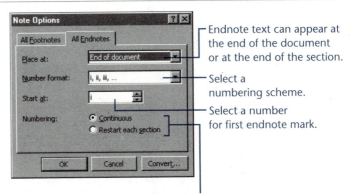

Endnote text can appear at the end of the document or at the end of the section.

Select a numbering scheme.

Select a number for first endnote mark.

Use continuous numbering throughout document, or restart numbering at the beginning of each section.

Creating a Table of Figures

Technical documents often contain a listing of all the figures or illustrations that appear in the document, in addition to a table of contents. Word can generate a table of figures for you. You can use the same method to generate a table of equations or a table of tables.

TIP

When you're creating a table of figures, keep in mind that Word doesn't search floating captions—or any content in text boxes, for that matter. This means that any floating text or text in text boxes won't appear in the table of figures. To include it, make sure the figure and its caption are not floating above the text.

SEE ALSO

"Creating Captions" on the facing page for information about adding captions to your figures.

Create a Table of Figures

1 Add captions to all your figures.

2 Click in the document where you want the table of figures to appear.

3 Choose Index And Tables from the Insert menu to display the Index And Tables dialog box.

4 Click the Table Of Figures tab.

5 Select Figure as the caption label.

6 Select a format for the table.

7 If it's not already turned on, turn on the option to show page numbers.

8 If it's not already turned on, turn on the option to include caption label and number.

9 Click OK.

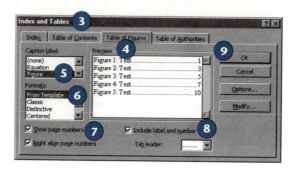

Creating Captions

Figures, tables, equations, and other similar elements in a technical document often need captions that number and identify them. Word can label and number these items, and can then re-number the entire sequence automatically if you add or delete an item.

Figure 1: Transportation issues

SEE ALSO

"Creating a Floating Caption" on page 258 for more information about working with captions.

TIP

To change the appearance of the caption's text, modify the Caption style.

Create a Caption

1. Select the item to be captioned.

2. Choose Caption from the Insert menu to display the Caption dialog box.

3. Select the type of caption.

4. Select a location.

5. Type the caption text.

6. Click OK.

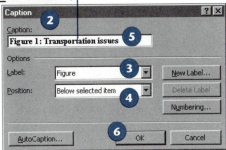

Word provides the label and number, and you provide the description.

Create a New Caption Type

1. Choose Caption from the Insert menu.

2. Click the New Label button to display the New Label dialog box.

3. Type a new label, and click OK.

4. Complete the caption.

5. Click OK.

The label you create...

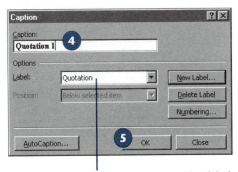

...becomes a new caption label.

7

Creating Cross-References

Cross-references are valuable tools in a long and informative document, but you have to be *very* well organized if you're going to insert them manually, especially if you do a lot of editing and re-writing. It's much easier to let Word do the work for you. Word will keep track of all your cross-references, and will keep all the information current. Word can even insert your cross-references as hyperlinks in an online document.

Create a Cross-Reference

1 Type the beginning text of your cross-reference.

2 Choose Cross-Reference from the Insert menu to display the Cross-Reference dialog box.

3 Select the type of item to be cross-referenced.

4 Select the type of cross-reference to be inserted.

5 Select the cross-reference.

6 Click Insert.

7 Continue using the Cross-Reference dialog box to insert cross-references.

8 Click Close.

Reference can be numbered item, heading, bookmark, footnote, endnote, equation, table, or any caption label you create.

Reference changes depending on the reference type selected.

Adds "above" or "below" to reference (available only for certain types of reference).

Available references in your document

Turn on if document is to be read on line. Clicking the cross-reference takes reader directly to the referenced item.

Numbering Headings

People who create long technical documents commonly number each heading level so that it's easy to refer to sections when the document is being technically reviewed or is being discussed at a meeting. Word uses the outline-level setting for each style as the basis for the numbering hierarchy.

SEE ALSO

"Organizing with Styles" on page 106 for information about setting outline levels.

"Numbering Lines" on page 156 for information about numbering the lines in a technical document.

"Creating a Numbered Outline" on page 158 for information about creating and printing a numbered outline.

Number the Headings

1 Verify that all headings have the correct heading styles applied.

2 Choose Select All from the Edit menu.

3 Choose Bullets And Numbering from the Format menu to display the Bullets And Numbering dialog box.

4 Click the Outline Numbered tab.

5 Select one of the numbering schemes shown in the bottom row.

6 Click OK.

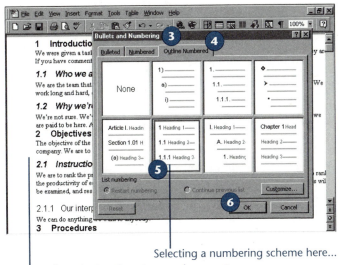

Selecting a numbering scheme here...

...numbers the headings in your document.

Numbering Lines

It's a nice convenience to be able to number the lines in a technical document for easy reference when the document is being reviewed or discussed. Word will number the lines for you in whatever increments you want, and will skip any paragraphs in which you *don't* want the line numbering to appear.

TIP

You can set a style's paragraph formatting to suppress line numbers if paragraphs of that style are never to be numbered.

TIP

You won't see the line numbering on your screen; it appears only in the printed document and in Print Preview.

Number a Document

1. Choose Page Setup from the File menu.

2. Click the Layout tab.

3. Select Whole Document in the Apply To list.

4. Click the Line Numbers button.

5. Turn on the Add Line Numbering option.

6. Set the options you want.

7. Click OK.

8. Click OK.

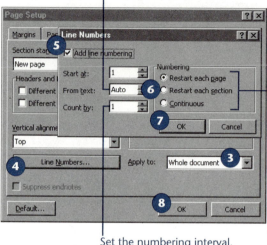

Set the distance between number and text.

Set the numbering interval.

Use continuous numbering throughout the document, or restart numbering at the beginning of each page or section.

In your long document, number the headings. Insert a Continuous section break before each Level 1 heading. Set up all the heading styles you use to suppress line numbers. Turn on the line numbering for the whole document, restarting the numbering at each new section. Click the Print Preview button, display a single page, and click it to zoom in. Use the browser on the vertical scroll bar to browse by heading. Note that when the document is printed you'll be able to refer to a specific line number under a specific topic number.

Exclude Paragraphs from Numbering

1 Select the paragraphs whose lines are not to be numbered.

2 Choose Paragraph from the Format menu.

3 Click the Line And Page Breaks tab.

4 Turn on the Suppress Line Numbers option.

5 Click OK.

Running heads are not numbered...

...but headings and titles are numbered.

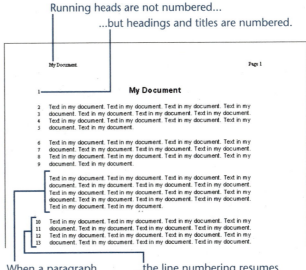

When a paragraph is formatted to suppress line numbers...

...the line numbering resumes in the next paragraph that isn't formatted to suppress line numbers.

Creating
a Numbered
Outline

Word's Outline view is an excellent tool for organizing a document, but let's say you want to create a printed outline from an existing document—to use as an agenda at a meeting, perhaps. Here's a great way to do it. You create a specialized table of contents, designate which headings are to be shown, and then format it with the look you want.

SEE ALSO

"Creating a Table of Contents" on page 133 for information about creating a table of contents.

"Numbering Headings" on page 155 for information about numbering headings.

"Wandering and Wondering Through Word's Fields" on page 185 for information about fields.

Create an Outline

1. Number the headings, using one of the outline-numbering schemes.

2. Click in your document where you want the outline to appear.

3. Choose Index And Tables from the Insert menu, and click the Table Of Contents tab.

4. Click the Options button, designate the appropriate heading levels, and click OK.

5. Turn off the Show Page Numbers option, and click OK.

Save the Outline as a New Document

1. Select the entire table of contents. (Because it's a *field*, the selection color is gray with white text instead of black with white text.)

2. Press Shift+Ctrl+F9 to make the text normal text instead of a field.

3. Click the Cut button, start a new document, and paste the copied text.

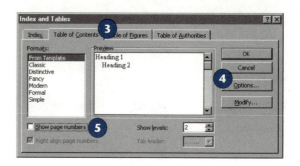

1 **Introduction**
  1.1 Who we are
  1.2 Why we're here

2 **Objectives**
  2.1 Instructions received
  2.2 Our interpretation

3 **Procedures**
  3.1 What we did
  3.2 How we did it

4 **Results**
  4.1 Expected
  4.2 Unexpected

5 **Discussion**
  5.1 What went wrong
  5.2 Why it went wrong
  5.3 What we can do about it

Modifying the TOC styles in your new document emphasizes the outline structure.

Creating a Chart

A chart can make the results of your data more instantly understandable than can a spreadsheet of figures that presents the same information. And, while a spreadsheet tends to put your readers to sleep, a chart makes them sit up and take notice. You can use Microsoft Graph, an accessory program that comes with Word, to produce a variety of different charts based on your data.

SEE ALSO

"Crunching Data" on page 165 for information about using a chart created in Microsoft Excel.

TIP

Are you wondering why the Chart command opens a program called Graph? So are we!

Create a Chart

1. Point to Picture on the Insert menu, and choose Chart from the submenu.

2. Replace the sample data in the worksheet with your own data. Use the toolbars to format the data.

3. Close the worksheet.

4. Select individual components of the chart, and use the toolbars and menus to format the chart components.

5. Click outside the chart area when you've finished.

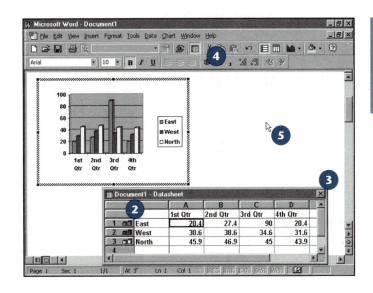

Edit the Chart

1. Double-click the chart to activate it.

2. Edit the data and the chart.

3. Click outside the chart area when you've finished.

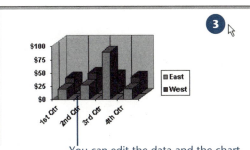

You can edit the data and the chart formatting when you activate the chart.

Summing Table Rows and Columns

Word, as its name suggests, is much more literary than it is mathematical—but it can do some simple table summarizing for you. For more complex calculations, you'll want to insert a Microsoft Excel worksheet.

TIP

If you're going to do some math in a table, don't split or merge any of the cells that contain data, or any cells in which there is more than one entry— you might get some surprising results!

TIP

The AutoSum button tries to guess what you want to calculate, but it usually decides to sum the column. When it does, it inserts the formula =SUM(ABOVE). If its guess is incorrect, you can edit the formula in the Formula dialog box.

Sum Columns

1. Display the Tables And Borders toolbar.

2. Create a table containing your data, with a blank row at the bottom and a blank column at the right.

3. Click in the blank cell in the bottom row that is to contain the sum of the cells above it.

4. Click the AutoSum button.

5. Move through the remaining blank cells, clicking the AutoSum button.

Item	Cost	Handling	Total
A1223	$23.95	$18.00	
B3312	$6.95	0	
XY9989	$234.50	$25.00	
Total	$265.40		

Put only one entry in a cell.

Use zeros for blank entries.

With the =SUM( ) formula, you can also use the word BELOW to place the sum of a column in the top row, and the word RIGHT to place the sum of a row in the left column.

"Using Toolbars" on page 22 for information about displaying toolbars.

"Calculating Values Outside a Table" on page 163 for information about calculating results from individual cells.

Sum Rows

1 Click in a blank cell whose row is to be summed.

2 Choose Formula from the Table menu to display the Formula dialog box.

3 Set the formula to sum the cells to the left.

4 Click OK.

5 Move through the remaining blank cells, repeating steps 3 and 4.

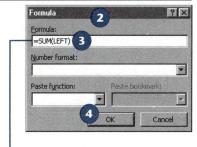

Item	Cost	Handling	Total
A1223	$23.95	$18.00	$41.95
B3312	$6.95	0	$6.95
XY9989	$234.50	$25.00	
Total	$265.40	$43.00	

Formula

Formula:
=SUM(LEFT)

Number format:

Paste function:

Paste bookmark:

OK   Cancel

Sums the cells to the left.

Edit the Table

1 Change any values in the table.

2 Choose Select Table from the Table menu to make sure all formulas are updated.

3 Press the F9 key to update the calculations.

Selecting the entire table...

Item	Cost	Handling	Total
A1223	$23.95	$18.00	$41.95
B3312	$6.95	$3.95	$10.90
XY9989	$234.50	$30.00	$264.50
Total	$265.40	$51.95	$317.35

...lets you update all the calculations at one time.

Calculating a Value

When you need to make a calculation, Word can do the math for you. Your calculation can be as simple as adding two numbers or as complex as using functions. You can place the results anywhere in your document, but they usually fit best in a table.

TIP

Additional functions are available, some of which can produce fairly complex calculations. See Word's Help for more detailed information.

SEE ALSO

"Calculating Values Outside a Table" on the facing page for information about putting the results of calculations into your text.

Do the Arithmetic

1 Click in your document where you want to place the result of your calculation.

2 Choose Formula from the Table menu.

3 If a formula is displayed, delete it except for the equal (=) sign.

4 Enter your calculation.

5 Choose a number format.

6 Click OK.

Use Functions

1 Click in your document where you want to show the result.

2 Choose Formula from the Table menu.

3 If a formula is displayed, delete it except for the equal (=) sign.

4 Choose a function from the Paste Function list.

5 Insert the values inside the parentheses.

6 Select a number format.

7 Click OK.

Use + for addition, - for subtraction, * for multiplication, / for division, and { } to group operations.

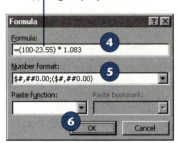

You wanted a quick estimate, so here it is: $ 82.80

Calculated result inserted into your document.

COMMONLY USED FUNCTIONS FOR CALCULATIONS

Example	Result
AVERAGE(10,20,33)	The average value of the numbers
INT(123/7)	The integer value of the result
MOD(17,3)	The remainder after the first number is divided by the second number (modular arithmetic)
PRODUCT(10,20,30)	The value of multiplying the numbers together
ROUND(22/7,4)	The result of the first calculation rounded to the nearest four decimal places
SUM(1,2,3,4,5,6)	The value of adding all the numbers together

Calculating Values Outside a Table

If you want to calculate values in a table and then place the results in your regular text, you name the table, and then refer to individual cells or a range of cells within the table.

TIP

To refer to a single cell, use the SUM function, and reference the table name and the one cell you want.

TIP

Use a colon (:) to separate a range of cells, and a comma (,) to separate individual cell references.

Name the Table

1. Select the entire table.

2. Choose Bookmark from the Insert menu to display the Bookmark dialog box.

3. Type a name for the table.

4. Click Add.

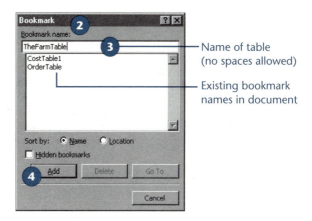

Name of table (no spaces allowed)

Existing bookmark names in document

Calculate the Value

1. Click in your text where you want to show the value of the cell.

2. Choose Formula from the Table menu.

3. Use the Paste Function list to insert any functions you want to use.

4. Use the Paste Bookmark list to insert the name of the table into the formula.

5. Type the reference to the cell or cells, enclosed in square brackets.

6. Click OK.

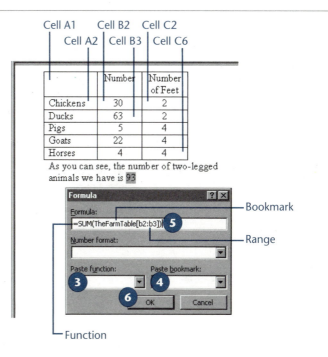

Cell A1 Cell B2 Cell C2
Cell A2 Cell B3 Cell C6

=SUM(TheFarmTable[b2:b3])

Bookmark

Range

Function

Creating an Equation

Mathematical equations can be difficult to construct on a computer. For simple equations, you can generally use standard characters and formatting, but for more complex equations, you'll want to use Microsoft Equation Editor 3.0. Be aware, though, that you are simply *constructing* the equation. Word doesn't do any calculations based on the equation.

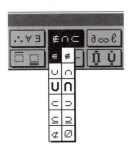

Create an Equation

1 Choose Object from the Insert menu.

2 Click the Create New tab, select Microsoft Equation 3.0 from the list, and click OK.

3 Use the template menus to insert the symbols with the correct configuration, and use the keyboard to enter characters, keeping these points in mind:

   ◆ Work from left to right; that is, from the outside of the equation to the inside.

   ◆ Use the Tab and Shift+Tab keys to move to different elements and levels.

4 Click outside the equation area when you've finished.

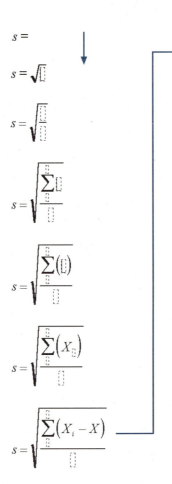

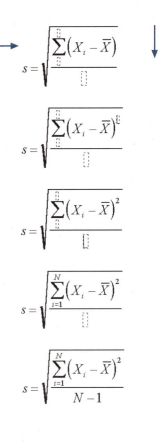

Crunching Data

Word is great for presenting information and doing simple calculations, but if you want to do some more advanced number crunching, add a Microsoft Excel worksheet to your document. You'll be using the power of Excel for the number crunching and the finesse of Word for the presentation.

TIP

Microsoft Excel must be installed on your computer for you to be able to insert an Excel worksheet.

SEE ALSO

"Adding Components" on page 294 for information about installing programs.

Add a Worksheet

1 Click in your document where you want to place the worksheet.

2 Click the Insert Microsoft Excel Worksheet button.

3 Drag the mouse to select the number of rows and columns to be included.

4 Complete the worksheet as you would any Excel worksheet.

5 Drag an outside border to change the number of worksheet cells displayed.

6 Click outside the worksheet area.

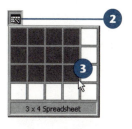

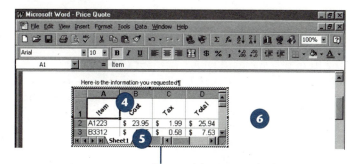

Drag a sizing square to change the number of cells displayed.

Edit a Worksheet

1 Double-click the worksheet.

2 Change any values or calculations.

3 Format the cells in any way you want: add borders and shading, for example, or rotate the text in the column headings.

4 Click outside the worksheet area.

Here is the information you requested:

Item	Cost	Tax	Total
A1223	$ 23.95	$ 1.99	$ 25.94
B3312	$ 16.95	$ 1.41	$ 18.36
XY9989	$234.50	$ 19.46	$ 253.96

Copying Data from Excel

If you want to include information that is stored in a Microsoft Excel worksheet, you can copy the data and then insert it into Word in the form of a standard table rather than as a worksheet.

Get the Data

1 Open the Excel worksheet.

2 Select the cells you want to copy.

3 Choose Copy from the Edit menu.

4 Switch to Word.

Only selected cells are copied.

	A	B	C	D	E	F	G
1	Subject	Test 1	Test 2	Test 3	Average	SD	
2	1	55	77	61	64.3	11.37	
3	2	66	55	64	61.7	5.86	
4	3	44	56	61	53.7	8.74	
5	4	54	62	65	60.3	5.69	
6	5	64	44	60	56.0	10.58	
7							

Insert the Data

1 Click in your document where you want to place the data.

2 Click the Paste button on the Standard toolbar.

3 Use the Tables And Borders toolbar to format the table.

Here are the test results:

Average	SD
64.3	11.37
61.7	5.86
53.7	8.74
60.3	5.69
56.0	10.58

Format the table as you would any other Word table.

Connecting to Excel Data

If you want to include data from a Microsoft Excel worksheet, and the data is likely to change periodically, you can link your document to the Excel worksheet. Then, whenever the data changes in the worksheet, the information in your document will be updated automatically.

TIP

Save the workbook before linking to Word, and don't move the workbook from its folder after you've created the link.

TIP

Microsoft Excel must be installed on your computer for you to be able to link your Word document to the Excel worksheet.

SEE ALSO

"Adding Components" on page 294 for information about installing programs.

Link to the Data

1. Open the Excel worksheet.

2. Select the cells that you want to copy.

3. Choose Copy from the Edit menu.

4. Switch to Word.

5. Click in your document where you want to place the data.

6. Choose Paste Special from the Edit menu to display the Paste Special dialog box.

7. Select the Paste Link button. Verify that the Formatted Text (RTF) option is selected.

8. Click OK.

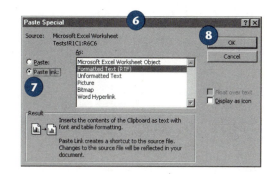

Subject	Test 1	Test 2	Test 3	Average	SD
1	55	77	61	64.3	11.37
2	66	55	64	61.7	5.86
3	44	56	61	53.7	8.74
4	54	62	65	60.3	5.69
5	64	44	60	56.0	10.58

Although the data is contained in a Word table, it will change if the data in the Excel worksheet changes.

Adding an Excel Chart

If you have the final results of your data in a Microsoft Excel worksheet, but you want to display the data as a chart, you can copy it into your Word document. The chart resides in Word, so you can edit the chart as necessary, and you no longer need the original Excel document.

TIP

Microsoft Excel must be installed on your computer for you to be able to edit the chart.

SEE ALSO

"Adding Components" on page 294 for information about installing programs.

Get the Chart

1 In Excel, use the Chart Wizard to create the chart as a chart object.

2 Select and copy the object.

3 Switch to Word.

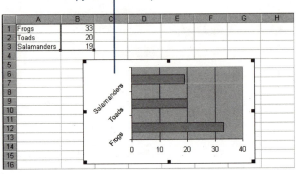

Copy the chart object.

Insert the Chart

1 Click in your document where you want to place the data.

2 Click the Paste button on the Standard toolbar.

Chart object in Word

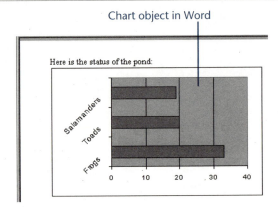

Here is the status of the pond:

Edit the Chart

1. Double-click the chart.

2. Use the toolbar buttons to make your changes to the chart.

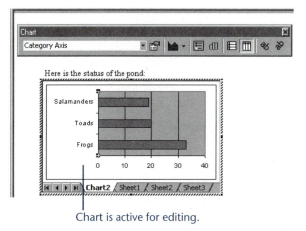

Chart is active for editing.

Edit the Data

1. Click the worksheet that contains the data.

2. Make your changes.

3. Click the Chart tab.

4. Click outside the chart area.

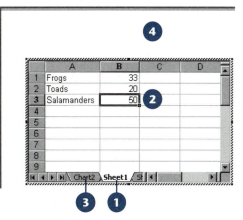

Connecting to an Excel Chart

When you insert a chart from Microsoft Excel, and the data the chart is based on changes, the chart will be updated automatically in your document. If you ever want to update the chart manually, however, the original Excel worksheet must be available to you.

Insert the Chart

1 In Excel, use the Chart Wizard to create the chart as a chart object.

2 Save the workbook.

3 Select and copy the object.

4 Switch to Word.

5 Click in your document where you want to place the data.

6 Choose Paste Special from the Edit menu to display the Paste Special dialog box.

7 Select the Paste Link option.

8 Click OK.

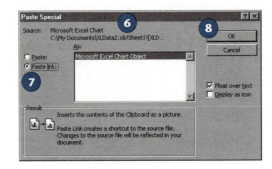

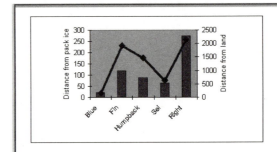

Creating an Organization Chart

An organization chart is a graphical representation of how your group is organized. In very little time, you can create an impressive chart that illustrates the chain of command—and you can change it even faster than people can move up or down the corporate ladder.

TIP

If Organization Chart 2.0 isn't in the Object Type list, you'll need to install it.

SEE ALSO

"Adding Components" on page 294 for information about installing components.

Create the Chart

1 Choose Object from the Insert menu.

2 Click the Create New tab, select MS Organization Chart 2.0 from the list, and click OK.

3 Complete the chart:

♦ Replace the placeholder text.

♦ Add any comments.

♦ Add new elements.

♦ Format the lines and borders.

4 Choose Update Document from the File menu.

5 Choose Exit And Return To Document from the File menu.

Use the buttons to add components.
Format the boxes to add emphasis.
Replace placeholder text.

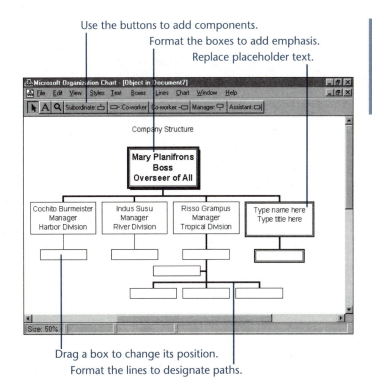

Drag a box to change its position.
Format the lines to designate paths.

Opening Files of Different Types

You can use the information contained in *foreign-format* files—that is, files that were created in a program other than Word—provided you have the correct *converter*. Converters transform diverse files into formats that Word can read. Some converters are installed automatically when you install Word, and there are others that you can install optionally. In some cases, you might need to get specific converters from Microsoft or from other sources.

TIP

If you don't have the correct converter installed, rerun Setup and make sure that you've installed all the available converters. If a converter you need isn't listed in Setup, check the Microsoft Office Web site for additional converters.

Open a Foreign-Format File

1 Choose Open from the File menu to display the Open dialog box.

2 Select the file type from the Files Of Type list.

3 Select the file.

4 Click Open.

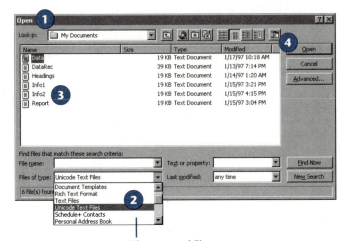

The types of files you can open depend on the converters that are installed.

Saving Files in Different Formats

As hard as it might be to believe, not everyone uses Word. Many programs, however, can read Word documents. If you need to transfer information to a program that can't read your Word documents, you can save the information in a different format. When you do, you're likely to lose much of your formatting and possibly your graphical information, but at least you won't have to retype everything.

TIP

If you're not sure which format you need, and if your document isn't too long, create several versions of it, each with a different format. It's a good idea to include a Text Only version, too, just to be safe.

Use a Different Format

1 Open the document in Word.

2 Choose Save As from the File menu to display the Save As dialog box.

3 Enter a short name (a maximum of eight characters) for the file.

4 Select a different format.

5 Click Save.

After you select a format type, all the files in the folder of that type are listed

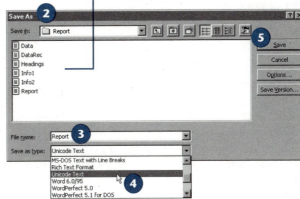

Creating an Index

Word simplifies and automates the sometimes arduous task of indexing a long document. You select the words or phrases in your document that will be the main index entries, changing the wording if necessary. You can add several levels of subentry to direct readers to other relevant topics. Choose among several styles for your index, and then let Word compile it for you, assigning the correct page numbers.

TIP

When you're creating an index, keep in mind that Word doesn't search text boxes for index entries. You can either decide not to put items in text boxes if you want them indexed or you can add text-box index entries manually after you've compiled the final index.

TIP

Index entries are marked with a hidden-text field. Click the Show/Hide ¶ button to see and, if necessary, edit the entry.

Tag the Entries

1. Choose Index And Tables from the Insert menu, and click the Mark Entry button on the Index tab.

2. In your document, select the text to be indexed.

3. Modify the wording or capitalization of the main entry, if necessary.

4. Type any subentries. To specify more than one level of subentry, separate each subentry level with a colon.

5. Select index-entry options and page-number formatting

6. Click Mark.

7. Repeat steps 2 through 6 until the entire document is tagged.

8. Press Ctrl+End to move to the end of the document, and choose Index And Tables from the Insert menu.

9. On the Index tab, select an index type and style, and click OK

Type the topic to be referenced.

Select for page number to be entered.

Select, and then select bookmark that marks entire range to show first and last page of topic.

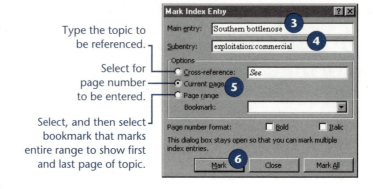

Letter separators are automatically inserted by some index styles.

Page range   Cross-reference

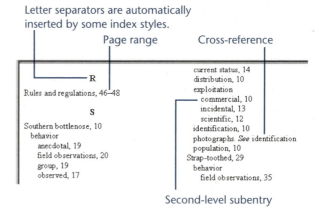

Second-level subentry

Creating Merged Documents

IN THIS SECTION

Creating Form Letters

Addressing Mailing Labels and Envelopes

Creating Awards

Creating a Data Source

Editing Data

Modifying a Data-Source Document

Incorporating Data from Excel or Access

Selecting Records to Merge

Merging Records in Order

Personalizing Merged Documents

Sending Merged Documents via E-Mail or Fax

Word's mail merge feature is a marvelous time-saver when you need to send the same information to a few individuals or to a large group of people. You provide a main document and a *data source,* and Word will combine, or merge, the information from your data source into your main document to create a new, personalized document. That new document might be a form letter that you send via the postal service, or an e-mail or fax document that you distribute electronically to a group of people. The data source can be any listing of items: names and addresses, employee records, data from a Microsoft Excel worksheet or an Access database, and so on.

You can use mail merge to address a big stack of envelopes or sheets of mailing labels, all created from the information in your database. You can find other uses for mail merge, too—if you want to have a little fun, try creating some personalized award certificates to present to friends or colleagues. Turn to page 186 for some ideas.

If you're reading this section because you want to know how to do a mail merge, or because you're stuck in the middle of one and don't know what to do next, you've come to the right place!

Creating Form Letters

When you want to create personalized, computer-generated form letters, you need two items: your *main document*, which is the letter that each person on your list will receive, and a *data source*, which is a list of the names and addresses of the people to whom you're sending your letter. You'll use the information in the data source for the inside address and salutation on each letter, and for the address on the envelopes or the mailing labels.

Start a Form Letter

1 Create and save a letter containing the information that will be the same in all letters. This is your *main document.*

2 Choose Mail Merge from the Tools menu.

3 Click the Create button.

4 Choose Form Letters.

5 Click the Active Window button.

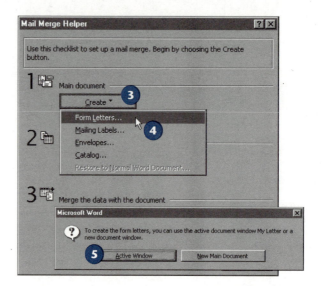

Get the Data

1 Click Get Data.

2 Choose a data source:

♦ Create Data Source to enter the data

♦ Open Data Source to use existing data

♦ Use Address Book to use data from an address book

♦ Header Options to use separate documents for the data and the data header

3 Click Edit Main Document.

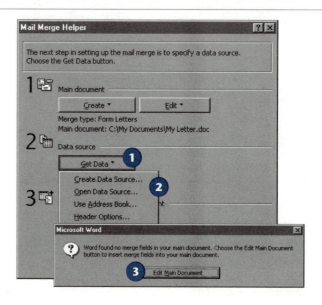

Specify the Merged Data

1. Click where you want to add information from your data source.

2. Click the Insert Merge Field button, and select the type of data to be included.

3. Repeat steps 1 and 2 until all the merged data is specified.

All merge fields are inserted with the Insert Merge Field button.

Merge fields specify which data is inserted and where it's placed.

Form letter goes to all recipients.

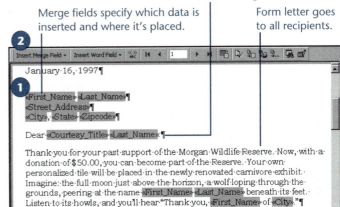

Create the Letters

1. Look the document over and correct any errors.

2. Click the Mail Merge button to display the Merge dialog box.

3. Make your settings.

4. Click Merge.

Specify which records are used, based on testing their values.

Select to merge to printer, new document, e-mail, or fax.

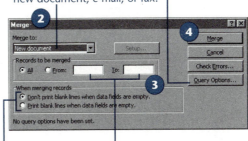

Specify which records to merge if you're not merging all records.

Control how the merge handles blank lines.

Reviewing Mail Merged Documents

What could be worse than printing a big batch of mail merged documents and then discovering an error in the setup or in your text? Before you print a whole mail merge, you should always test your setup, print a couple of samples, and inspect the results. It's well worth the extra few minutes, and can save you time, money, and frustration.

Inspect the Merge

1. Create the main document, and attach your data source.

2. Click the View Merged Data button, and review the merged document.

3. Click the Next Record button, and review the merged document.

4. Repeat step 3 for a series of records.

Simulate the Merge

1. Click the Mail Merge button.

2. Make your settings.

3. Click the Check Errors button.

4. Select the option to simulate the merge.

5. Click OK.

6. Click Merge.

7. Read any error messages, and correct your main document as necessary. Repeat steps 1 through 6 until all you've corrected all errors.

8. Close the Mail Merge Helper dialog box.

You can see your merged data instead of the merge fields.

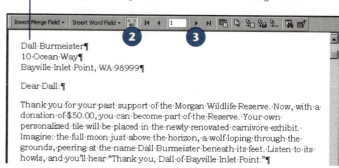

Dall·Burmeister¶
10·Ocean·Way¶
Bayville·Inlet·Point,·WA·98999¶

Dear·Dall:¶

Thank·you·for·your·past·support·of·the·Morgan·Wildlife·Reserve.·Now,·with·a· donation·of·$50.00,·you·can·become·part·of·the·Reserve.·Your·own· personalized·tile·will·be·placed·in·the·newly·renovated·carnivore·exhibit.· Imagine:·the·full·moon·just·above·the·horizon,·a·wolf·loping·through·the· grounds,·peering·at·the·name·Dall·Burmeister·beneath·its·feet.·Listen·to·its· howls,·and·you'll·hear·"Thank·you,·Dall·of·Bayville·Inlet·Point."¶

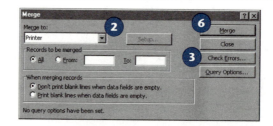

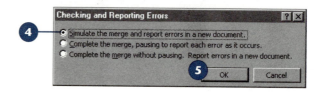

Test the Merge

1. Click the Mail Merge button to display the Merge dialog box.

2. Enter a range that includes two records, using data records from the middle of your data set.

3. Select Printer from the Merge To list.

4. Click Merge.

5. Proofread the printed document, make any corrections, and save the document.

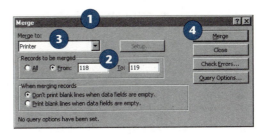

Addressing Mailing Labels

When you mail certain types of information to a list of people, it's often more practical or more economical (or both) to attach mailing labels than to use envelopes. Word can use your data source to create those mailing labels for you.

SEE ALSO

"Creating Mailing Labels" on page 69 for information about creating labels using a single address.

Set Up the Labels

1 Start and save a new blank document.

2 Choose Mail Merge from the Tools menu.

3 Click the Create button, and choose Mailing Labels. Click the Active Window button when asked which document window to use.

4 Click the Get Data button, and choose your data source. Click the Set Up Main Document button when prompted.

5 Select a label type and location.

6 Click OK.

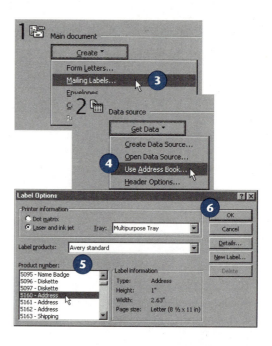

Insert the Address

1 Click Insert Merge Field, and click the data field you want to include.

2 Add any spaces or punctuation, and press Enter to start new lines as necessary.

3 Repeat steps 1 and 2 until you've completed the label information.

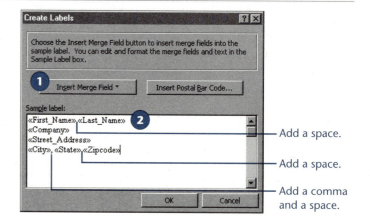

Add a space.

Add a space.

Add a comma and a space.

Add a Postal Bar Code

1. Click the Insert Postal Bar Code button in the Create Labels dialog box.

2. Specify the field that contains the ZIP code.

3. Specify the field that contains the street address.

4. Click OK.

Create the Labels

1. Proofread the address, and correct any errors.

2. Click OK in the Create Labels dialog box.

3. Click Merge in the Mail Merge Helper dialog box.

4. Make your settings.

5. Click Merge.

Select Printer or New Document.

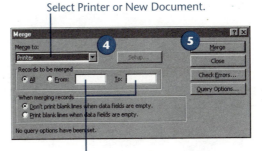

Specify a range of records if you're not printing all the records.

8

Addressing Envelopes

If your printer can print envelopes, you can quickly address a stack of envelopes based on a list of names and addresses.

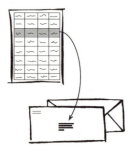

TIP

Feed Me! *If your printer supports it, set the Feed From option to feed from a tray or from an envelope feeder rather than to manual feed.*

Set Up the Envelopes

1 Start and save a new blank document.

2 Choose Mail Merge from the Tools menu.

3 Click the Create button, and choose Envelopes. Click the Active Window button when Word asks you which document window to use.

4 Click the Get Data button, and choose your data source. Click the Set Up Main Document button when prompted.

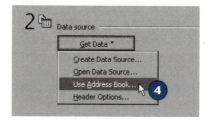

Set Up the Main Document

1 If necessary, make any changes on the Envelope Options and the Printing Options tabs, and click OK.

2 Use the items from the Insert Merge Field button to complete the address.

3 Add a postal bar code if necessary. Click OK to close the Insert Postal Bar Code dialog box.

Click, and choose a data field...

...to insert the merge field here.

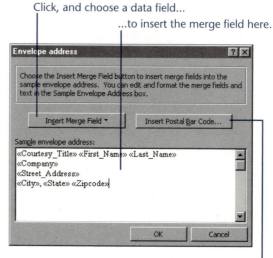

Click to insert a postal bar code.

SEE ALSO

"Addressing an Envelope" on page 70 for information about creating envelopes one at a time.

"Reviewing Mail Merged Documents" on page 178 for information about testing your setup before you print the whole mail merge.

"Addressing Mailing Labels" on page 180 for information about inserting a postal bar code.

"Printing Envelopes Without a Return Address" on page 184 for information about addressing envelopes that have pre-printed return addresses.

"Selecting Records to Merge" on page 194 for information about merging only specific records.

Create the Envelopes

1. Proofread the address, and correct any errors.

2. Click OK in the Envelope Address dialog box.

3. Click Merge in the Mail Merge Helper dialog box.

4. Make your settings.

5. Click Merge.

Select Printer or New Document.

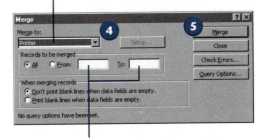

Specify a range of records if you're not printing all the records.

8

Printing Envelopes Without a Return Address

When you address a stack of envelopes using mail merge, your return address is automatically added to the upper left corner of the envelope. You'll want to prevent it from printing if your envelopes are preprinted with your return address.

SEE ALSO

"Addressing Envelopes" on page 182 for information about setting up and creating envelopes.

TIP

If you never want a return address printed on any of your envelopes, you can delete the user information. Choose Options from the Tools menu, click the User Information tab, and delete the Mailing Address information.

Delete the Return Address

1. Start and save a new blank document.

2. Choose Mail Merge from the Tools menu.

3. Set up a main document for the envelopes.

4. Click the Edit button, and choose your main document.

5. Delete the return-address information.

6. Click Merge.

7. Create the envelopes.

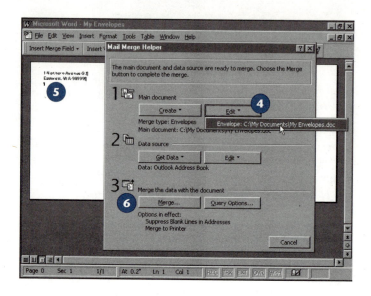

Wandering and Wondering Through Word's Fields

The term *field* can be confusing: it has different meanings depending on how it's used.

◆ A field in Word is usually a placeholder—often containing a bit of programming code—for information that gets automatically updated, such as a date or a page number.

◆ A merge field is another type of field—also a placeholder—which is used exclusively to get information from a data source.

◆ A field in a data source refers to a single item in a data record.

Anatomy of a Field

Most of the time, you're not aware of the fields that might be in your document. You generally see the *results* of fields: the current date, perhaps, or the summing of a table. If, however, your document is suddenly transformed into a chaotic riddle of strange characters, you're seeing the other side of fields: their *code*.

Field characters enclose a field. These are special characters—they're not the { and } characters on your keyboard.

{ FILLIN "Enter your closing." \d "Have a pleasant day." }

Field name   Field instructions

Anatomy of a Merge Field

A merge field is used only during a mail merge, in which you combine—or merge—a main document with a data source. Merge fields are usually visible in your main document before it's printed. If you show the full field codes for these fields, you'll see that the merge field is a special form of a field: the MERGEFIELD field.

Merge-field characters enclose the merge field.

«MonthlyDonation» — Merge-field name is the name of the data field.

{ MERGEFIELD MonthlyDonation } — A merge field is just a special type of field.

Anatomy of a Data Field

Database programs also use the term *field*, but a data field is different from a field in Word. A data field is a specific item in a *data record*. A data record is one complete set of information contained in the data source. If your data source contained addresses, a single data record would be the address information for an individual, and a single field in that data record would be one component of the address: the city or the ZIP code, for example.

The first row lists the names of each data field.   A column is one data field.

First	Last	Address	City	State	ZIP	Monthly Donation	YTD Donation
Harry	Planifrons	3 Kerguelen Place	Crozet Basin	WA	98999	65	175
Dall	Burmeister	10 Ocean Way	Bayville Inlet Point	WA	98999	50	120
Dusky	Cruciger	1090 West Oceanside	West Sound Inlet Cove	WA	99998	100	400
Indus	Susu	101 Ocean Way	Bayville Inlet Point	WA	98999	300	900

A row is one data record.   A cell is a data field for a specific record.

Creating Awards

Everyone deserves an award once in a while, whether it's for a crowning accomplishment or just for fun. You can use Word to create a basic award document, with blank places for the recipient's name and the achievement that is being recognized. If several people are being honored for different reasons, you can create a list of names and awards, and Word will insert them into the award document for you.

Create the Data

1 Start a new blank document, and create a table with two columns and two rows.

2 Place a label, or title, for each column in the top row.

3 Type the name of the recipient and the type of award.

4 Press Tab to start a new row, and type the next recipient's name and award.

5 Repeat step 4 until you've listed all recipients and their awards, and then save and close the document.

Column title becomes the Merge Field name.

Employee¤	Award¤	¤
Harry·Planifrons¤	Perfect·Attendance¤	¤
Dusky·Cruciger¤	Writing·the·Longest·Report¤	¤
Dall·Burmeister¤	Having·the·Cleanest·Office¤	¤
¤	¤	

Create an Award Certificate

1 Start a new blank document, and use Word's tools to create a handsome certificate.

2 Insert and format a paragraph mark for the recipient's name.

3 Insert and format a paragraph mark for the award.

4 Save the document.

Blank paragraph for recipient's name

Blank paragraph for award

TIP

A catalog-type document is any document that doesn't fit the criteria for form letters, mailing labels, or envelopes. It's usually a generic sort of document with few specialized features, such as the award described here.

TIP

You can't merge a catalog-type document to a fax. If you want to fax the awards, merge them to a single document, divide the document into separate documents, and fax each document individually.

SEE ALSO

"Creating Stylized Text" on page 268 for creating a dramatic heading.

"Adding an Art Border Around a Page" on page 273 for information about adding a border around the award.

Set Up the Documents

1. Choose Mail Merge from the Tools menu.

2. Set up the document:
   - ◆ Click the Create button and choose Catalog.
   - ◆ Use the active window.

3. Click the Get Data button, and use the data-source document you created previously.

4. Set up the document when prompted.

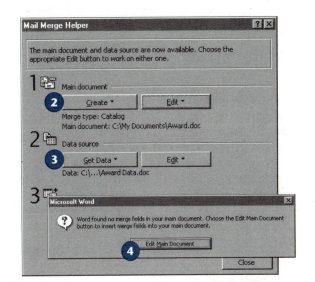

Create the Awards

1. Click where you want the recipient's name.

2. Click Insert Merge Field, and choose the recipients-column title.

3. Click where you want the award title.

4. Click Insert Merge Field, and choose the awards-column title.

5. Click the Merge To Printer (or Merge To Document) button.

6. Hand out the awards!

Creating a Data Source

When you're creating mail merged documents, you need two things: a main document and a data source. If the data you want to use is not already organized in an easily accessible form, you can create a data-source document and enter your data there.

SEE ALSO

"Modifying a Data-Source Document" on page 191 for information about changing the structure of a data-source document.

"Incorporating Excel Data" on page 192 for information about using data from Microsoft Excel.

"Incorporating Access Data" on page 193 for information about using data from Microsoft Access.

Create a Data Source

1 With the document you're using as your main document open, choose Mail Merge from the Tools menu to display the Mail Merge Helper dialog box.

2 Click the Create button and choose the type of document you want. Use the active window for your main document.

3 Click the Get Data button, and choose Create Data Source.

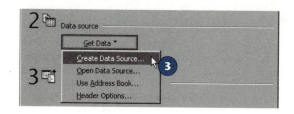

Define the Data Fields

1 Modify the list of field names:

◆ Select and delete the fields you don't want.

◆ Type and add any new fields.

◆ Select and move fields to change their order.

2 Click OK.

3 Save the document.

Type new field name, and click Add Field Name to add new fields to the list.

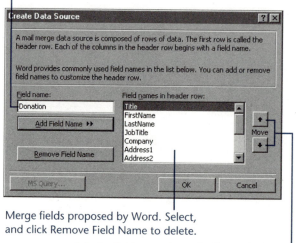

Merge fields proposed by Word. Select, and click Remove Field Name to delete.

Select a field name from the list, and click to move the field up or down in the list.

After you've created your data-source document and completed the main document, save and close both documents. Then click the Open button on the Standard toolbar, and open the data-source document. Note that the document is a standard Word table, with the names of the fields in the top row and the data you entered in the rows below. Close the document without making any changes.

Enter the Data

1 Click the Edit Data Source button.

2 Enter the data for each line. Press the Tab key to move to the next line.

3 Click Add New after each set of entries.

4 Press the Tab key to move to the next line, and enter a new record. Continue adding and completing records until you've completed the last record.

5 Click OK.

6 Complete the main document.

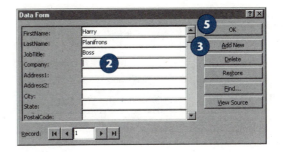

8

Editing Data

If the data for one or more records in your data-source document is incorrect or needs to be updated, you can edit the data. You can also add new records and delete old ones.

TIP

If your data resides in another program, such as an address book or an Access database, close the main document, edit and save the data in its own program, and then reopen the main document to get the updated information.

SEE ALSO

"Modifying a Data-Source Document" on the facing page for information about adding or deleting data records.

Find a Record

1. If it isn't already open, open the main document for which the data source was created.

2. Click the Edit Data Source button.

3. Click the Find button.

4. Type the information you're looking for.

5. Select the field in which it occurs.

6. Click Find First. If the found record isn't the one you want, click the Find Next button. Repeat until you've found the record.

7. Click Close.

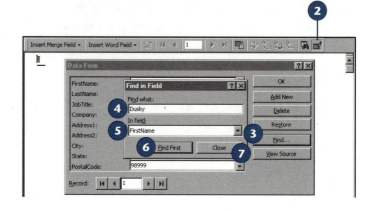

Edit a Record

1. Do any of the following:

   ◆ Edit the text in any of the fields.

   ◆ Add new records.

   ◆ Delete records.

2. Click OK when you've finished.

Add, delete, or edit text in any field.

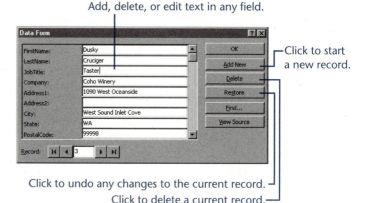

Click to start a new record.

Click to undo any changes to the current record.

Click to delete a current record.

Modifying a Data-Source Document

When you want to change the number of fields or the names of the fields in an existing data-source document, you can edit the data-source document directly. Because the data source is a table, it's a simple matter to add or delete columns when you want to add or delete fields of data.

> **TIP**
>
> *The data-source document contains all the information in a single table. Turn on the gridlines if they're not displayed so that you can see the boundaries of each data field.*

Edit the Data-Source Document

1. If it isn't already open, open the main document for which the data source was created.

2. Click the Edit Data Source button.

3. Click the View Source button.

4. Modify the fields and records:

   - Delete a column to remove a data field.

   - Add a column and fill it with data to add a data field.

   - Change data-field names by changing text in the first row.

   - Sort the records in alphanumeric order.

5. Save the document.

6. Click the Mail Merge Main Document button.

Click in table, and then click button to sort records.

Edit name to change the field name.

Click to return to main document.

Delete a column to remove a field.

Add a column to add a new field.

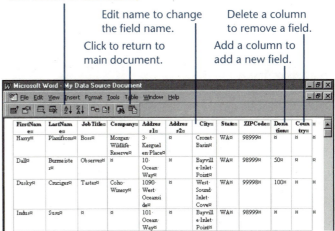

8

Incorporating Excel Data

When the data you want to use is contained in a Microsoft Excel worksheet, you can use the worksheet as your data source when you're creating mail merged documents.

TIP

Microsoft Excel must be installed on your computer for you to be able to incorporate Excel data.

SEE ALSO

"Adding Components" on page 294 for information about installing Microsoft Excel.

Prepare the Data

1. Open the workbook in Excel.

2. Organize the worksheet data so that each row is a data record and each column is a data field.

3. Save and close the worksheet.

Verify that the top row of the data contains the field name for each column.

To use only part of the worksheet, select and name a range. The field names must be in the top row of the named range.

Get the Data

1. In Word, use Mail Merge to create a main document.

2. Click the Get Data button, and choose Open Data Source.

3. Select MS Excel Worksheets.

4. Double-click the worksheet to open it.

5. Select a named range or the entire worksheet.

6. Click OK.

7. Edit the main document, and use the Insert Merge Field button to insert the data fields.

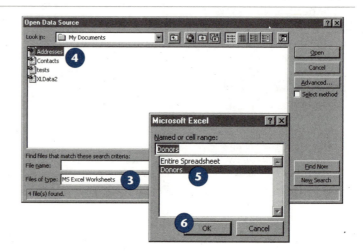

Incorporating Access Data

If you want to create mail merged documents using information contained in a Microsoft Access database, you can use a table from the database as your data source, or you can customize the data by using a query and then use the query as the data source.

Get the Data

1 In Word, use Mail Merge to create a main document.

2 Click the Get Data button, and choose Open Data Source.

3 Select MS Access Databases.

4 Double-click the database.

5 Select the table or query that contains the data.

6 Click OK.

7 Edit the main document, and use the Insert Merge Field button to insert the data fields.

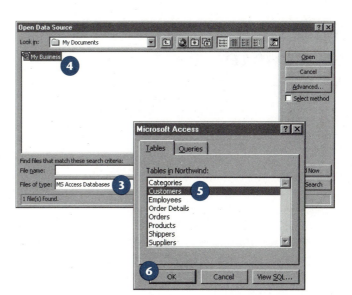

8

Selecting Records to Merge

There might be occasions when you want to use only the records in your data source that match certain criteria: addressing envelopes to clients who live in a specific ZIP code, for example, or sending letters to only the most generous donors. You can specify which records are used by testing the data in a field against data that you specify.

Limit the Records

1. Prepare your completed main document for merging.

2. Click the Mail Merge button to display the Merge dialog box.

3. Specify the range of records to be merged.

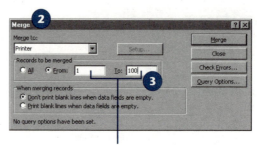

Only the records you specify will be merged.

Specify a Test

1. Click the Query Options button in the Mail Merge Helper dialog box to display the Query Options dialog box.

2. Select the field to be tested.

3. Select the type of comparison.

4. Type the data you want to test against.

Only records showing a monthly donation of $100 or more will be merged.

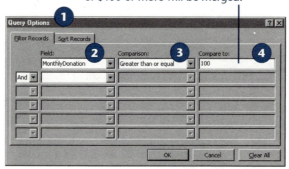

Logical Confusion. *Using the And/Or logic can be very confusing. Always test your merge with records that both pass and fail the test before you run the full merge.*

The Or in this query is not an exclusive Or. The test is satisfied if either condition or both conditions are met.

Add Tests

1 Select the relationship between the two tests.

2 Select the field to be tested.

3 Select the type of comparison.

4 Type the data you want to test against.

5 Continue adding tests until you've defined the data records to be used.

6 Click OK.

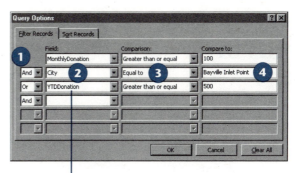

Merged documents will be generated for anyone in Bayville Inlet Point who contributed $100 or more per month, or for anyone, anywhere, who contributed $500 or more this year.

8

Merging Records in Order

Word normally merges records in the order in which they occur in your data source. If you want to merge them in a different order, you can sort the records. For example, you might want your envelopes sorted by ZIP code so they comply with bulk-mailing regulations.

SEE ALSO

"Addressing Mailing Labels" on page 180 and "Addressing Envelopes" on page 182 for information about bulk mailings.

Sort the Records

1. Prepare your completed main document for merging.

2. Click the Mail Merge button.

3. Click the Query Options button to display the Query Options dialog box.

4. Click the Sort Records tab.

5. Select the field you want to sort by.

6. Specify whether the sort is to be ascending or descending.

7. Add any secondary sorts.

8. Click OK.

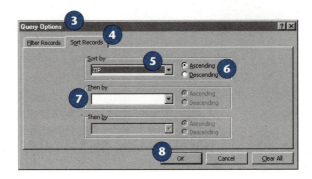

Merging Conditionally

You can change the text of a merged document based on conditions in your data source. For example, you can insert one message for the most generous donors, and a different one for contributors of smaller amounts of money, provided your data source has a column that lists individual donations.

TIP

Conditional tests can be tricky. Always review the document and its results before you conduct the full merge.

SEE ALSO

"Reviewing Mail Merged Documents" on page 178 for information about testing your setup before you print the whole mail merge.

Create the Test

1 Use Mail Merge to create a main document. Connect to your data source, and add the merge fields you want Word to complete for you.

2 Click in the document where you want to insert the conditional text.

3 Click the Insert Word Field button, and choose If…Then…Else from the drop-down menu.

4 Create the test.

5 Type the text to be inserted if the test result is true.

6 Type the text to be inserted if the test result is false.

7 Click OK.

8 Click the Mail Merge button and create your documents.

Select the field name that contains the data to be tested.

Select the type of comparison.

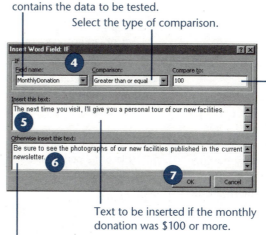

Type the data you want to test against.

Text to be inserted if the monthly donation was $100 or more.

Text to be inserted if the monthly donation was less than $100.

Personalizing Merged Documents

Sometimes you might want to insert different personalized messages into a few documents in a mail merge. You can do this by having Word fill in all the fields that are the same in all the documents, and then pausing to ask you for the personalized information.

TIP

If you need to edit the text of your prompt or the default text after you've completed the field information and clicked OK, you'll need to edit the Fill-In field that is created.

SEE ALSO

"Wandering and Wondering Through Word's Fields" on page 185 for information about working with fields.

Create a Dialog Box

1. Use Mail Merge to create a main document, and connect to your data source.

2. Add the merge fields you want Word to complete for you.

3. Click in the document where you want to place the personalized information.

4. Click the Insert Word Field button, and choose Fill-In from the drop-down menu.

5. Type the prompt you want to see when Word asks for the personalized message.

6. Type the default text for the personalized message.

7. Click OK.

8. Click Cancel if Word immediately asks for the personalized message.

9. Save the main document.

Turn on if you want to fill in the information only once, after which Word will insert the message into every document.

Personalize the Message

1 Start the merge.

2 Type a different personalized message and click OK, or click OK to accept the proposed message.

Word proposes the default text.

Type new text for a different personalized message.

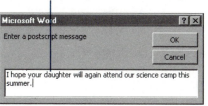

The message appears in the merged document.

Harry·Planifrons¶
• Lead·Trainer¶
• Morgan·Wildlife·Reserve¶

PS·I·hope·your·daughter·will·again·attend·our·science·camp·this·summer.¶

8

E-Mailing Merged Documents

When you distribute your merged documents by electronic mail, you can specify whether the document is to be sent as the body of the e-mail text or as an enclosure. An enclosed document can be opened as a Word document by the recipient, with the document's formatting intact. When the document is sent as the body of the e-mail message, some of its formatting might be lost, depending on the e-mail system.

Set Up the Merge

1 Prepare your completed main document for merging.

2 Click the Mail Merge button to display the Merge dialog box.

3 Select Electronic Mail.

4 Click the Setup button.

5 Select the field with the e-mail name.

6 Type a subject line.

7 Click OK.

Click to send as a Word document.

Skip Missing E-Mail Addresses

1 Click the Query Options button in the Merge dialog box to display the Query Options dialog box.

2 Select the field with the e-mail name.

3 Set the comparison to Is Not Blank.

4 Click OK.

5 Click Merge.

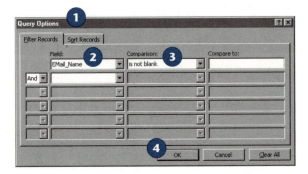

Faxing Merged Documents

You can distribute your merged documents electronically by fax, provided your computer has faxing capabilities. You can merge your main document only with the records in your data source that have fax-number entries.

SEE ALSO

"E-Mailing Merged Documents" on the facing page for information about creating a comparison to test whether a number is blank.

Set Up the Merge

1. Prepare your completed main document for merging.

2. Click the Mail Merge button.

3. Select Electronic Fax.

4. Click the Setup button.

5. Select the field with the fax number.

6. Type a subject line.

7. Click OK.

8. Create a query to skip records with missing fax numbers.

9. Click Merge.

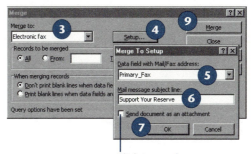

Click to send as a Word document.

8

Working with Your Workgroup

IN THIS SECTION

Sharing Templates

Sending Documents Out for Comments or Edits

Routing and Reviewing Documents

Adding Comments to Documents

Highlighting Text

Tracking Changes to Documents

Limiting Access to Documents

Reading Documents On Line

Summarizing Documents

The ability to work efficiently and harmoniously as part of a team is an important requirement in today's busy offices, where speed, accuracy, and security are all important factors in the daily exchange of information.

When you're a member of a workgroup—that is, when you and your coworkers are connected over a network—"working well with others" becomes a lot easier. Everyone in the workgroup has access to the same information, so no one is accidentally left out of the loop when important information is distributed. Everyone who needs it has access to the group's style sheet of approved terminology, for example, so that all the documents produced by the group use consistent wording. Everyone who creates documents can access the appropriate templates so that all the documents produced by the group have a consistent look. Documents can be circulated electronically for everyone's comments, which can be added as text or as sound recordings, or for more detailed content editing. When the comments or edits are returned, they can be easily combined into a single document so that you (or the person who makes the final decisions) can see all the comments in one place. If you prefer to review the comments separately, you can do that, too.

Sharing Templates

When everyone in a workgroup works on the same types of documents, you can all use the same templates so that all the documents produced in the group have the same general appearance. And if a template needs to be updated, only the shared templates need to be replaced.

Set Up the Templates

1 Create a templates folder on a server or workgroup computer that is accessible to everyone in your workgroup.

2 Create folders in the templates folder to classify the template types.

3 Place the templates to be shared in the folders.

Connect to the Templates

1 On your own computer, choose Options from the Tools menu, and click the File Locations tab.

2 Select Workgroup Templates.

3 Click Modify.

4 In the Modify Location dialog box, locate the templates folder.

5 Click OK.

6 Click OK in the Options dialog box.

Folders with unique names create new tabs in the New dialog box.

Main workgroup folder

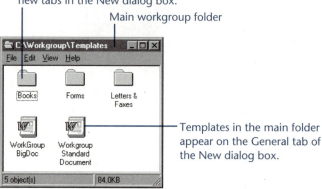

Templates in the main folder appear on the General tab of the New dialog box.

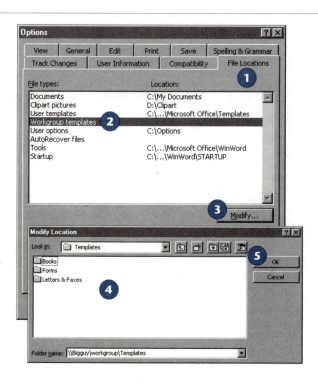

Use a Workgroup Template

1 Choose New from the File menu to display the New dialog box.

2 Locate and double-click the template.

Workgroup templates and local computer templates are displayed on the same tab if the folders have the same name.

Workgroup templates are displayed on separate tabs if they are stored in folders with unique names.

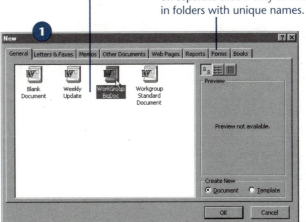

Sending a Document Out for Comments

When you send a document out to be reviewed, you can "protect the document for comments." What this rather unintuitive phrase means is that the only thing reviewers can do to the document is add comments—they can't make any actual changes. (They can, if they want, highlight the topics on which they're commenting.) When the document is returned, you can read the comments and consider the suggestions.

TIP

Always use a password to protect a document. If you don't use a password, anyone can unprotect the document and make changes to it. But remember to note the password and keep it in a safe place!

Distribute a Document

1 Create and save the document.

2 Choose Protect Document from the Tools menu.

3 Protect the document for comments.

4 Enter a password.

5 Click OK.

6 Confirm the password and click OK.

7 Choose Save As from the File menu, and save the document under a different name.

8 Send the new copy of the document to reviewers in any of the following ways:

◆ Route it via e-mail to have it automatically circulate among individuals.

◆ Mail copies to individuals via e-mail.

◆ Post it to a common mail folder.

◆ Post it to a network location.

◆ Copy it to a floppy disk.

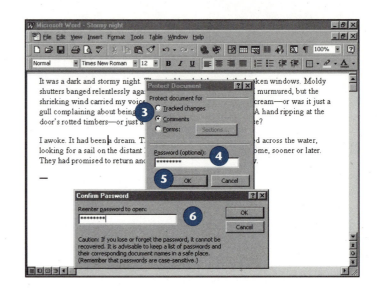

Review the Comments

1 Open the returned document.

2 If Word asks you if you want to merge documents, click the appropriate button:

◆ Click OK, and specify the original document if you want to gather the comments from this reviewer and, later, other reviewers into one document.

◆ Click Cancel if you simply want to review the comments in the returned documents.

3 Display the Reviewing toolbar if it's not already displayed.

4 Click the Next Comment button.

5 Read the comment.

6 Repeat steps 4 and 5 until you've read all the comments.

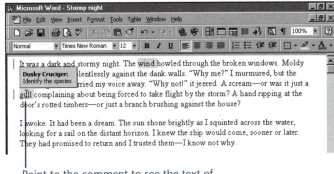

Point to the comment to see the text of the comment and the reviewer's name.

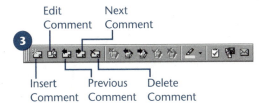

Edit Comment Next Comment

Insert Comment Previous Comment Delete Comment

9

Sending a Document Out for Editing

When you want reviewers to be actively involved in *changing* the content of a document rather than simply making comments about it, you can distribute the document for editing. All the changes are marked on the document, and you can accept or reject each change.

SEE ALSO

"Tracking Changes to a Document" on page 215 for information about the various ways to mark edits.

Protect a Document

1. Create and save a document.

2. Choose Protect Document from the Tools menu.

3. Protect the document for tracked changes.

4. Type a password.

5. Click OK.

6. Confirm the password, and click OK.

7. Save and distribute the document.

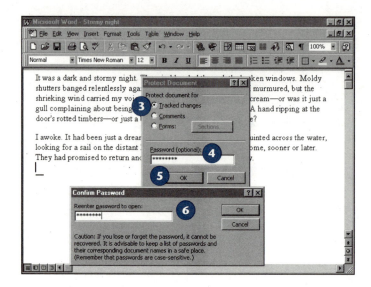

Review the Edits

1 Open the returned document.

2 If Word asks if you want to merge documents

- ◆ Click OK, and specify the original document to gather the comments from this reviewer and, later, other reviewers into one document.

- ◆ Click Cancel if you simply want to review the comments in the returned document.

3 If the document is protected, choose Unprotect Document from the Tools menu.

4 Display the Reviewing toolbar if it's not already displayed.

5 Click the Next Change button to locate the first edit.

6 Click Accept Change to use the edit, or Reject Change to discard the edit.

7 Continue to locate and accept or reject the edits. Then save the document.

It was a dark and stormy night. The wind just howled through the shattered broken windows. Moldy shutters banged relentlessly against the dank walls. "Why me?" I murmured, but the shrieking wind carried my voice away. "Why not!" it jeered. A scream—or was it just a bird gull complaining about being forced to fly in take flight by the storm? A hand ripping at the door's rotted timbers—or just a branch brushing against the house?

I awoke. It had been just a dream. The sun shone brightly as I squinted across the water, looking for a sail on the distant horizon. I knew the ship would come, sooner or later. They had promised to return and I trusted them—I know not why.

Colored strikethrough text is a deletion by a reviewer.

Colored underlined text is an insertion by a reviewer.

Vertical bar indicates that something has been changed on that line.

9

Routing a Document

If everyone in your workgroup has Word 97 installed, you can circulate a document for review using your e-mail system. You can route the document to a series of people or to everyone at once. You need a MAPI- or VIM-compatible e-mail system such as Microsoft Exchange or Lotus cc:Mail.

TIP

A routed document is sent in Word 97 format, regardless of the format you saved it in. To send the document in a format other than Word 97 format, save the file in the format you want it in, close it, and use your e-mail system to send it.

SEE ALSO

"Sending a Document Out for Comments" on page 206 and "Sending a Document Out for Editing" on page 208 for information about preparing a document for comments or editing.

Distribute a Document

1. Prepare the document to be distributed for comments or editing.

2. Point to Send To on the File menu, and choose Routing Recipient from the submenu.

3. Add the recipients' names.

4. Type a subject line.

5. Type a message to be included with the document.

6. Specify whether to send the document in sequence or to everyone at once.

7. Turn the routing options on or off.

8. Click Route.

9. Save and close the document.

Click to use your address books...
...to add names to the routing slip.

Routing Slip

From: George
To:
1 - Harry
2 - Indus
3 - Risso
4 - Dusky

Add Slip
Cancel
Route
Move
Clear

Address... Remove

Subject:
Routing: Dark Night review

Message text:
Please review and make your comments ASAP.

Route to recipients
⊙ One after another
○ All at once

☑ Return when done
☑ Track status
Protect for: Tracked changes

Turn on to receive a mail message each time the document is forwarded to the next recipient.

Select the level of protection (not available if the document is already protected with a password).

Incorporate Returned Changes

1. Open the returned document.

2. Click OK when asked if you want to merge changes into the original document.

3. Find and open the original document.

4. Display the Reviewing toolbar if it's not already displayed.

5. Use the Reviewing toolbar buttons to review and incorporate comments or changes.

6. Save the document.

Open the document that has the changes you want to include.

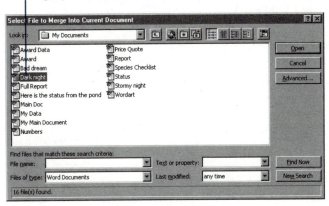

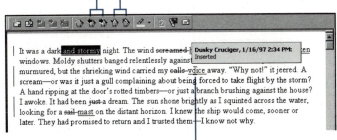

Jump to previous or next change.   Accept or reject change.

Point to a change to see who made it.

9

Reviewing a Routed Document

When a document has been routed to you with a routing slip, you can review the document and then pass it on to the next person in the list or back to the sender. The changes you can make to the document depend on whether the document was protected by the original sender and, if so, what level of protection was specified.

SEE ALSO

"Routing a Document" on page 210 for information about circulating a document via e-mail with a routing slip.

Review the Document

1 Open the document that was routed to you.

2 Display the Reviewing toolbar if it's not already displayed.

3 Edit the document as allowed:

◆ Add comments and highlighting if the document is protected for comments.

◆ Edit the text and add comments if the document is protected for tracked changes.

◆ Complete the online form if the document is protected for forms.

◆ Make any changes you want to the document if it has not been protected.

4 Click the Next Routing Recipient button on the Reviewing toolbar.

Tools that you use to change the document are unavailable when the document is protected for comments.

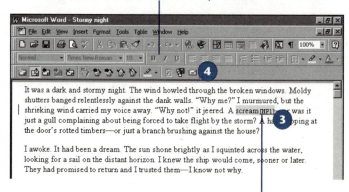

The initials of the person who made the comment are displayed whenever the comment area is open or whenever hidden text is displayed.

Adding Comments to a Document

When you're reviewing a document on line, you can add your comments to the document as text or as a sound recording.

TIP

Get to the Point! *A sound recording can make a document very large very fast. When you include sound comments, make them succinct! Be very cautious about using sound comments if you're e-mailing the document—it could become too large to be mailed by your system.*

Add a Text Comment

1. Display the Reviewing toolbar if it's not already displayed.

2. Select the text you want to comment on.

3. Click the Insert Comment button.

4. Type your comment.

5. Click Close.

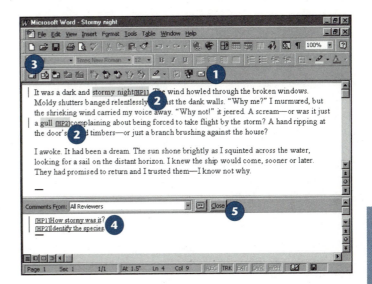

Add a Sound Comment

1. Select the text you want to comment on.

2. Click the Insert Comment button.

3. Click the Insert Sound Object button.

4. Record or insert a sound file.

5. Click the Play button and check your comment.

6. Choose Exit & Return from the File menu.

7. Click Close.

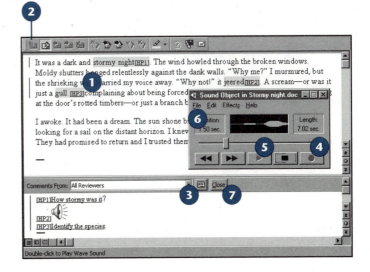

Highlighting Text

When you're reviewing a document on line, you can highlight text in a variety of colors to call attention to certain information. Then, when you're looking through the document at a later date, you can use the Find command to stop at every instance of highlighted text for you—it's so much faster than having to scroll through the entire document searching for the material yourself.

Highlight Text

1. Select the text to be highlighted.

2. Click the down arrow at the right of the Highlight button to open the color menu.

3. Select the highlight color.

4. Select the next text to be highlighted.

5. Click the Highlight button to apply the same color highlight.

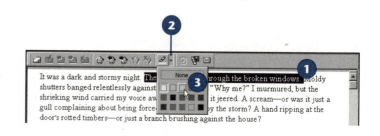

Find Highlighted Text

1. Choose Find from the Edit menu.

2. Click the More button if it's displayed.

3. Click the Format button, and choose Highlight.

4. Click Find Next.

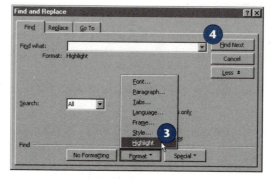

Tracking Changes to a Document

When a document is going to be edited, by you or by others in your workgroup, you can track the changes and set up the document for various ways of marking the changes.

> **TIP**
>
> **Colorful Comments.** *If the document is going to be edited by more than one person, leave the color options set to By Author and Word will automatically choose a different color for each reviewer's edits.*

> **TIP**
>
> *If the document has been protected for tracked changes, all changes are tracked and the Track Changes button is not available. You must unprotect the document to turn off the tracking.*

Choose a Marking Scheme

1 Choose Options from the Tools menu, and click the Track Changes tab.

2 Select the marks and colors for inserted text, deleted text, and changed formatting, and the color and location for the lines that indicate where changes occurred.

3 Click OK.

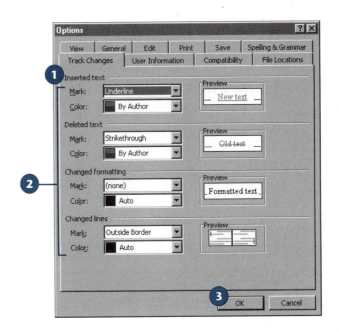

Make Your Mark

1 Display the Reviewing toolbar.

2 Click the Save Version button to save an unedited copy of the document.

3 Click the Track Changes button.

4 Edit the text.

5 Click the Save Version button again to save an edited copy of the document.

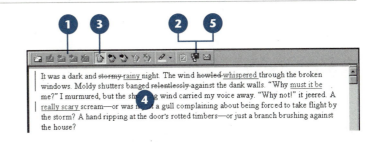

Limiting Access to a Document

If your document is posted in an area where others can access it, but you want to limit who can open it and who can make changes to it, you can use a password to control access.

Assign a Password

1. Choose Options from the Tools menu, and click the Save tab.

2. Type and confirm a password to limit who can open the document.

3. Type and confirm a password to limit who can save changes to the document.

4. Click OK.

5. Save the document.

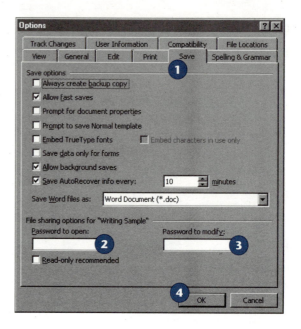

Reading a Document On Line

If documents were easier to read on a computer screen, we might be a little closer to the day when the promise of the paperless office becomes a reality. Most of us still feel that a printed document is easier on the eye than its screen version. However, if you'd like to save a few trees, consider Word's Online Layout View. It reformats a document to fit your screen: the fonts are larger, the page length is set to one screenful, and the document's readability is really greatly improved. Try it—you might like it.

TIP

Change of Scene. *To change views, choose a different view from the View menu.*

View a Document On Line

1. Click the Online Layout View button at the bottom left of the window.

2. Use the Document Map to find the section you want to read.

3. Click the Document Map button to close the Document Map.

4. Review the document.

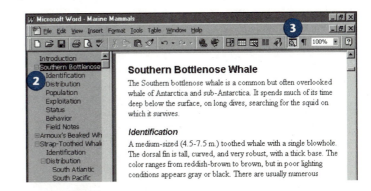

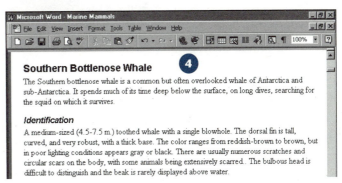

Set Up Online Layout View

1. Choose Options from the Tools menu, and click the View tab.

2. Set the Window options, and click OK.

Enlarge small fonts to improve onscreen readability.

Summarizing a Document

When you receive a long document to review, and your time is short, you can get Word to help you cut through some of the clutter by adding highlighting to the key points. Word won't always find all the important items, and it might highlight some unimportant material, but its highlighting capability is a very good starting point.

TIP

If the document is long and complex, Word might take a few minutes to summarize it.

SEE ALSO

"Creating a Summary" on page 136 for information about summarizing a long document.

Summarize a Document

1. With the document open, choose AutoSummarize from the Tools menu.

2. Select the Highlight Key Points option.

3. Select the size of the summary.

4. Click OK.

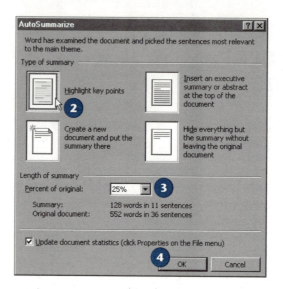

Review the Summary

1. Scroll through the document and review the key points.

2. Use the AutoSummarize toolbar:

   ◆ Click the Highlight/Show Only Summary button to display the summary only.

   ◆ Drag the bar to adjust the size of the summary in 1% increments.

3. Click Close when you've finished reviewing the document.

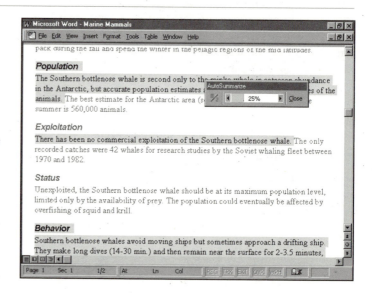

Working On Line

IN THIS SECTION

Using Word in Outlook E-Mail

Faxing Several People

Creating Hyperlinks

Converting Text into Hyperlinks

Making Text Stand Out

Adding Voice Messages, Video Clips, and Sound Clips

Getting a Document from the Internet

Creating an Online Word Document

Jumping to a Web Site

Creating a Web Page

If you're a member of a workgroup, you've already expanded your work area beyond your desktop. Now you can expand your work area ever outward to include not only your workgroup but your entire company, and, with Internet access, the whole world. The possibilities are endlessly exciting!

You can use a special form of Word—WordMail—as your e-mail editor. This means that you can use Word's features to format your e-mail, check the spelling and grammar, and so on. You can also send faxes to many people at once.

You can create hyperlinks that, with a single mouse-click, let you "jump" instantly to another part of your current document, to a specific part of any Microsoft Office document, to a completely different document or folder, or to any Web page, whether it's located on your company's intranet or on the worldwide Internet. Your mobility is swift and far-reaching, and your access to vast amounts of information is mind-boggling.

If you want to create documents for an intranet or for the Internet, you'll find that Word works very closely with Internet Explorer. When you create a jump in Word to a Web page, Internet Explorer displays the page. When you download a Word document from a Web page, Word displays the document.

Using Word in Outlook E-Mail

When you turn on WordMail in Outlook, you can use all the powerful features of Word—formatting, spelling and grammar checking, AutoText, and so on—in your e-mail messages. You can even format your signature in the font of your choice and have Word add it automatically to your messages.

Turn On WordMail

1. In Outlook, choose Options from the Tools menu, and click the E-Mail tab.

2. Turn on the Use Microsoft Word As The E-Mail Editor option.

3. Click the Template button, select the template to use, and click Select.

4. Click OK.

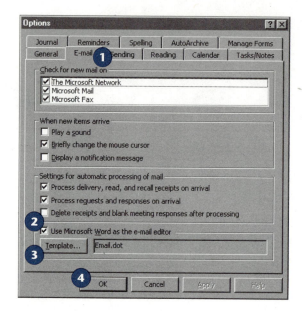

Create Your Signature

1. In Outlook, start a new mail message.

2. Type, format, and select the text you want for a signature line.

3. Choose AutoSignature from the Tools menu to display the AutoSignature dialog box.

4. Click Yes.

Compose a Message

1 In Outlook, start a new mail message.

2 Address the message.

3 Compose your message using Word's features.

4 Click the Send button.

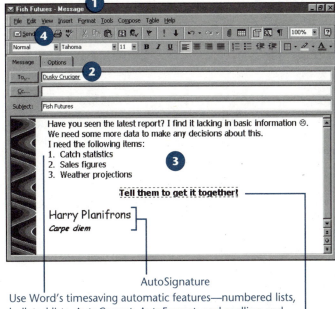

AutoSignature

Use Word's timesaving automatic features—numbered lists, bulleted lists, AutoCorrect, AutoFormat, and spelling and grammar checking—when you write messages.

Use Word's paragraph formatting, text formatting, and special effects.

10

Faxing Several People

If you send faxes from your computer rather than from a fax machine, you can send the same fax simultaneously to several different people. You give Word a list of who is to receive the fax, and Word creates and sends separate cover sheets for each recipient, along with the attached document.

SEE ALSO

"Creating a Fax Cover Sheet" on page 52 for information about creating a cover sheet for use with a fax machine.

"Faxing Merged Documents" on page 201 for information about faxing documents you've creating using external data sources.

TIP

If you're sending a fax to only one address, you won't see the Mail Merge toolbar.

Address the Fax

1 Open the document you want to send.

2 Point to Send To on the File menu, and choose Fax Recipient from the submenu.

3 Work your way through the Fax Wizard, specifying the document to be faxed and the fax software to be used.

4 Specify the recipients.

5 Complete the remaining steps of the Fax Wizard, but don't click the Send Fax Now button yet.

Map shows you the steps of the wizard.

Click to get names and fax numbers from one of your address books.

Type a name, get a name from an address book, or open the list to select a previously used name.

Type the Text

1 In the cover sheet, type the text that is the same for all recipients.

2 Double-click to check the appropriate boxes.

3 Type other information, as desired.

Merge fields inserted by Word—do not delete.

Information inserted by Word
Complete these items.

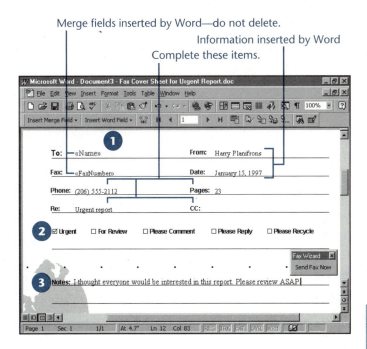

Review the Results

1 Click the View Merged Data button.

2 Verify that the data that replaces the merge fields is correct.

3 Click the Next Record button, and review the data.

4 Repeat step 3 until you've looked at all the fields.

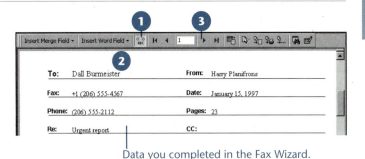

Data you completed in the Fax Wizard.

Click to send the fax from your computer to all recipients, and then close the document.

10

Creating a Hyperlink to a Document

You can create a *hyperlink* to refer to another document, and by clicking the hyperlink you can *jump* to that document. You can also create jumps to different types of files—sound or video files, for example.

TIP

"Hyperlink" is a "techie" term for a jump. You've used this type of jump if you've ever used a help system; when you click an underlined word or phrase, you're activating a hyperlink that "jumps" you to another part of the help file or to a location in a different file.

SEE ALSO

"Converting Text into Hyperlinks" on page 230 for information about creating hyperlinks from text.

Create a Hyperlink

1. Type and select the text to be used for the hyperlink.

2. Save the document.

3. Click the Insert Hyperlink button.

4. Click the Browse button to locate the file you want to jump to.

5. Click OK.

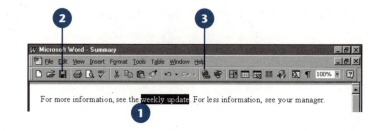

Location and name of document

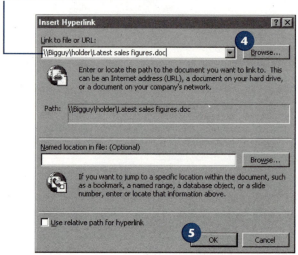

When you're distributing a document that contains hyperlinks, remember that the recipients must have access to the servers or folders where the hyperlinked material resides for the jumps to work.

The Use Relative Path For Hyperlink option is useful if you're referring to a file on your computer. Turn the option on if you intend to move your documents in their folders to a new location. Leave the option turned off for files that won't be moved.

Jump Around

1. Display the Web toolbar if it's not already displayed.

2. Click the hyperlink.

3. Read the material.

4. Click the Back button to return to the original document.

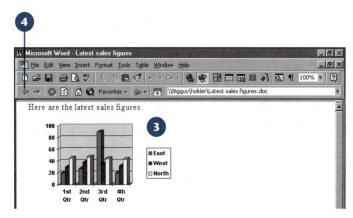

10

Jumping to Part of a Document

You can jump to a specific part of any Office document: a group of cells in an Excel worksheet or a slide in a PowerPoint presentation, for example. If the section to be used as a hyperlink is large, copy only the beginning: the heading in a Word document, the first cell in an Excel worksheet, a slide in a PowerPoint presentation, and so on. When the hyperlink is in place, click it to jump to that part of the document.

TIP

If you want to copy a slide from a PowerPoint presentation, switch to Slide Sorter view, and select and copy the slide.

Create a Hyperlink

1. Open the document that contains the item you want to jump to.

2. Select the area you want to jump to.

3. Click the Copy button.

4. Switch to your Word document, and click where you want to insert the hyperlink.

5. Choose Paste As Hyperlink from the Edit menu.

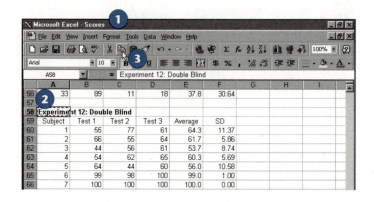

Hyperlink created by using the Paste As Hyperlink command

Change the Hyperlink Text

1. Click just at the left of the hyperlink.

2. Drag the mouse to the right to select the entire hyperlink.

3. Type new descriptive text for the jump.

Jumping to a Folder

You can create a hyperlink to a Windows folder, whether it's a folder on your computer, a shared folder in your workgroup, or a folder on a server. When you click the hyperlink, a window for the folder opens, giving you ready access to all the items contained in the folder.

SEE ALSO

"Jumping to Part of a Document" on the facing page for information about changing the text of a hyperlink.

Create a Hyperlink

1 Open Windows Explorer if it's not already open. Arrange your programs so that both Word and Explorer are visible.

2 In Explorer, locate the folder.

3 Hold down the right mouse button, drag the folder, and drop it into your document.

4 Choose Create Hyperlink Here from the shortcut menu.

Hold down the right mouse button, drag this folder...

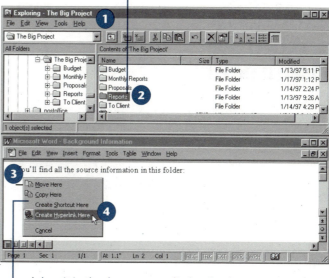

...and drop it in the document to display the shortcut menu.

Hyperlink to the folder is created.

Jumping Around in a Word Document

Whether you're circulating a document, placing it on an intranet, or using it as the basis for a Web page, you can use hyperlinks to jump to different areas within your document.

SEE ALSO

"Creating Cross-References" on page 154 for information about an alternative way to jump to other topics in your document.

"Creating a Hyperlink to a Document" on page 224 for information about creating a hyperlink.

Name a Destination

1. Click at the beginning of the area you want to jump to.

2. Choose Bookmark from the Insert menu.

3. Type a name for the location or select an existing bookmark name and redefine it so that it points to the current location.

4. Click Add to define the bookmark and close the Bookmark dialog box.

5. Save the document.

Name of selected area

Names of other areas in the document

Create a Hyperlink

1 Click in the document where you want the hyperlink to appear. Type and then select the text for the hyperlink.

2 Click the Insert Hyperlink button on the Standard toolbar.

3 Click Browse to specify the name and location of the current document.

4 Click Browse to specify the named location.

5 Select the name of the location you want to jump to.

6 Click OK.

7 Click OK.

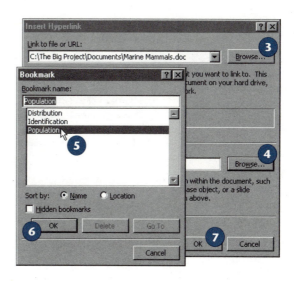

10

Converting Text into Hyperlinks

You can change the cryptic names, or *paths,* of network or Internet locations into easy-to-use hyperlinks, and then you can jump to a location by clicking the hyperlink. You convert text into a hyperlink using Word's AutoFormat and AutoFormat As You Type features.

SEE ALSO

"Jumping to Part of a Document" on page 226 for information about changing the hyperlink text.

TIP

If you don't want to format the entire document, select the part of the document that you do want to format before you choose AutoFormat.

Change Text into a Hyperlink

1 Enclose any path or location name that has any spaces in it with a less-than sign (<) before and a greater-than sign (>) after the name. (The signs won't appear in the hyperlink text.)

2 Choose AutoFormat from the Format menu to display the Auto-Format dialog box.

3 Click the Options button.

4 Turn on the Internet And Network Paths With Hyperlinks check box if it's not already checked.

5 Click OK.

6 Click OK.

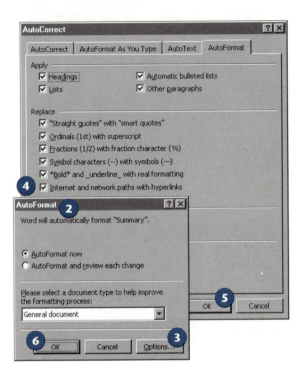

SEE ALSO

"Controlling Automatic Changes" on page 280 for information about setting other AutoFormat options.

Type a Hyperlink

1 Choose AutoCorrect from the Tools menu, and click the AutoFormat As You Type tab.

2 Turn on the Internet And Network Paths With Hyperlinks check box if it's not already checked, and click OK.

3 Type a less-than sign (<) if the location has any spaces in its name.

4 Type the location.

5 Type a greater-than sign (>) if you typed a less-than sign before the location.

6 Press the Spacebar.

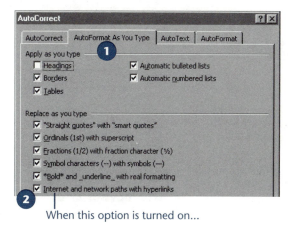

When this option is turned on...

...typing this text...   ...creates this hyperlink.

http://www.microsoft.com   http://www.microsoft.com

Making Text Stand Out

When you're creating documents on line, you can draw your readers' attention to specific parts of the document by adding special effects to the text. Some of these effects will be printed if you decide to print the document, but text effects are designed primarily to stand out on your screen, especially when you've added a background to the document or shading to the text.

SEE ALSO

"Creating a Background" on page 234 for information about adding a background to enhance an online document.

Add Text Effects

1. Select the text that will have the special effect.

2. Choose Font from the Format menu, and click the Font tab.

3. Select an effect.

4. Click OK.

This text has a shadow.
This text is outlined.
This text is embossed.
This text is engraved.

Add Moving Effects

1. Select the text that will have the special effect.

2. Choose Font from the Format menu, and click the Animation tab.

3. Select an animation effect.

4. Click OK.

This text has a blinking background.
Las Vegas lights surround this text.
This text has marching ants.
This text shimmers.
This text sparkles.

Change Text Color

1 Select the text you want to color.

2 Click the down arrow on the Font Color button.

3 Choose a color.

Add Borders and Shading

1 Select the text.

2 Display the Tables And Borders toolbar if it's not already displayed.

3 Select a border line style.

4 Select the weight (thickness) of the border line.

5 Click the Border Color button, and choose a color.

6 Click the down arrow on the Borders button, and select a border.

7 Click the down arrow on the Shading Color button, and select a shading color.

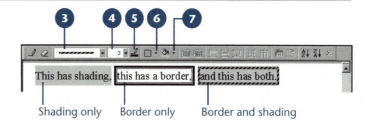

Shading only   Border only   Border and shading

10

Creating a Background

When you're creating a document that's going to be viewed using Word's Online Layout view, you can add an interesting background to enhance your text: colors, gradients, patterns that come with Word, or even an existing picture.

TIP

A background is visible only in Online Layout view; it will not be printed if you print the document.

TIP

Enticing Effects. *The Gradient tab lets you choose a predesigned gradient background or create your own gradient. The Pattern tab lets you use a patterned background in the color of your choice. The Picture tab lets you insert a background picture that fills the entire document window.*

Add a Solid Background

1. Point to Background on the Format menu.

2. Choose a color.

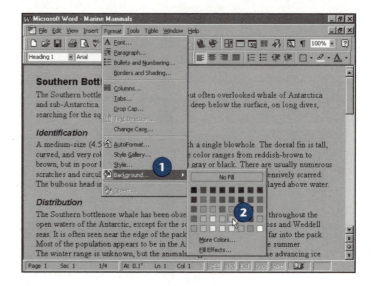

Add a More Interesting Background

1. Point to Background on the Format menu.

2. Choose Fill Effects from the submenu.

3. Click the appropriate tab, and select the type of background you want.

4. Click OK.

5. Format your text so that it's visible on top of the background.

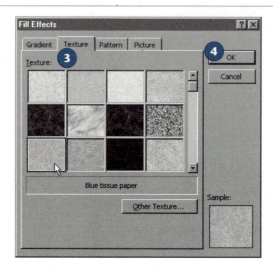

Recording a Message

If text and pictures just aren't adequate, you can include a voice message, or any other sounds you want to record, in your document. You need a sound card in your computer and an attached microphone to be able to record sounds, and whoever receives the document needs a sound card and speakers to play back the sounds.

SEE ALSO

"Adding Comments to a Document" on page 213 for information about adding voice comments to a document.

"Adding a Sound Clip" on page 238 for information about adding a sound clip to a document.

TIP

Sound Recorder is a Windows accessory. If Wave Sound isn't listed, see Windows Help for information about adding components.

Record a Message

1 Click in the document where you want to insert the sound.

2 Choose Object from the Insert menu, and click the Create New tab.

3 Select Wave Sound.

4 Click OK.

5 Click the Record button.

6 Speak, sing, or otherwise make noise in front of your microphone.

7 Click Stop.

8 Choose Exit & Return from the File menu.

9 In your document, double-click the icon to hear the sound.

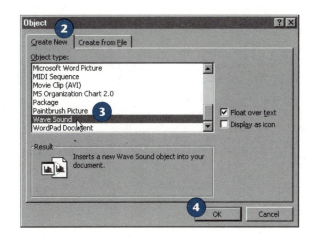

10

Adding a Video Clip

A video clip can add a great deal of interest and drama to a document—at the cost of considerable disk space, of course. You can add to the video clips that come with Microsoft Office 97 by importing video clips from other sources and storing them in the Clip Gallery.

TIP

If you haven't installed the Clip Gallery, you can still add video clips by choosing Object from the Insert menu and specifying the video file on the Create From File tab of the Object dialog box.

SEE ALSO

"Getting Free Stuff" on page 298 for information about adding items to the Clip Gallery from the Microsoft Web site.

Add a Video Clip

1 Click in the document where you want to insert a video clip.

2 Point to Picture on the Insert menu, and choose Clip Art from the submenu.

3 Click the Videos tab.

4 Select a video clip.

5 Click Insert.

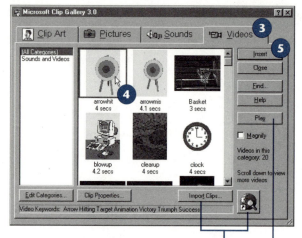

Click to import videos into your Clip Gallery.

Click to preview the selected video before adding it to your document.

*To play a video, you need
Media Player—a Windows
Multimedia accessory pro-
gram—installed on your system.
And, unless you like silent
movies, you'll need a sound
card and speakers, too, for any
videos that have sound.*

Change the Video Playback

1. With the video clip selected, point to Video Clip Object on the Edit menu, and choose Edit from the submenu.

2. Choose Options from the Edit menu.

3. Change the playback options.

4. Click OK.

5. Click outside the video window.

Media Player menus and controls appear in the Word window.

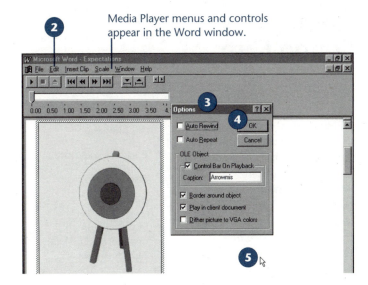

Change the Size

1. Drag the sizing handles to resize the image and the playback window.

2. Double-click the video window to play the video.

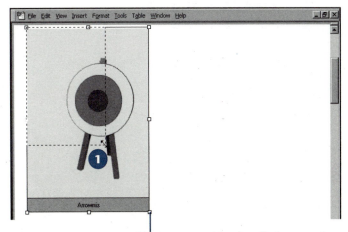

Drag a corner sizing handle to prevent distortion of the video window.

10

Adding a Sound Clip

A sound clip—music or other sound effects—can add another dimension to an online document. You can use two kinds of sound files: Wave Sound files, which contain digitally recorded sounds, and MIDI (Musical Instrument Digital Interface) Sequence files, which contain synthesized sounds.

SEE ALSO

"Adding Clip Art" on page 90 for information about adding items to the Clip Gallery.

"Creating a Hyperlink to a Document" on page 224 for information about creating a hyperlink to a sound or video clip.

TIP

To play a sound, you need Sound Recorder or Media Player—Windows Multimedia accessory programs—installed on your system, along with a sound card and speakers.

Add a Sound Clip

1 Click in the document where you want to insert a sound.

2 Point to Picture on the Insert menu, and choose Clip Art from the submenu.

3 Click the Sounds tab.

4 Select a sound clip.

5 Click Insert.

6 In your document, double-click the icon to hear the sound.

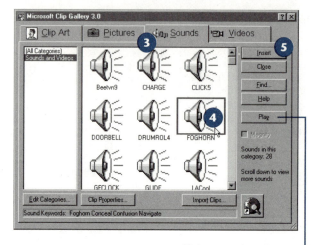

Click to preview the sound.

Getting a Document from the Internet

One of the easiest and most commonly used ways to get a document from the Internet is to use the FTP (File Transfer Protocol) method. You can access and download FTP documents directly into Word.

TIP

Who Goes There? *When you log on as an anonymous user, many FTP sites will require your user name as a password.*

TIP

Click the Search The Web button to locate specific sites whose address you don't know.

Define a Location

1. Choose Open from the File menu.

2. In the Files Of Type box, select the type of document you want to open.

3. Open the Look In box, and select Add/Modify FTP Locations.

4. Type the name of the FTP site.

5. Log on as an anonymous or a specific user.

6. Complete the user name and password areas if logging on as a specific user.

7. Click OK.

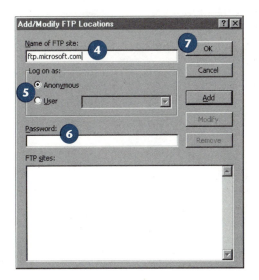

Get the Document

1. In the Open dialog box, double-click the site.

2. Select the type of file.

3. Navigate to find the document, and then double-click it.

4. Wait for the document to download, choose Save As from the File menu, and save the document using the name and location you want.

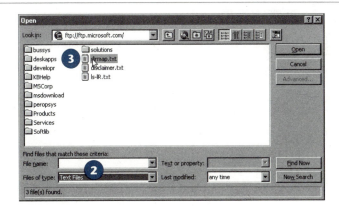

10

Creating an Online Word Document

A Word document becomes an effective online document when you design it for that purpose. Word provides all the tools and features you need to create an interesting, attention-getting online document. The people who access the document can read it in Word instead of using a Web browser.

SEE ALSO

"Creating Cross-References" on page 154 for information about an alternative way of jumping to other topics in a document.

"Creating a Hyperlink to a Document" on page 224 for information about adding hyperlinks to a document.

"Creating a Background" on page 234 for information about adding a background to a document.

Create a Document

1. Switch to Online Layout View.

2. Add a background to the page.

3. Add your content.

4. Add hyperlinks for jumps within the document, and for jumps to Web pages and other documents.

5. Save and close the document.

6. Place the document on the server.

7. In Windows Explorer, change the file's properties to Read Only.

8. Create hyperlinks to this document from other documents so that people can find and use your document.

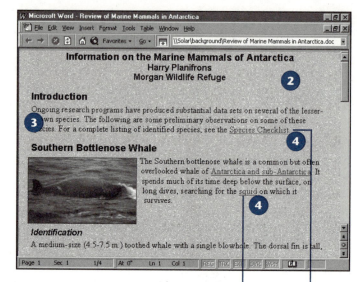

Hyperlink to another part of this document

Hyperlink to another document

Jumping to a Web Site

You can place jumps in your document that take your online reader to a Web page. The reader must have a connection to the Web (the Internet or an intranet) and a Web browser.

TIP

Because Word 97 was built to work closely with Microsoft's Internet Explorer, this example assumes that you're using Internet Explorer as your default Web browser.

Create a Hyperlink

1. Use Microsoft's Internet Explorer to find the Web site you want.

2. Click the Add To Favorites button, and add the site to your Favorites folder.

3. Type and select the text you want to use for the jump.

4. Choose Hyperlink from the Insert menu.

5. Click the Browse button.

6. Click the Look in Favorites button.

7. Select Internet Files in the Files Of Type list.

8. Double-click the Web site you want.

9. Click OK.

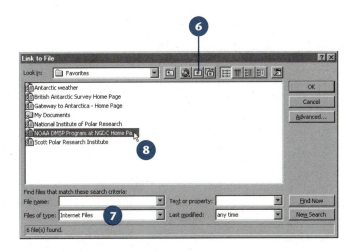

Get the Internet address from your Favorites folder.

10

Creating a Web Page

Web pages, whether posted on the Internet or on your organization's intranet, are wonderful—and often quite entertaining—ways to disseminate information to a large number of people. Word provides the Web Page Wizard, which makes short work of creating spectacular Web pages. After you create your page, contact your system administrator or your Internet Service Provider (ISP) for instructions on posting your Web page on the Web server.

TIP

When you select or change a page type or style, the page on your screen changes immediately so that you can preview the results.

TIP

If you don't see the Web Page Wizard, run Word Setup again, and install the Web Page Authoring option.

Use the Wizard

1 In Windows, create a folder for your Web page.

2 Choose New from the File menu.

3 Click the Web Pages tab of the New dialog box, and double-click Web Page Wizard.

4 Specify the type of Web page.

5 Click Next.

6 Select a style for the page.

7 Click Finish.

8 Save the document in the new folder you created. Be sure to save the document as an HTML document.

Modify the Content

1 Scroll through the document and insert your content:

  ◆ Click the placeholder text, and insert your own text.

  ◆ Copy and paste elements to create additional elements.

  ◆ Delete elements you don't need.

  ◆ Add hyperlinks.

2 Save your document frequently as you work.

Hyperlinks jump to different parts of this document.

Replace placeholder text with your own text.

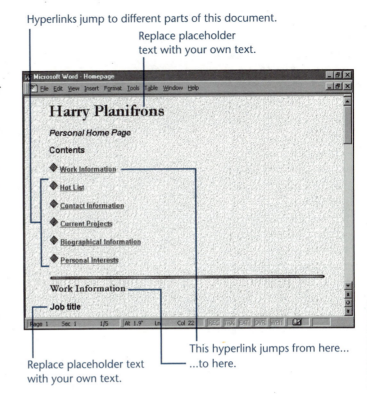

This hyperlink jumps from here... ...to here.

Replace placeholder text with your own text.

10

Converting a Document to a Web Page

If you want to create a Web page without using the Web Page Wizard, you can start by creating a document and then have Word convert the document into the HTML (Hypertext Markup Language) format used in Web pages. Once that's done, you can add some interesting HTML features to the document: decorative elements, hyperlinks, and even text that scrolls a message horizontally across the screen.

SEE ALSO

"Creating a Web Page" on page 242 for information about using the Web Page Wizard to create a Web page.

TIP

Keep the content simple in the Word document—many of Word's features aren't supported in HTML documents.

Create the Web Page

1. In Windows, create a folder for your page.

2. Open the Word document you want to convert to a Web page.

3. Choose Save As HTML from the File menu, and save the HTML document in the new folder.

4. Click where you want to place an element.

5. From the Insert menu, choose an element:
   - ◆ Horizontal Line
   - ◆ Picture
   - ◆ Video
   - ◆ Background Sound
   - ◆ Forms

6. From the Format menu, choose an element:
   - ◆ Font And Font Size
   - ◆ Bullets And Numbering
   - ◆ Text Color
   - ◆ Background

Add a decorative horizontal line.

Use a table to help lay out the page.

Add hyperlinks to other parts of your document.

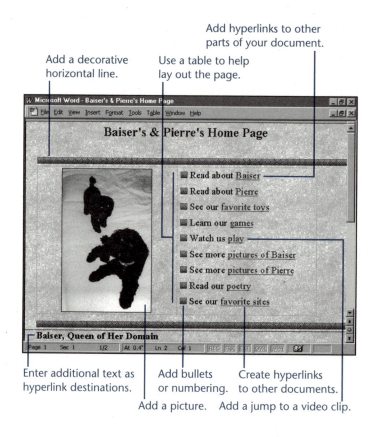

Enter additional text as hyperlink destinations.

Add bullets or numbering.

Create hyperlinks to other documents.

Add a picture.

Add a jump to a video clip.

Add Scrolling Text

1 Start a new paragraph where you want the scrolling text.

2 Format the blank paragraph with the font you want to use.

3 Choose Scrolling Text from the Insert menu to display the Scrolling Text dialog box.

4 Type the text you want to scroll.

5 Specify Background Color and Animation (Behavior, Direction, and Loop).

6 Set the speed of the scrolling text.

7 Click OK.

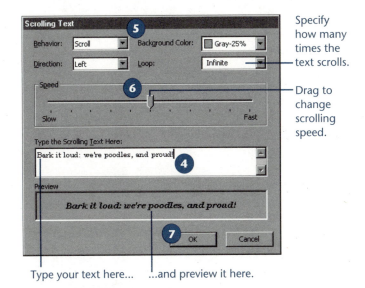

Specify how many times the text scrolls.

Drag to change scrolling speed.

Type your text here...   ...and preview it here.

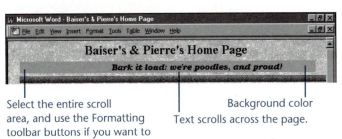

Select the entire scroll area, and use the Formatting toolbar buttons if you want to change the text formatting.

Background color

Text scrolls across the page.

10

Desktop Publishing

Wrapping Text

Creating Drawings

Positioning Objects

Creating Callouts, Captions, Drop Caps, Pull Quotes, and Margin Notes

Flowing Text

Creating Side-by-Side Paragraphs

Working with AutoShapes

Creating Stylized Text

Writing Text Sideways

Creating Page Borders

Creating a Watermark

Fine-Tuning a Document

Desktop publishing requires neither a desktop (a kitchen table or a lap will do) nor a publisher. Desktop publishing is simply a collection of tools and techniques that let you design and lay out pages so that they look the way you want.

Word gives you many of the features you'll find in most commercial desktop publishing programs, so, unless you need to do really specialized tasks, you can use Word to perform the most frequently used publishing techniques. For example, you can wrap text around pictures or other objects; add sidebars, pull quotes, callouts, dropped capital letters, and borders; and twist text into fantastic shapes using WordArt.

You'll encounter a few new terms in this section. Some tasks involve working with *text boxes* and objects that *float* above the text. Text boxes give you the freedom to put text inside a *speech balloon* or to *flow* text between columns on different pages. An object that floats is on a different *layer* from that of other objects; you can put a floating object on top of your text or behind it to create special effects.

This section of the book will show you how to use the power of Word to enhance your own creativity. We hope it will spark your imagination and free you to come up with new ideas and new approaches in your work.

Wrapping Text Around an Object

When you insert a picture, a graph, or any object that *floats* above the text, you can specify how you want the text to *wrap* around the object. It can be a lot of fun to try out the different looks you can create with Word's Text Wrapping feature.

SEE ALSO

"Adding Clip Art" on page 90 and "Adding a Picture" on page 91 for information about inserting clip art and pictures into a document.

Set the Wrap

1. Click the picture to select it.

2. Choose Picture (or Object) from the Format menu, and click the Wrapping tab.

3. Select the type of wrap you want.

4. Select the wrapping style.

5. Specify the distance from text.

6. Click OK.

7. Drag the picture to the location you want.

We have three new staff members and twelve new four-legged residents. Meet the entire staff, including our annual Zebra and fundraiser, just been open for Our crew has ducks to new start expanding game room. We new director, at the (Black-and-White) Ball The new gift shop has been completed and will business next week. now started moving the quarters, so the staff can the snack bar and video are having plans drawn up for the Morgan Wildlife Refuge Children's Theatre. Thanks to a generous grant from the city council, the theatre will soon become a reality.

— Square wrap

We have three new staff members and twelve new four-legged residents. Meet the entire staff, at the annual Zebra (Black-fundraiser. The new completed and week. Our crew ducks to new quarters, expanding the snack bar We are having plans drawn Wildlife Refuge Children's from the city council, the including our new director, and-White) Ball and gift shop has just been will open for business next has now started moving the so the staff can start and video game room. up for the Morgan Theatre. Thanks to a generous grant theatre will soon become a reality.

— Tight wrap

We have three new staff members and twelve new four-legged residents. Meet the entire staff, at the annual Zebra (Black-fundraiser. The new completed and week. Our crew ducks to new quarters, expanding the snack bar are having plans drawn up Refuge Children's Theatre. council, the theatre will including our new director, and-White) Ball and gift shop has just been will open for business next has now started moving the so the staff can start and video game room. We for the Morgan Wildlife Thanks to a generous grant from the city soon become a reality.

— Through wrap

We have three new staff members and twelve new four-legged residents. Meet the entire staff, including our new director, at the annual Zebra (Black-and-White) Ball and fundraiser. The new gift shop has just been completed and open for business next week. Our crew has now ducks to new quarters, so the staff can start expand and video game room. We are having plans drawn for Wildlife Refuge Children's Theatre. Thanks to a generous grant from the city council, the theatre will soon become a reality.

— No wrap

We have three new staff members and twelve new four-legged

residents. Meet the entire staff, including our new director, at the annual Zebra (Black-and-White) Ball and fundraiser. The new gift shop has just been completed and will open for business next week. Our crew has now started moving the ducks to new quarters, so the staff can start expanding the snack bar and video game room. We are having plans drawn up for the Morgan Wildlife Refuge Children's Theatre. Thanks to a generous grant from the city council, the theatre will soon become a reality.

— Top And Bottom wrap

It's a Wrap. *Change the wrapping outline to make small adjustments to the text wrap. Change the type of wrap or combine with AutoShapes to make major changes to the wrap.*

Square, Tight, and Through wraps give you additional choices: depending on where the picture is positioned within your text, you can choose to wrap text around both sides of the picture, on the left side only, on the right side only, or—for a picture that isn't centered in the text—on the side that has the most text.

"Creating a Drawing" on page 250 for information about working with AutoShapes.

Change the Wrapping Shape

1 Display the Picture toolbar if it's not already displayed.

2 Click the picture to select it if it's not already selected.

3 Click the Text Wrapping button on the Picture toolbar, and choose Edit Wrap Points.

4 Change the wrapping points.

5 Click outside the picture to deselect it.

Drag the wrapping line to create a wrapping point.

Drag a wrapping point to change the wrapping outline.

Change the wrapping outline...

We have three new staff members and twelve new four-legged residents. Meet the entire staff, at the annual Zebra (Black-fundraiser. The new gift completed and week. Our crew ducks to new quarters, expanding the snack bar We are having plans drawn Wildlife Refuge Children's from the city council, the including our new director, and-White) Ball and shop has just been will open for business next has now started moving the so the staff can start and video game room. up for the Morgan Theatre. Thanks to a generous grant theatre will soon become a reality.

We have three new staff members and twelve new four-legged residents. Meet the entire staff, at the annual Zebra and fundraiser. The completed and week. Our crew ducks to new quarters, expanding the snack bar We are having plans drawn Wildlife Refuge Children's grant from the city council, including our new director, (Black-and-White) Ball new gift shop has just been will open for business next has now started moving the so the staff can start and video game room. up for the Morgan Theatre. Thanks to a generous the theatre will soon become a reality.

...to control the way text wraps around the picture.

11

Creating a Drawing

For those of us who aren't great artists, Word's drawing tools provide a quick and easy way to create a variety of professional-looking drawings directly on the page. For an extremely complex drawing, you'll probably want to use a drawing program and then insert the picture, but try Word's tools out first. As nonartists, we were really astonished at some of the lively effects we created.

TIP

Use the Zoom Control on the Standard toolbar if you want to see a highly detailed view of your drawing when you're working with small shapes.

TIP

You can combine your drawing with other objects, such as pictures or graphs.

Create a Drawing

1. Display the Drawing toolbar if it's not already displayed.

2. Click AutoShapes, point to a type of AutoShape, and click the shape you want.

3. Drag the mouse to create the shape in the dimensions you want. Hold down the Shift key while dragging to draw the shape without distortion.

4. Use the adjustment handle, if present, to modify the shape.

5. Format the shape using the tools on the Drawing toolbar.

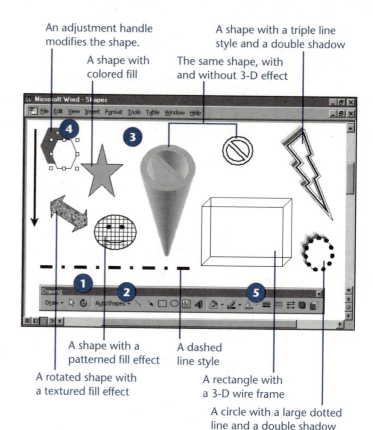

An adjustment handle modifies the shape.

A shape with colored fill

A shape with a triple line style and a double shadow

The same shape, with and without 3-D effect

A shape with a patterned fill effect

A dashed line style

A rotated shape with a textured fill effect

A rectangle with a 3-D wire frame

A circle with a large dotted line and a double shadow

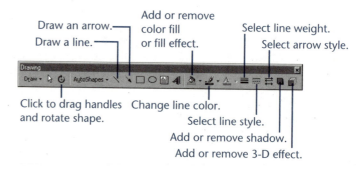

Draw an arrow.

Draw a line.

Add or remove color fill or fill effect.

Select line weight.

Select arrow style.

Click to drag handles and rotate shape.

Change line color.

Select line style.

Add or remove shadow.

Add or remove 3-D effect.

TRY THIS

Draw an AutoShape, choose Fill Effects from the Fill Color button, and add a picture to the shape. Draw a second AutoShape that you'll use as a background shape, and add a fill color. Stack and group the shapes.

SEE ALSO

"Aligning Objects" on pages 254–255 for information about "nudging" objects into position.

Combine Drawings

1 Create and format additional AutoShapes.

2 Drag the objects (the drawings) to arrange them.

3 Right-click an object, choose Order from the shortcut menu, and change the stacking order of the object. Continue rearranging until the objects are in the desired sequence.

4 Click the Select Objects button, and drag to enclose all the objects in the selection rectangle.

5 Click the Draw button, and choose Group.

6 Drag the drawing to the location you want.

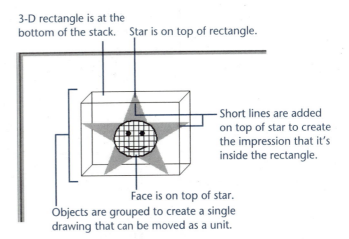

3-D rectangle is at the bottom of the stack.

Star is on top of rectangle.

Short lines are added on top of star to create the impression that it's inside the rectangle.

Face is on top of star.

Objects are grouped to create a single drawing that can be moved as a unit.

11

Positioning Objects on a Page

An object—whether it's a picture, an AutoShape, a graph, or any other type of object—is associated with, or *anchored to,* the paragraph nearest where you inserted the object. It's quite simple to position objects where you want them. If the paragraph moves to a different page, any object anchored to the paragraph moves with it.

TIP

If you can't move an object into the position you want, check to make sure that the object is not set to snap to the grid.

SEE ALSO

"Aligning Objects" on page 254 for information about using the grid.

Move an Object into a Relative Position

1 Display the Drawing toolbar if it's not already displayed.

2 Click the object to select it.

3 Click the Draw button, point to Align Or Distribute, and choose Relative To Page from the submenu.

4 Click the Draw button, point to Align Or Distribute, and choose left, center, or right alignment.

5 Click the Draw button, point to Align Or Distribute, and choose top, middle, or bottom alignment.

6 Click the Text Wrapping button on the Picture toolbar, and adjust the wrap as desired.

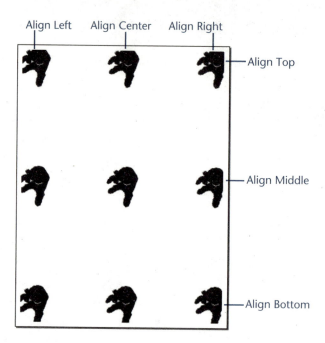

Align Left   Align Center   Align Right

Align Top

Align Middle

Align Bottom

TRY THIS

In Page Layout view, choose Options from the Tools menu. Click the View tab, turn on the Object Anchors check box, and click OK. Turn on the Show/Hide ¶ button on the Standard toolbar. Click an object, and you'll see an anchor symbol in the left margin next to the paragraph the object is anchored to. To anchor the object to a different paragraph, click to select the object, drag the anchor, and drop it next to the paragraph where you want it.

Fine-Tune the Object's Position

1 Click the Format Picture or Format Object button on the Picture toolbar, and click the Position tab.

2 Specify the horizontal position.

3 Specify where the distance is to be measured from (Column, Page, or Margin).

4 Specify the vertical position.

5 Specify where the distance is to be measured from (Margin, Page, or Paragraph).

6 Turn the Move Object With Text option on or off.

7 Turn the Lock Anchor option on or off.

8 Click OK.

Turn on to keep object in same relative position to the paragraph it's anchored to. The vertical distance must be measured from the paragraph.

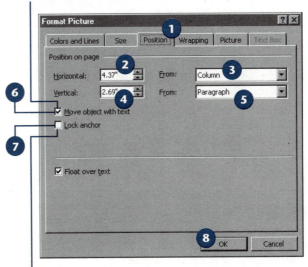

Turn on to keep the object on the same page as the paragraph it's anchored to, even if the horizontal and vertical measurements are from the page or margin.

11

Aligning Objects

When you insert objects—pictures, videos, or graphs, for example—aligning them properly on the page can often be quite tricky. Word has several tools that can help you position all the objects exactly where you want them.

Line Up the Objects

1. Display the Drawing toolbar if it's not already displayed.

2. Click the Draw button, and choose Grid.

3. Set the dimensions for your layout grid.

4. Turn on the Snap To Grid option.

5. Click OK.

6. Drag the object and drop it near where you want it to align. It will snap to the closest gridlines.

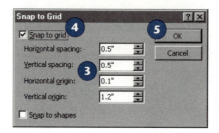

Although the grid is invisible, Word uses it to align objects.

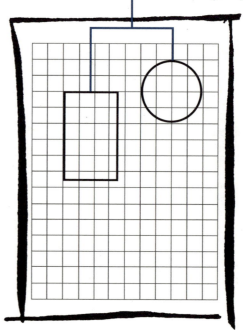

Positioning Objects on a Page on page 252 and _Flowing Text Between AutoShapes_ on page 265

TIP

Drag the little title-bar area of the Nudge submenu to turn the submenu into a floating toolbar.

SEE ALSO

"Positioning Objects on a Page" on page 252 for information about anchoring an object to a paragraph.

"Flowing Text Between AutoShapes" on page 265 for information about drawing and working with AutoShapes.

Fine-Tune the Position

1 Click the Draw button, point to Nudge, and choose a direction from the submenu.

2 Click the Draw button, choose Grid, and decrease the dimensions of the grid.

3 Use the Nudge command to move the object to different gridlines.

4 Click the Draw button, choose Grid, and turn off the Snap To Grid option.

5 Use the Nudge command to move the object one pixel at a time.

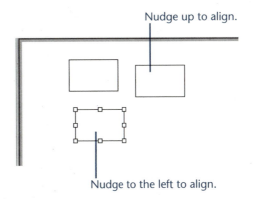

Nudge up to align.

Nudge to the left to align.

Connect AutoShapes

1 Click the Draw button, and choose Grid.

2 Turn on the Snap To Shapes option, turn off the Snap To Grid option, and click OK.

3 Drag a shape and drop it near another shape. It will snap to a border of the shape.

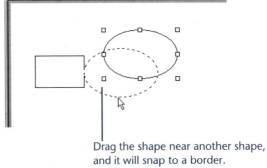

Drag the shape near another shape, and it will snap to a border.

11

Creating a Callout

A callout is a combination of a graphics element and a text box. Although its purpose is similar to that of a caption—to annotate, draw attention to, or explain the content of illustrations and other types of graphics—a callout is also a part of the graphic, whereas a caption is placed outside the graphic.

TIP

Callouts have built-in text boxes, so you can do anything in a callout that you can do in a text box.

SEE ALSO

"Flowing Text in Sidebars" on page 266 for information about working with text boxes.

Create a Callout

1. Display the Drawing toolbar if it's not already displayed.

2. Click the AutoShapes button, point to Callouts, and choose the type of callout you want from the submenu.

3. Drag the mouse to create the shape for the callout in the dimensions you want.

4. Type the text for the callout, using the text, paragraph, or style formatting you want.

5. Resize the text box to fit the text.

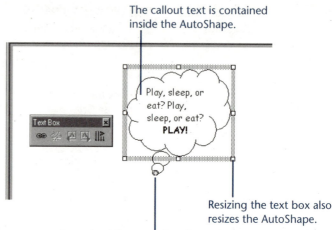

The callout text is contained inside the AutoShape.

Resizing the text box also resizes the AutoShape.

Drag the adjustment handle to elongate or reposition the "tail" of the AutoShape.

Format the Callout

1 Click the callout if it's not already selected.

2 Use any of the formatting tools on the Drawing toolbar:

- ◆ Rotate the callout.
- ◆ Add a fill color, gradient, texture, pattern, or picture.
- ◆ Change the line color.
- ◆ Change the line style.
- ◆ Add a shadow.

3 Move the callout where you want it.

4 Drag the callout line where you want it.

5 Group the callout with its associated object.

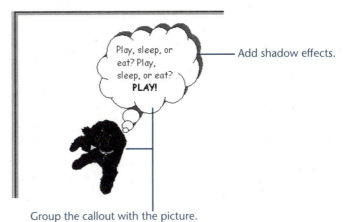

Add shadow effects.

Group the callout with the picture.

Creating a Floating Caption

When you have inserted an object—a picture or a graph, for example—that *floats,* or moves, above the text so that you can wrap text around the object, you can also create a caption that will float with the object.

SEE ALSO

"Creating Captions" on page 153 for information about creating captions.

"Wrapping Text Around an Object" on page 248 for information about text wrap.

"Flowing Text in Sidebars" on page 266 for information about working with text boxes.

TIP

When you're creating any type of table of contents or an index, remember that Word doesn't search text boxes, so items in text boxes won't be included. If you want to reference any text in a caption, you'll have to create a caption that doesn't float, or manually add the caption text to your index or TOC.

Create a Caption

1. Display the Drawing toolbar if it's not already displayed.

2. Click the object to select it.

3. Choose Caption from the Insert menu.

4. Type the caption text, and click OK.

5. Size and position the caption text box if necessary.

6. Click the Select Objects button.

7. Drag a selection rectangle around the object and the caption text box.

8. Click the Draw button, and choose Group.

9. Set the text wrap for the grouped object.

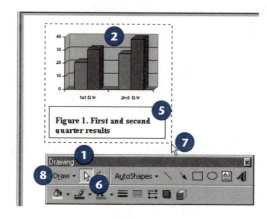

Figure 1. First and second quarter results

Creating a Dropped Capital Letter

A *drop cap*, sometimes called a "fancy first letter," adds style and interest to a document, and attracts the reader's eye to the page. Drop caps are typically used at the beginning of chapters or sections, as in this book.

Create a Drop Cap

1. Click at the left of the first letter of your paragraph.

2. Choose Drop Cap from the Format menu to display the Drop Cap dialog box.

3. Select a drop cap style.

4. Select a font.

5. Specify a size.

6. Specify the horizontal distance from text.

7. Click OK.

A three-line drop cap in the text

It was a dark and stormy night. The wind howled through the broken windows. Moldy shutters banged relentlessly against the dank walls. "Why me?" I murmured, but the shrieking wind carried my voice away. "Why not!" it jeered. A scream—or was it just a gull complaining about being forced to take flight by the storm? A hand ripping at the door's rotted timbers—or just a branch brushing against the house?

A three-line drop cap in the margin

It was a dark and stormy night. The wind howled through the broken windows. Moldy shutters banged relentlessly against the dank walls. "Why me?" I murmured, but the shrieking wind carried my voice away. "Why not!" it jeered. A scream—or was it just a gull complaining about being forced to take flight by the storm? A hand ripping at the door's rotted timbers—or just a branch brushing against the house?

11

Creating a Pull Quote

A pull quote is a short piece of text extracted from the document that calls attention to the content of the page and adds visual interest. You'll want to set the pull quote off from the rest of the text by surrounding it with some white space in the shape of your choice.

SEE ALSO

"Positioning Objects on a Page" on page 252 for information about placing an object relative to a paragraph or to the page.

Draw the Area

1. Select and copy the text you want to use for the pull quote.

2. Display the Drawing toolbar if it's not already displayed.

3. Click the AutoShapes button, point to a type of AutoShape, and click the shape you want.

Add the Text

1. Right-click the AutoShape, and choose Add Text from the shortcut menu.

2. Paste and format the copied text, and resize the AutoShape if necessary.

3. Position the pull quote where you want it.

4. Set the text wrapping to Tight, and adjust the shape and the position of the pull quote if necessary.

Use an AutoShape to define the way the text wraps around the pull quote.

It was a dark and wind howled through windows. Moldy relentlessly against the me?" I murmured, but carried my voice it jeered. A scream— stormy night. The the broken shutters banged dank walls. "Why the shrieking wind away. "Why not!" or was it just a gull complaining about being forced to take flight by the storm? A hand ripping at the door's rotted timbers—or just a branch brushing against the house?

Remove the AutoShape's line; or use a line style, color, and fill for dramatic effects.

It was a dark and stormy night. The wind howled through the broken windows. relentlessly against "Why me?" I shrieking wind away. "Why scream—or was complaining to take flight by the ripping at the door's branch brushing against the house? Moldy shutters banged the dank walls. murmured, but the carried my voice not!" it jeered. A it just a gull about being forced storm? A hand rotted timbers—or just a

"Why me?" I murmured. "Why not!" it jeered.

Flowing Text in Columns

You can flow text through multiple columns on a page, like the columns in a newspaper or magazine. By dividing a page into separate sections, you can even vary the number of columns in each section of the page.

SEE ALSO

"Setting Up the Page" on page 44 for information about changing the margins and page orientation within a document.

"Using Different Layouts in a Document" on page 130 for information about changing the layout of existing text.

"Flowing Text Between AutoShapes" on page 265 and "Flowing Text in Sidebars" on page 266 for information about using text boxes to flow text to different locations.

TIP

Columns don't balance automatically if you've inserted a column break.

Specify the Number of Columns

1. Press Enter at the end of your last paragraph.

2. Choose Break from the Insert menu.

3. Select Continuous for the type of section break, and click OK.

4. Choose Columns from the Format menu.

5. Specify the arrangements of the columns.

6. Click OK.

Use a predesigned setup...

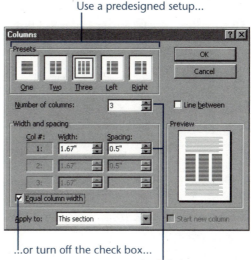

...or turn off the check box...

...and design your own column arrangement.

Add the Content

1. Type your text. The text flows automatically into the next column.

2. Control the text flow:

   ◆ Press Shift+Ctrl+Enter to create a column break and start text in the next column.

   ◆ Insert a section break to distribute the text equally between the columns.

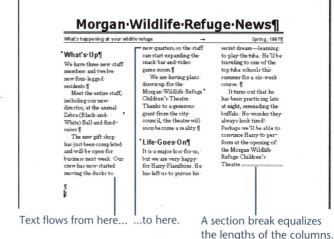

Text flows from here... ...to here.

A section break equalizes the lengths of the columns.

Creating Margin Notes

A popular design for many documents is to create wide outside margins, and then use them to place notes—tips or cross-references as in this book, for example—that are separate from the flow of your main content.

SEE ALSO

"Setting Up the Page" on page 44 for information about changing the width of the margins.

TIP

If you'll be printing on both sides of the page, turn on the Mirror Margins option when you're setting up the page. If you'll be printing on only one side of the page, turn off the Mirror Margins option and position the frame on the left or right side of the page.

Create a Layout

1 Set the margins so that the document will have wide outside margins.

2 Press Enter to insert a new paragraph.

3 Choose Style from the Format menu, click the New button, and name the style.

4 Click the Format button, and choose Frame.

5 Under Text Wrapping, select None.

6 Under Horizontal, set Position to Outside and Relative To to Page.

7 Set the horizontal Distance From Text to the amount of space you want between the note and the main text column of the document.

8 Under Size, set the Width to Exactly, and the At setting to the width of your note.

9 Click OK. Format the paragraph and font as desired, and close the dialog boxes.

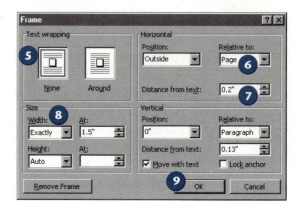

Because the margin note is a paragraph, you can add borders and shading as you can with any paragraph.

A margin note is anchored to a specific paragraph. To move the margin note, drag its anchor to a different paragraph, and then reapply the margin-note style.

"Positioning Objects on a Page" on page 252 for information about viewing and moving anchors.

Create a Margin Note

1 Click at the beginning of the paragraph that you want the margin note to be next to.

2 Press Enter.

3 Move back to the empty paragraph and type the text of the margin note.

4 Apply the margin-note style.

Text with margin-note style appears in the outside margins of the document.

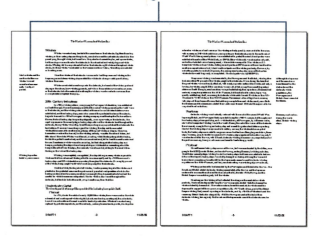

11

Creating Side-by-Side Paragraphs

Side-by-side paragraphs are often used to present an item in one paragraph—a picture, a title, or a topic, for example—and a description or an explanation of the item in the adjoining paragraph. You can create this type of layout using a Word table.

SEE ALSO

"Putting Information in a Table" on page 76 for more information about creating a table.

Create the Layout

1. Click the Insert Table button on the Standard toolbar, and drag out a one-row-by-two-column table.

2. Resize the columns to the size you need.

3. Format each cell with the appropriate paragraph style.

4. Remove any table borders, and choose Show Gridlines from the Table menu.

5. Enter your side-by-side paragraphs.

6. To add another row, click in the last cell, press Tab, and enter your content. Repeat until you've inserted all the content.

Use paragraph formatting to add a little vertical space after the paragraph.

Who we are	We are the team that brought you seventeen products, three of which actually made it to the shelves. We work long and hard, and we let everybody know it.
Why we're here	We're not sure. We've been asking the same question for three weeks, and I guess the answer is that we are paid to be here. And our boss told us to be here.
What we do	Sometimes we work hard. Other times we sit around and eat pizza. Whatever looks like fun we do, and whatever looks boring we assign to others.

Paragraphs are always side by side regardless of the length of the previous paragraph.

Flowing Text Between AutoShapes

AutoShapes can contain text, and you can flow text—or anything else that can be inserted into a text box—between the shapes to create all sorts of interesting and high-impact designs.

TIP

You can link a maximum of 32 text boxes.

TIP

Is This a Mistake? *Always proofread your flowed text to verify that it matches the original text. (In this case, there's no mistake—there really are two people named Kari on the team.)*

Add Text to a Shape

1 Display the Drawing toolbar if it's not already displayed.

2 Draw an AutoShape.

3 Right-click the shape, and choose Add Text from the shortcut menu.

4 Paste or type the text.

Flow Text into Another Shape

1 Draw another AutoShape.

2 Right-click the shape, and choose Add Text from the shortcut menu.

3 Click the first shape to select it.

4 Click the Create Text Box Link button on the Text Box toolbar.

5 Click the text-flow mouse pointer inside the second shape.

6 Continue creating AutoShapes and flowing text between them.

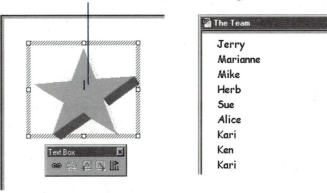

Add all the text here, even though it won't all fit.

The Team

Jerry
Marianne
Mike
Herb
Sue
Alice
Kari
Ken
Kari

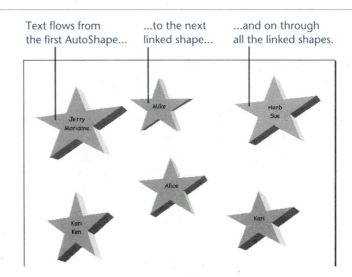

Text flows from the first AutoShape...

...to the next linked shape...

...and on through all the linked shapes.

11

Flowing Text in Sidebars

You can create text that flows from one location to another by placing the text in a text box and linking that text box to a second one. As you edit the text, it ebbs and flows between the text boxes. This is very useful for items such as sidebars or columns that often continue on another page.

SEE ALSO

"Inserting Frequently Used Information" on page 96 for information about creating AutoText entries.

"Creating a Floating Caption" on page 258 for information about formatting a text box.

"Flowing Text Between AutoShapes" on page 265 for information about adding text to AutoShapes.

Create the Flow

1. Choose Text Box from the Insert menu.

2. Drag out a text box to the dimensions you want for the sidebar.

3. Format the text box and place it where you want it. Either place the text box in a wide margin area or use text wrapping to isolate the text box from the main text of the document.

4. Create, format, and place a second text box where the sidebar text will continue.

5. Select the first text box.

6. Click the Create Text Box Link button.

7. Click the text-flow mouse pointer in the second text box.

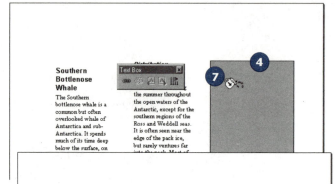

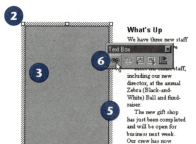

TIP

If you're going to use the same sidebar design several times in a document, or in different documents, save the formatted text box as an AutoText entry before you place any text in it.

TIP

To select all the text in linked text boxes, click in one of the text boxes and choose Select All from the Edit menu.

Add the Content

1. In a separate document, create the text for the sidebar.

2. Select and copy the text.

3. Click in the first text box and paste the text.

4. Add any other elements to the first or second text box.

Text pasted here...

...continues here.

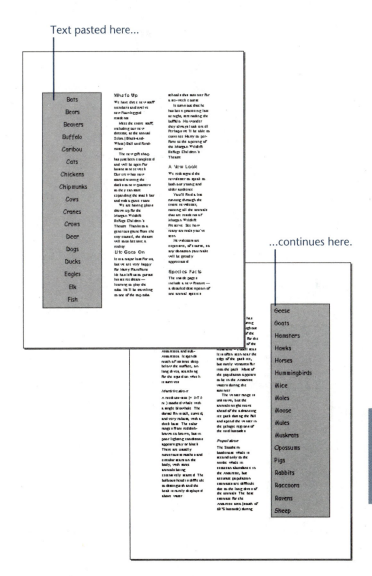

11

Creating Stylized Text

You can create some *spectacular* text effects by creating text as art. Word uses a special accessory program called WordArt that lets you twist your text into all sorts of weird and wonderful shapes and three-dimensional configurations, and then inserts the results into your document as an object.

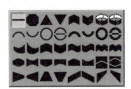

Create Word Art

1 Display the Drawing toolbar if it's not already displayed.

2 Click the Insert WordArt button to display the WordArt Gallery.

3 Select a WordArt style.

4 Click OK.

5 Select a font, a font size, and any emphasis.

6 Type your text.

7 Click OK.

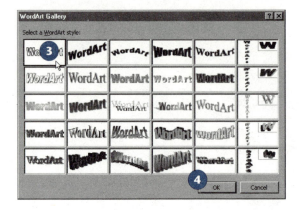

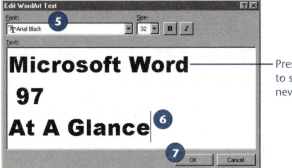

Press Enter to start a new line.

Fine-Tune the Result

1 Use the WordArt toolbar to

- ◆ Change the text.
- ◆ Choose another style.
- ◆ Change the fill color or effect.
- ◆ Change the shape.
- ◆ Rotate text to any angle.
- ◆ Equalize character height.
- ◆ Change alignment.
- ◆ Adjust character spacing.

2 Use the Drawing toolbar to

- ◆ Add or change a shadow.
- ◆ Apply 3-D effects.
- ◆ Stack and group the WordArt with any other objects.

3 Place the WordArt where you want it, and set the text wrap.

Button (Pour) shape with 3-D effect, rotated and tilted

Double Wave 1 shape with 3-D effect, rotated and tilted

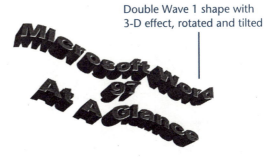

Deflate Inflate Deflate shape with wire frame 3-D effect

Fade Up shape with shadow

11

Writing Text Sideways

You can write any text sideways by placing the text in a text box and then rotating the text.

TIP

If you forget which buttons or tools are which, just hold the mouse pointer over any of them to see an identifying tooltip.

SEE ALSO

"Changing Paragraph Alignment" on page 31 for information about using the alignment buttons on the Formatting toolbar, and "Indenting Paragraphs" on page 34 for information about controlling the horizontal alignment of paragraphs.

"Creating Stylized Text" on page 268 for information about creating text as art.

Create a Text Box

1. Choose Text Box from the Insert menu.

2. Drag out a text box to the dimensions you want.

3. Format the text box and place it where you want it. Either place the text box in a wide margin area or use text wrapping to isolate the text box from the main text of the document.

4. Click in the text box so that an insertion point is visible.

5. Type or paste the text you want to run sideways.

6. Click the Change Text Direction button on the Text Box toolbar.

7. Format the text, and adjust the paragraph alignment, indents, and spacing as necessary.

Use the alignment buttons on the Formatting toolbar to control the vertical alignment within the text box.

Use paragraph spacing settings to control the horizontal alignment within the text box.

Text box has black fill and white text.

Creating an Inline Heading

Many document designs use *inline headings*—that is, the first sentence, or part of the first sentence, of a paragraph is formatted as a bold or italic subheading. An inline heading is also called a *run-in* heading because, unlike more prominent headings, it doesn't have its own paragraph. Just as you create main headings with a paragraph style, you create inline headings with a style, which is called a *character* style.

SEE ALSO

"Using Standard Paragraph Formats" on page 39 for information about quick ways of applying styles.

Create a Style

1 Choose Style from the Format menu.

2 Click the New button to display the New Style dialog box.

3 Enter a name for the style.

4 Select Character as the style type.

5 Turn on the Add To Template option so that the style becomes part of the template.

6 Click Format, and design the heading.

7 Click OK.

8 Click Close to close the Style dialog box.

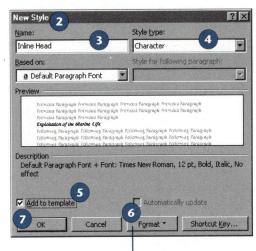

Specify font, language, border, and shading, as desired.

Create the Inline Heading

1 Start a new paragraph, using the correct paragraph style.

2 Choose the inline heading style.

3 Type the heading text.

4 Press Ctrl+Spacebar to turn off the character style, and then type the remaining text.

A character style formats only the characters it's applied to, not the entire paragraph.

Life Goes On. It is a major loss for us, but we are very happy for Harry Planifrons. He has left us to pursue his secret dream—learning to play the tuba. He'll be traveling to one of the top tuba schools this summer for a six-week course.

11

Adding a Line Border Around a Page

You can create a very nice "finished" look by placing a border around an entire page. Word provides a variety of formal and informal line styles that you can easily apply and that you can use to custom-design your own line borders.

Create a Page Border

1. Choose Borders And Shading from the Format menu, and click the Page Border tab.

2. Select a setting.

3. Select a line style.

4. Select a line color.

5. Select a line width.

6. Select the part of the document that will have this border.

7. Click OK.

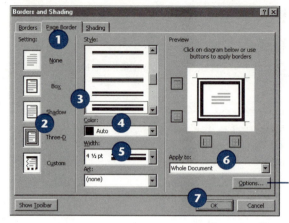

Click to change distance of border from edge of page or from text.

Create a Custom Border

1. Choose Borders And Shading from the Format menu, and click the Page Border tab.

2. Click None to remove any existing border.

3. Select a line style for one side of the page border.

4. Click the border button for that side.

5. Repeat steps 3 and 4 to add the line styles of your choice to the other sides of the page border.

6. Click OK.

Preview shows the arrangement of the border line styles.

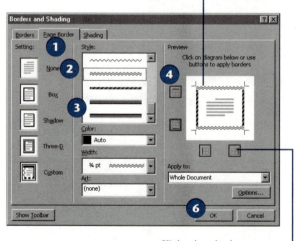

Click a border button to add or remove a border.

Adding an Art Border Around a Page

You can go beyond line borders and add one of Word's attractive and fanciful art borders around a page. How about a border of cupcakes or ice-cream cones for a party invitation, palm trees for a travel brochure, or ladybugs for an environmental newsletter? It's hard to resist playing with the different looks you can create with this huge collection of art borders, and it's so easy!

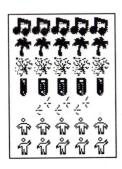

Create an Art Border

1 Choose Borders And Shading from the Format menu, and click the Page Border tab.

2 Select the art you want to use.

3 Specify the size of the art.

4 Look at the preview. If you want the border on only two or three sides of the page, click the appropriate border button to remove that side of the border. To put it back, click the button again.

5 Select the part of the document that will have the selected border.

6 Click the Options button if you want to change the distance of the border from the page edge or from the text.

7 Click OK.

Selected art forms the border.

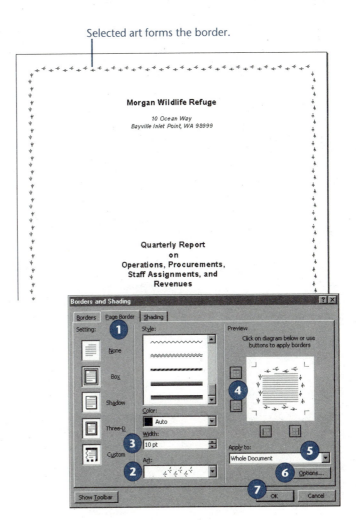

Morgan Wildlife Refuge

10 Ocean Way
Bayville Inlet Point, WA 98999

Quarterly Report
on
Operations, Procurements,
Staff Assignments, and
Revenues

11

Creating a Watermark

Watermarks are pictures or text (such as a company logo) that sit "behind" the main text. They appear on every page as if they were part of the paper. In a dedicated desktop publishing program, you create a watermark by placing a graphic on the background of the page. In Word, you place the graphic that you want as a watermark on the header and footer layer.

Add a Picture

1. Choose Header And Footer from the View menu.

2. Click the Show/Hide Document Text button.

3. Change the Zoom Control setting on the Standard toolbar to Whole Page.

4. Point to Picture on the Insert menu, choose From File from the submenu, and insert the picture.

5. Drag the picture sizing handles to create the watermark in the size you want.

6. Drag the picture and position it where you want it.

Make sure the picture is outside the Header and Footer areas.

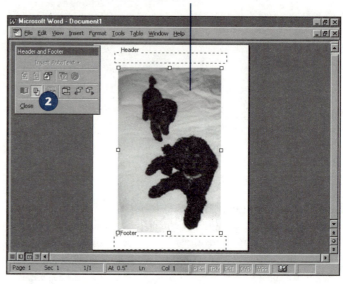

Make It a Watermark

1 Click the Image Control button on the Picture toolbar, and choose Watermark.

2 Click the Text Wrapping button on the Picture toolbar, and choose None.

3 Click Close on the Header And Footer toolbar.

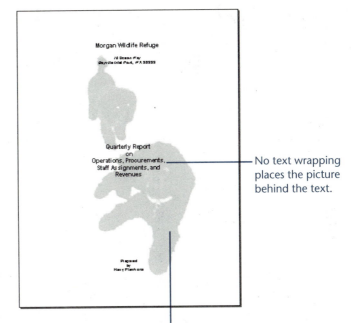

Morgan Wildlife Refuge

70 Ocean Way
Bayville Inlet Peak, CA 92222

Quarterly Report
on
Operations, Procurements,
Staff Assignments, and
Revenues

Prepared
by
Harry Planticans

No text wrapping places the picture behind the text.

The Image Control Watermark setting makes the picture light enough not to interfere with the text.

Fine-Tuning a Document

After composing your document, you can adjust the text and the text flow to improve the look of the document. Word does much of this automatically, but you can make a few adjustments yourself.

Control Widows and Orphans

1. Choose Style from the Format menu.

2. Select a style you've used for body text, and click the Modify button.

3. Click the Format button, and choose Paragraph.

4. Click the Line And Page Breaks tab.

5. Turn the Widow/Orphan Control option on or off.

6. Click OK.

7. Repeat steps 2 through 5 for any other body-text styles.

With Widow/Orphan Control turned off, the text extends to the bottom margin, regardless of whether it creates a widow or an orphan.

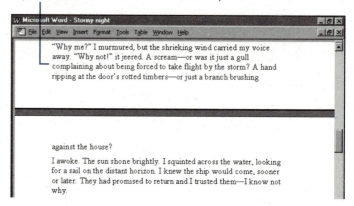

With Widow/Orphan Control turned on, the page breaks before the text reaches the bottom margin...

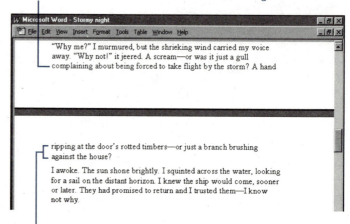

...so that there will always be at least two lines of a paragraph at the top or bottom of a page.

Break Lines

1. Switch to Page Layout view if you're not already using it.

2. Turn off automatic hyphenation if it's turned on.

3. Adjust the Zoom Control setting on the Standard toolbar so that you can see the entire length of the lines of text.

4. Adjust the way the lines break by pressing

   ◆ Ctrl+Hyphen (-) to create an optional hyphen that will occur only when the whole word won't fit on the line.

   ◆ Ctrl+Shift+Hyphen (-) to create a nonbreaking hyphen that will keep a whole hyphenated word on one line.

   ◆ Ctrl+Shift+Spacebar to create a nonbreaking space that will keep two words that can't be separated on the same line.

   ◆ Shift+Enter to create a manual line break.

The story before fine-tuning

I awoke. The sun shone brightly. I squinted across the water, looking for a sail on the distant horizon. I knew the ship would come, sooner or later. They had promised to return and I trusted them—I know not why.

All I had for company was a broken radio, a waffle iron, and my 3-D glasses. The land provided for all my needs, but none of my wants.

The sand stood in sweeping mounds as if to mock me. As I fell upon a dune, the sand poured through my fingers like the sands of an hourglass. I knew, however, my wait would not be measured in hours.

The sand grew in front of me, a 25 cm. testament to the time I have lost and will never regain.

Insert a line break.

Replace this hyphen with a nonbreaking hyphen.

Insert an optional hyphen.

Replace this space with a nonbreaking space.

The result after a little tweaking

I awoke. The sun shone brightly. I squinted across the water, looking for a sail on the distant horizon. I knew the ship would come, sooner or later. They had promised to return and I trusted them—I know not why.

All I had for company was a broken radio, a waffle iron, and my 3-D glasses. The land provided for all my needs, but none of my wants.

The sand stood in sweeping mounds as if to mock me. As I fell upon a dune, the sand poured through my fingers like the sands of an hour-glass. I knew, however, my wait would not be measured in hours.

The sand grew in front of me, a 25 cm. testament to the time I have lost and will never regain.

Ideally, paragraph edges should have the shape of a backward letter "C."

11

Adjusting the Spacing Between Characters

Sometimes you'll need to squeeze more text into a line; sometimes you'll want to spread the text out to fill up a line. Perhaps you want to create a special look in a heading by condensing or expanding the text. You can achieve all of these effects by adjusting the width of characters and the spaces between words.

SEE ALSO

"Creating Stylized Text" on page 268 for information about adjusting character spacing in WordArt.

TIP

As a side effect of increasing or decreasing the character spacing, the spacing between words is adjusted too.

Adjust the Spacing

1 Select the text to be adjusted.

2 Choose Font from the Format menu, and click the Character Spacing tab.

3 Change the settings to adjust the spacing:

◆ In the Scale list box, select or type a percentage to expand or condense the width of each character.

◆ In the Spacing list box, select Expanded or Condensed, and in the By text box enter a value to expand or condense the spacing between characters.

4 Turn on the Kerning For Fonts option to decrease the spacing between certain pairs of letters.

5 Click OK.

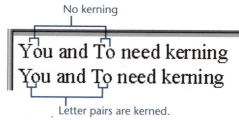

This text is not adjusted.

This text is scaled to 80%.

This text is scaled to 150%.

This text is condensed by 1 pt.

This text is expanded by 1 pt.

This text is scaled to 80% and condensed by 1 pt.

This text is scaled to 150% and expanded by 1 pt.

No kerning

You and To need kerning
You and To need kerning

Letter pairs are kerned.

Automating Your Work

IN THIS SECTION

Controlling Automatic Changes

Watching Your Grammar

Working with Spelling Dictionaries

Changing What Gets Proofed

Finding Alternative Wording

Keeping Track of Documents

Inserting Document Information

Working with Online Forms

Converting Documents into Word 97 Format

Getting More Help

Getting Free Stuff

Early in this book, we talked about using Word as a smart typewriter or as a *thought processor*. Although Word can't do any original thinking for you, you can set certain features so that Word knows what you want done in a given situation. You can then leave it to Word to execute on its own the actions it knows you want done.

For example, you can have Word check your spelling and make the appropriate corrections to certain misspellings or transpositions "on the fly"—that is, as you're typing. You can type four or five letters of a long word or phrase, and have Word automatically enter the rest— a wonderful time- and keystrokes-saver, especially if you use a lot of scientific, medical, or other difficult-to-type words or phrases. You can change the level of the proofreading that Word does for you so that it uses different criteria for business letters, technical reports, and the novel you're writing in your spare time. And Word will convert any documents that were saved in a different format into the Word 97 format.

And finally, in the unlikely event that you can't find the information you need in this book or in Word Help, and you have Internet access, we'll show you the way to Microsoft Online Support for Word, where you'll find the answers to the most arcane questions you can come up with.

Controlling Automatic Changes

Automatic text formatting, automatic insertion of long words or complete phrases, and automatic correction of common misspellings or transpositions are wonderful time-savers—provided they work the way you want them to. To make these tools do your bidding, you have to tell Word what (and what not) to do.

Set AutoFormat Options

1 Choose AutoCorrect from the Tools menu, and click the AutoFormat As You Type tab.

2 Turn options on or off to include or exclude formatting features.

Replaces characters with special characters, and applies character formatting.

Creates special formats.

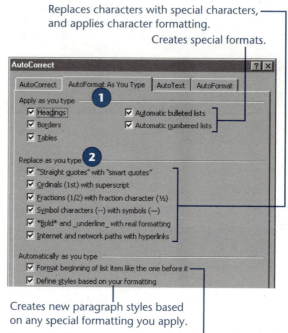

Creates new paragraph styles based on any special formatting you apply.

Automatically repeats any special character formatting applied to the beginning of a list item.

Control AutoComplete Tips

1 Click the AutoText tab.

2 Turn on the Show AutoComplete Tip For Autotext And Dates option if you want to see AutoComplete tips on the screen, or turn it off to disable the AutoComplete feature.

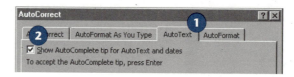

TRY THIS

Make sure that all the options on the AutoCorrect tab are turned on. Type the following: THis is due tuesday. will it be done? :-). Try to figure out which AutoCorrect feature caused which change!

SEE ALSO

"Word's Behind-the-Scenes Magic" on page 46 for information about the AutoCorrect, AutoFormat, and spelling- and grammar-checking features, and "Inserting Frequently Used Information" on page 96 for information about the AutoText feature.

TIP

Thought Processor? *If you type a word that immediately changes into a completely different word, an AutoText entry is probably responsible. For example, if you type* beer *and it changes to* champagne, *someone probably added an AutoText entry as a gentle hint!*

Set AutoCorrect Options

1 Click the AutoCorrect tab.

2 Turn options on or off to include or exclude the AutoCorrect features.

3 Click the Exceptions button to add or delete exceptions to Word's automatic correction of two initial capital letters or capitalization of a noncapitalized first letter after the apparent end of a sentence.

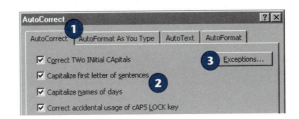

Modify AutoCorrections

1 Do either of the following:

◆ Create a new entry by typing the item to be replaced, typing the replacement text, and then clicking Add.

◆ Delete an existing entry by clicking the entry in the list and then clicking Delete.

2 Click OK when you've finished.

Type text you usually type incorrectly...

...and type the correct replacement text.

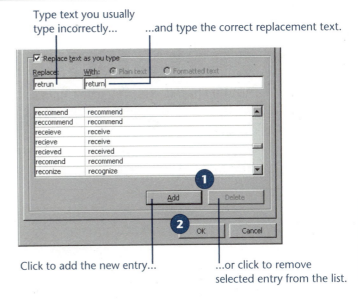

Click to add the new entry...

...or click to remove selected entry from the list.

12

Watching Your Grammar

We all know that nothing can take the place of human proofreaders and editors, but if you're not fortunate enough to have the services of a wordsmith or grammarian at your disposal, Word's grammar-checking feature is the next best thing. Not only will it help you polish your writing, but it can be tailored to specific *types* of writing so that it will react differently depending on whether you're writing a casual letter or a scientific report. You set the rules.

SEE ALSO

"Word's Behind-the-Scenes Magic" on page 46 for information about Word's grammar-checking feature.

Change the Rules

1   Choose Options from the Tools menu, and click the Spelling & Grammar tab.

2   Click the Settings button.

3   Select the writing style for which the rules are to be changed.

4   Turn off the grammar and style rules you don't want Word to remind you about, and turn on those you do want to observe.

5   Repeat steps 3 and 4 for each writing style you want to modify.

6   Click OK.

7   Select the writing style for the current document.

8   Click OK.

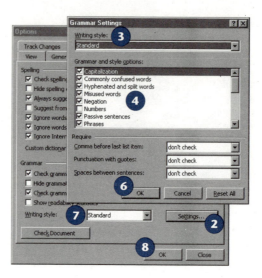

Correcting Your Spelling Dictionary

When Word tells you that a word is misspelled, and you then correct it and add it to the list of correctly spelled words, that word is stored in your personal dictionary. Word uses both its standard dictionary and your personal dictionary for correct spellings. If you've inadvertently added any incorrectly spelled words to your personal dictionary, Word won't identify those misspellings. However, you can easily edit the contents of your personal dictionary to correct such errors. (Note that you can't edit the standard dictionary.)

SEE ALSO

"Word's Behind-the-Scenes Magic" on page 46 for information about Word's spelling-checker.

Edit a Dictionary

1. Choose Options from the Tools menu, and click the Dictionaries button on the Spelling & Grammar tab.

2. Select the dictionary to be edited if it's not already selected.

3. Click the Edit button.

4. Correct any misspellings. Make sure there is only one word per line.

5. Click the Save button.

6. Close the document.

7. Choose Options from the Tools menu, and turn the spelling- and grammar-checking options back on.

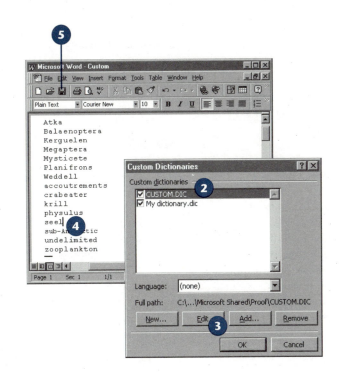

12

Adding or Creating a Custom Dictionary

You can add customized dictionary files to Word's spelling checker by creating a new dictionary or by using an existing one. Why use a customized dictionary? Let's say that in your work you use medical, legal, scientific, or other specialized words that might not be contained in your main dictionary. When you use a customized dictionary that contains those words, your spelling checker will recognize them and won't flag them as being incorrect.

TIP
If you purchased a commercially produced dictionary, follow its installation instructions. Some commercial dictionaries use a special format and won't be recognized by Word until an installation program is run.

Add or Create a New Dictionary

1. Choose Options from the Tools menu, and click the Dictionaries button on the Spelling & Grammar tab.

2. Click the New button or the Add button:
   - ◆ If you click Add, select the existing dictionary and click OK.
   - ◆ If you click New, name the new dictionary and click Save.

3. Select a language for the dictionary. Select (None) if you want the dictionary to be used for all text that is not formatted for a specific language.

4. Make sure that all the dictionaries you want to use are checked and that those you don't want to use are unchecked.

5. Click OK.

6. Select the dictionary to which you want to add any words.

7. Click OK.

Check only the dictionaries you want the spelling checker to use. The more dictionaries there are to check, the slower the spelling checker will be.

Creates a new dictionary.

Includes an existing dictionary.

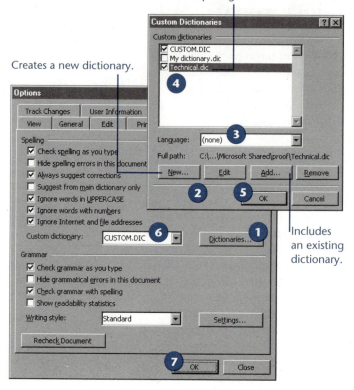

Changing What Gets Proofed

If you don't want some, or all, of your text checked for spelling or grammatical errors, or if there's text that you want checked using a different language dictionary, you can format that text to be handled differently from the rest of your document.

TIP

If you choose to use a different language, you must have a dictionary for that language installed.

SEE ALSO

"Adding or Creating a Custom Dictionary" on the facing page for information about assigning a language to your personal dictionary.

"Word's Behind-the-Scenes Magic" on page 46 for information about Word's spelling- and grammar-checking features.

Specify the Proofing Criteria

1. Choose Style from the Format menu, and click the New button.

2. Name and select a type of style:
   - ◆ Select Paragraph if the text will always be in whole paragraphs.
   - ◆ Select Character if the text will sometimes be only part of a paragraph.

3. Turn on the Add To Template option.

4. Click the Format button, and choose Language.

5. Specify the proofing:
   - ◆ Select (No Proofing) to turn off proofing.
   - ◆ Select a language to assign proofing to the dictionary for that language.

6. Click OK.

7. Click OK.

8. Click Close.

9. Apply the style to the text you don't want proofed or to the text to be proofed in a different language.

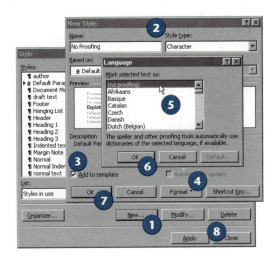

12

Finding Alternative Wording

If you find that you're using the same word repeatedly in one sentence or paragraph, or if a word you've used doesn't express your meaning precisely enough or provide the impact you want, Word's Thesaurus feature can come to your rescue. It will automatically provide you with a wide choice of similar words.

Select an Alternative Word

1 Click the word you want to replace.

2 Point to Language on the Tools menu, and choose Thesaurus from the submenu to display the Thesaurus dialog box.

3 Select the meaning the word has in the context of your sentence.

4 Select the most appropriate alternative word.

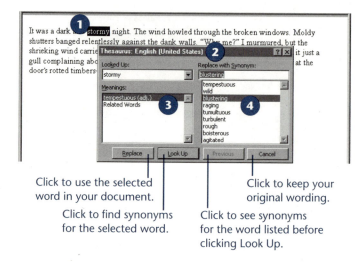

Click to use the selected word in your document.

Click to find synonyms for the selected word.

Click to keep your original wording.

Click to see synonyms for the word listed before clicking Look Up.

Keeping Track of Document Information

Word keeps track of a lot of information about your document. When you add your own information, you have an even more comprehensive record of the document and its history. You can then print this information for review and tracking purposes.

TIP

To have a different name automatically inserted into the Author box, choose Options from the Tools menu, and change the information on the User Information tab.

TIP

To print the properties whenever the document is printed, choose Options from the Tools menu, click the Print tab, and then turn on the Document Properties option.

Check the Document Information

1. Choose Properties from the File menu, and click the Summary tab.

2. Modify any incorrect information or add any missing information.

3. Review the information on the other tabs.

4. Click OK.

Print the Information

1. Choose Print from the File menu to display the Print dialog box.

2. In the Print What dialog box, choose Document Properties.

3. Click OK.

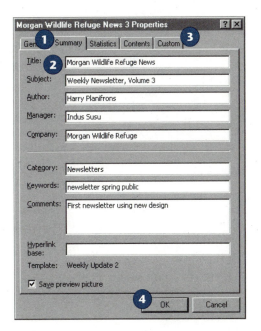

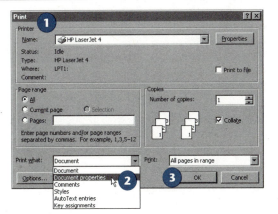

12

Inserting Document Information

Word can automatically insert all sorts of information about a document: its file size, the person who last worked on it, the number of words or pages, keywords, and so on. All you have to do is tell Word which information you want to include.

SEE ALSO

"Tracking Versions" on pages 134–135 for information about inserting document information into headers and footers.

TIP

To manually update the information in a field, right-click the field, and choose Update Field from the shortcut menu.

Insert the Information

1 Choose Field from the Insert menu to display the Field dialog box.

2 Select Document Information.

3 Select the field that provides the information you want to include.

4 Click the Options button.

5 Select the options you want.

6 Click Add To Field.

7 Click OK.

8 Click OK.

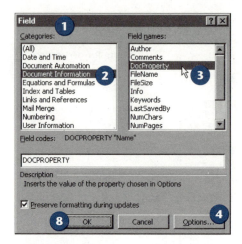

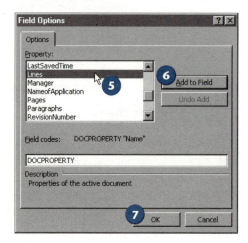

TIP

If the field codes print in your document, choose Options from the Tools menu, click the Print tab, and turn off the Field Codes options

TIP

If you don't see the most recent information in the field results when you print, choose Options from the Tools menu, click the Print tab, and turn on the Update Fields option. This will also update all your links to other files.

TIP

Frozen in Time. *To freeze a field result so that it no longer updates, convert the field result from a field into normal text. To do so, select the field, and press Shift+Ctrl+F9.*

Set the Display

1. Choose Options from the Tools menu.
2. Click the View tab, and do the following:
   - ◆ Turn off the Field Codes option.
   - ◆ Select When Selected in the Field Shading box.
3. Click OK.
4. Right-click a field in which the field code is displayed, and choose Toggle Field Codes from the shortcut menu.

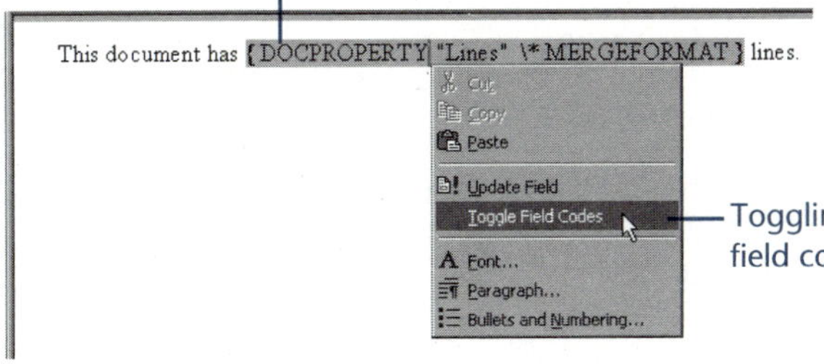

The field code is displayed instead of the field result.
This document has { DOCPROPERTY "Lines" * MERGEFORMAT } lines.
Cut
Copy
Paste
Update Field
Toggle Field Codes
Font...
Paragraph...
Bullets and Numbering...
Toggling the field code...

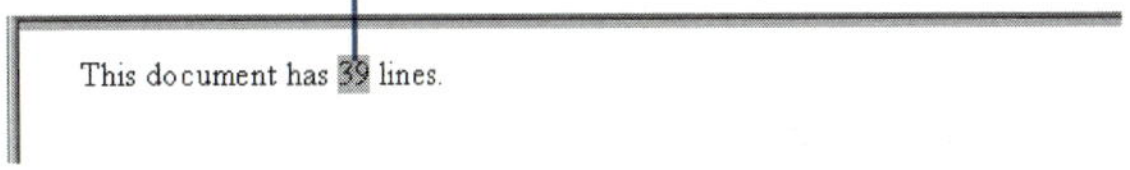

...displays the result of the field.
This document has 39 lines.

Creating an Online Form

Online forms are great when you need to complete the same information repeatedly, when you want to gather information from others on line, or when you need to print the information on a preprinted form. With an online form, you can ask specific questions and get the response in the format you want: text, an item selected from a list, or a checked box. You create your master form as a template, and then start a document to fill in the form. By protecting the document, you ensure that its main text can't be changed and that entries will be made in the form fields only.

SEE ALSO

"Creating Your Own Template" on page 58 and "Creating a Template from a Document" on page 62 for information about creating templates.

Add a Text Field

1. Start a new template.
2. Display the Forms toolbar.
3. Lay out the page, adding any explanatory text.
4. Click where you want the text-field box.
5. Click the Text Form Field button.
6. Click the Form Field Options button.
7. Change any of the options.
8. Click OK.

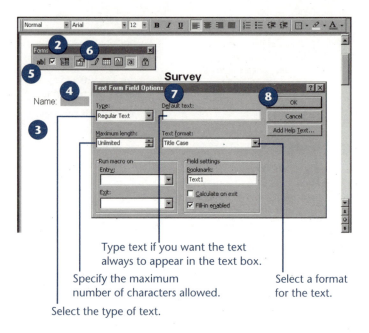

Type text if you want the text always to appear in the text box.

Specify the maximum number of characters allowed.

Select a format for the text.

Select the type of text.

Add a Drop-Down List

1. Click where you want to place the drop-down list.
2. Click the Drop-Down Form Field button.
3. Click the Form Field Options button.
4. Add items to the list.

Add an entry of spaces if you want the option of leaving the field blank.

Type text here, and press Enter to add it to the list.

Click to re-order items in the list.

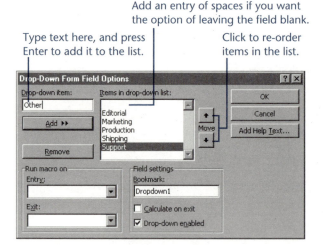

Add a Check Box

1 Click where you want
to place a check box.

2 Click the Check Box
Form Field button.

3 Type a label for the
check box.

Text box   Normal text is used for the label.

Create the Form

1 Choose Protect
Document from the
Tools menu to display
the Protect Document
dialog box.

2 Select the Forms option.

3 Type and confirm
a password.

4 Click OK.

5 Save and close the
template.

12

Using an Online Form

A predesigned form is a great tool for gathering information repeatedly in exactly the format you want. You can protect the form to allow entry in the form fields only. When the form has been completed, you can print it with all the content, or print only the completed data.

SEE ALSO

"Creating an Online Form" on page 290 for information about creating customized online forms.

TIP

If the completed information will always be printed on a preprinted form, set the appropriate print options in the template.

Complete the Form

1 Start a new document based on your form template.

2 Type text in a text field.

3 Select an item from a list.

4 Click a check box to add or remove a check mark.

5 Press the Tab key to move to the next field.

6 Save the completed form.

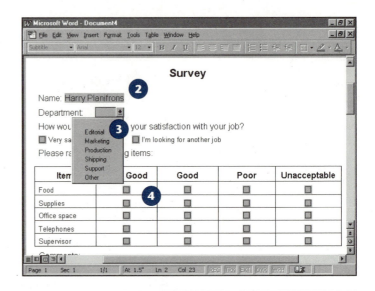

Print on a Preprinted Form

1 Choose Options from the Tools menu, and click the Print tab.

2 Turn on the Print Data Only For Forms option.

3 Click OK.

4 Click the Print button.

Converting a Document into Word 97 Format

When you open a document that was saved in a different format, Word converts the document into the Word 97 format. If you have several documents that need conversion, you can use a special wizard to convert all the documents at one time.

TIP

If Convert8 isn't available, install it by rerunning the Setup program. To install the Convert8 Wizard, turn on the Macro Templates check box under the Wizards And Templates option for Word.

If you installed Word as part of Office and you used the default folders, the path to Convert8 is C:\Program Files\Microsoft Office\Office\Macros.

SEE ALSO

"Adding Components" on page 294 for information about installing components.

Set Up the Conversion

1 In Windows, create a new folder. Move the documents to be converted into the folder.

2 Switch to Word. Choose Open from the File menu, select All Files from the Files Of Type List, navigate to the folder containing the Convert8 Wizard, and open the Convert8 Wizard.

3 Click the Enable Macros button if Word warns you that the document contains macros. Choose to conduct a batch conversion.

4 Step through the wizard:

   ◆ Select the type of document you're converting.

   ◆ Specify the location of files and where to save converted files.

   ◆ Select the documents to be converted.

   ◆ Click Finish to convert the documents.

   ◆ Wait while files are being converted.

5 Close the Convert8 document.

Select the type of document to be converted.

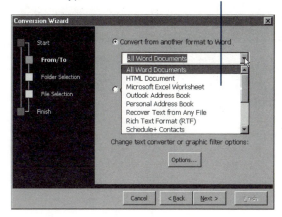

Select the type of files to be displayed in the list.

Double-click to add a file...

...or click to add all files.

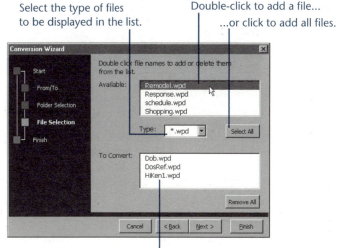

List of files that will be converted.

12

Adding Components

If, after you've installed Word, you find that you're missing components you need, you can run the Maintenance program to install the missing components. If you installed Word as part of Microsoft Office, you can also use the Maintenance program to install any Office component, including Microsoft Excel, Access, PowerPoint, and Outlook.

TIP

The Maintenance program will look different depending on the package from which Word was originally installed. If Word was automatically installed from your network, contact the network administrator for information about adding components.

TIP

Word and any other Office programs must be closed before you run Setup.

Add Components

1. In the Windows Control Panel, double-click Add/Remove Programs.

2. On the Install/Uninstall tab, select the package your Word program came in (Microsoft Office 97, for example), and click Add/Remove. Insert your program disk or CD if requested.

3. In the Setup dialog box, click Add/Remove.

4. Select Microsoft Word.

5. Click Change Option.

6. Turn on the options for the components you want to install; turn off the options for any components you want to remove, and click OK.

7. Click any other items you want to include, clicking the Change Option button as necessary to specify only selected components.

8. Click Continue.

9. Step through the remaining dialog boxes to complete Setup and install the components.

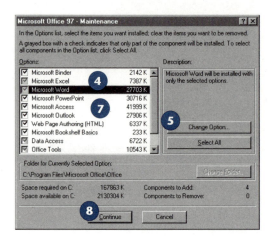

Getting System Information

If you ever need help for any problems you might encounter when you're using Word, the first thing you'll be asked for will be information about your system. This information is readily available on Word's Help menu, and it's a good idea to print it and keep it at hand—if your computer is misbehaving, you might not be able to access the information on screen when you need it.

SEE ALSO

"Getting More Help" on page 296 for information about the help resources that are available.

Get Information About Your System

1 Choose About Microsoft Word from the Help menu.

2 Click the System Info button.

3 With System selected, choose Copy from the Edit menu.

4 Close the Microsoft System Information dialog box and the About Microsoft Word dialog box.

5 Paste the system information into a Word document, and save it for reference.

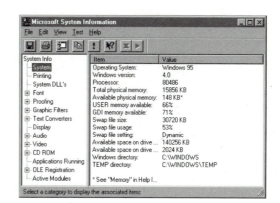

Getting More Help

What if you can't find the information you need in this book? And what if the Office Assistant and Word Help don't provide the answer? Don't despair. If you have access to the Internet, you have a wealth of additional resources at your fingertips.

Get Help from Microsoft

1. Point to Microsoft On The Web on the Help menu, and choose Online Support from the submenu.

2. Select the articles or items you want information about.

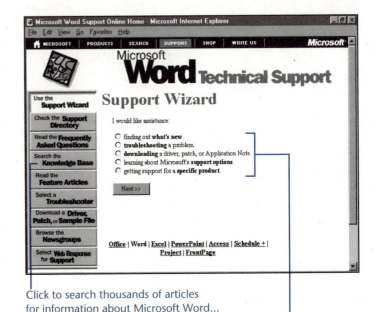

Click to search thousands of articles for information about Microsoft Word...

...or use the Support Wizard to navigate through the different sources available to find the information you want.

Get Help from Other Word Users

1 From the Microsoft Support Online page, click Browse The Newsgroups to go to the Word Newsgroups page.

2 Click the topic you want information about.

3 Post a message with full details of the problem, including the version of Word you're using and information about your system, if relevant.

4 Check back periodically for a reply.

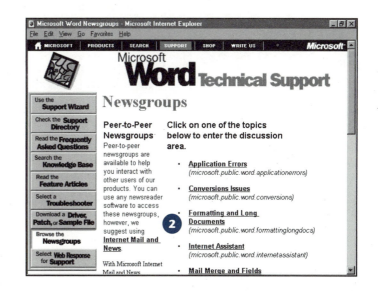

12

Getting Free Stuff

Want free stuff? Microsoft is giving away a variety of clip art, pictures, sound clips, and video clips that you can add to your Clip Gallery. All you need is an Internet connection, a browser, and a little time.

TIP

The Microsoft Word and Office Web sites have many links to additional free materials. To go directly to the download site, point to Microsoft On The Web on the Help menu, and choose Free Stuff from the submenu.

SEE ALSO

"Getting More Help" on page 296 for information about connecting to Microsoft Web sites.

Get the Clips

1 Point to Picture on the Insert menu, and choose Clip Art from the submenu.

2 Click the Connect To Web For Additional Clips button.

3 Step through the opening screens.

4 Click the type of clip you want.

5 Select a category.

6 Click Go.

7 Find the clip you want, and click its name to download it.

6 Exit the Clip Gallery Live, and see the picture you downloaded in your Clip Gallery.

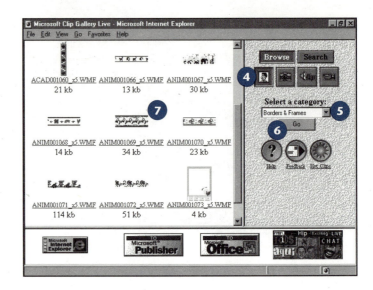

Index

Italicized page numbers refer you to information you'll find in a Tip or a Try This entry.

+ (addition operator) in formulas, 162
* (asterisk or multiplication operator)
    in filenames, 9
    in formulas, 162
    as wildcard character, *124*
\ (backslash) in filenames, 9
: (colon) in cell references, *163*
, (comma) in cell references, *163*
/ (division operator or forward slash sign)
    in filenames, 9
    in formulas, 162
= (equal sign) in formulas, 162
> (greater-than sign or right angle bracket)
    as bullets in lists, *40*
    enclosing hyperlink location names in, 230, 231
    in filenames, 9
    in Replace text, *146*
{ } (grouping operations sign) in formulas, 162
- (hyphen or subtraction operator)
    as bullets in lists, *40*
    in formulas, 162
    at line breaks, 277

< (less-than sign or left angle bracket)
    enclosing hyperlink location names in, 230, 231
    in filenames, 9
    in Replace text, *146*
| (pipe sign) in filenames, 9
? (question mark)
    in filenames, 9
    as wildcard character, *124*
[ ] (square brackets) in Replace text, *146*

A

About Microsoft Word command (Help menu), 295
Accept Change button (Reviewing toolbar), 209
Access. *See* Microsoft Access
accessory programs. *See also* components of Word; *names of specific programs*
    data as Word data source, *190*
    described, 94
    for playing videos, *237*

access to documents, limiting, 216. *See also* protecting documents
actions. *See also names of specific actions*
    keyboard compared with mouse, 98
    recording for macros, *99*
Add button (Bookmark dialog box), 228
Add button (Custom Dictionaries dialog box), 284
adding
    addresses to mailing labels, 180
    AutoShapes, 260
    backgrounds, 234
    blank lines, 36
    borders
        around pages, 272–73
        around paragraphs, 42–43
        around selected text, 233
        around tables, 82–83
    callouts, 256–57
    captions, 153, 256
    check boxes to online forms, 291
    clip art, 90

adding, *continued*
columns in documents, 25
columns in tables, 88–89
commands to menus, 100
comments to
documents, 213
components to Word, 294
Continuous section
breaks, *157*
data from Microsoft Access,
193, 194
data from Microsoft Excel,
165, 166, 167, 170, 192
dates and times in
footers, *117*
drop-down lists to online
forms, 290
endnotes, 151
fields
in data sources, 188
in form letters, *177*
in online forms, 290–91
footnotes, 148
graphics images to
documents, 91, 274
gutters, 113
hyperlinks, 25
information about
documents, 135,
288–89
macros to menus, 101
Microsoft Excel worksheets,
25, 165
MIDI sequences to
documents, 238
numbers in functions, 162
page breaks, 109, 276, *277*
page numbers, 129
parts of documents to other
documents, 119
passwords for document
access, 216
pictures to AutoShapes, *251*

adding, *continued*
shortcuts for inserting
symbols, 147
shortcuts for inserting
text, 97
sound clips to documents,
213, 235, 238
subdocuments, 140
symbols to documents, 145,
146–47
tables, 25
borders to, 82–83
columns in, 76, 88–89
rows in, 76, *77*, 88
shading to, 83
text in, 77
tabs in table cells, *77*
text
to AutoShapes, 265
to columns, 261
to documents, 8, 10
to sidebars, 267
text fields in online
forms, 290
toolbar items, 102
video clips to documents,
236–37
voice messages to
documents, 213
Word documents to other
documents, 118
ZIP codes to mailing
labels, 181
addition operator (+) in
formulas, 162
Add/Remove Programs dialog
box, 294
Address Book feature, *181*
addresses
creating address-book, *181*
on envelopes, 70–71, 182–84
in faxes, 222
on mailing labels, 69, 180–81

Add To Favorites button (in
Internet Explorer), 241
Add To Template option (Modify
Style dialog box), 64
Add To Template option (New
Style dialog box), 271
alien objects in Word, 94
alignment
of paragraphs, 24, 31, 32
snapping objects to grid,
252, 254–55
of tables, 86
of text, 270
Align Or Distribute submenu
(Draw button), 252
All Endnotes tab (Note Options
dialog box), 151
All Footnotes tab (Note Options
dialog box), 149
Alt key
+F9, *62*
hiding and displaying field
codes, *62*
moving toolbar buttons, *103*
anchors
of margin notes, *263*
on objects, 252, *253*
And/Or (logical operators), *195*
angle brackets (< >)
as bullets in lists, *40*
enclosing hyperlink location
names in, 230, 231
in filenames, 9
in Replace text, *146*
animated text on Web
pages, 245
Animation tab (Font dialog
box), 232
Appearance tab (Display
Properties dialog
box), *233*
applications. *See* programs
arrow keys, 77

art. *See* graphics images
Ask field (Insert Word Field
button), *199*
assigning passwords for
document access, 216
asterisk (*)
in filenames, 9
in formulas, 162
as wildcard character, *124*
author of document
editing information
about, *287*
AutoComplete feature, 96, *97*
AutoCorrect command (Tools
menu), 146
AutoCorrect dialog box, 146
AutoCorrect feature
described, 46
hyperlinks added
automatically, 231
list of spelling errors, 18, 281
options, 280, 281
symbols inserted
automatically, 146
using, *280*
AutoCorrect tab (AutoCorrect
dialog box), 281
AutoFormat As You Type tab
(AutoCorrect dialog box),
35, 231, 280
AutoFormat button (Tables And
Borders toolbar), 77
AutoFormat command (Format
menu), 45
AutoFormat dialog box, 45
AutoFormat feature. *See also*
paragraph formatting;
Table AutoFormat feature
converting text to hyperlinks
using, 230–31
creating lists with, *40*
described, 45–46

AutoFormat feature, *continued*
  formatting only parts of
      documents, *230*
  options, 280
Automatically Update The Style
    From Now On check box
    (Modify Style dialog
    box), *107*
AutoNumber option (Footnote
    And Endnote dialog
    box), 148
AutoShapes
  adding pictures to, *251*
  adding text to, 265
  adding to documents, 260
  choosing shapes from, 250
  resizing, 250
  rotating, *257*
  snapping to grid, 255
  wrapping text around, *249*
AutoShapes button (Drawing
    toolbar), 250, 256, 260
AutoShape shortcut menu,
    260, 265
AutoSignature command (Tools
    menu), 220
AutoSignature dialog box, 220
AutoSum button (Tables And
    Borders toolbar), 160, 161
AutoSummarize command
    (Tools menu), 136
AutoSummarize dialog box, 136
AutoSummarize toolbar, 218
AutoText command (Insert
    menu), 97
AutoText feature. *See also* text
  copying between
        templates, 66
  described, 96
  entries
    creating, 96, *97*
    editing, *281*
    list of, *97*
    saving, *267*

AutoText tab (AutoCorrect
    dialog box), 96, 97, 280
averaging numbers in
    functions, 162
awards, creating, 186–87

Background command (Format
    menu), 234
backgrounds
  adding, 234
  color on Web pages, 245
  for text, 232
  shapes as, *251*
backslash (\) in filenames, 9
Backspace key
  deleting text using, 10
  turning off bullets and
        numbering, 40
balloons (speech), 247, 256–57
bar codes (postal)
  on envelopes, *71*
  Insert Postal Bar Code dialog
        box, 182
  on labels, 69, 181
black-and-white images, *93*.
        See also graphics images
blank lines, adding or deleting,
        36. *See also* lines of text
blinking background for
        text, 232
Bold button, 24, 28
boldface. *See also* emphasizing
        text; fonts
  adding, 28
  applying to selected text
        only, *107*
  button on toolbar, 24, 28
Bookmark command (Insert
    menu), 163
Bookmark dialog box, 163, 228

bookmarks inserted by
    Word, *229*
Border Color button (Tables And
    Borders toolbar), 233
borders. *See also* Tables and
    Borders toolbar
  color selection, 233
  deleting, 43
  for drop caps, *259*
  for pages, 272–73
  for paragraphs, 42–43
  for selected text, 233
  for tables, 78, 82–83
  including in style, *42*
Borders And Shading command
    (Format menu), 272
Borders And Shading dialog box,
    272, 273. *See also* shading
Borders button (Tables And
    Borders toolbar)
  picture of, 24, 42
  using, *43, 83*
Borders menu, 42, 43
boundaries of tables, *76*. *See also*
    tables
boxes around text. *See* borders
Break command (Insert menu),
    132, 261
Break dialog box, 132
breaking lines, 277
breaking pages, 109, 276, *277*
Briefcase. *See* Windows Briefcase
Browse button
  in Insert Hyperlink dialog
        box, 224, 229
  on vertical scroll bar, 7
browsing through documents,
    options for, 120, 150. *See
    also* finding
bulleted lists. *See also* lists
  bullet types, *40*
  button on toolbar, 24, 41
  creating, 40, 41
  on Web pages, 244

Bullets And Numbering
    command (Format
    menu), 155
Bullets And Numbering dialog
    box, 155. *See also*
    numbering
Bullets button, 24, 41
buttons. *See also names of
    specific buttons or toolbars*
  dialog boxes compared
        with, *33*
  labeling, 111
  moving, 103
  pictures of, 6–7
  using, 22

calculations in functions, 162
callouts, 256–57. *See also*
    graphics images
capital letters, dropped, 259
Caption command (Insert
    menu), 153, 258
Caption dialog box, 153
captions. *See also* graphics
    images
  callouts compared with, 256
  creating, 153, 256
  floating, 258
  grouping with objects, 258
  numbering, 153
  in table of contents, *152*
  text in, *153*
catalog-type documents, *187*
Cell Height And Width dialog
    box, 86
Cell Height And Width
    command (Table
    menu), 86
Cell marker (in tables), 78

center alignment of paragraphs, 31, 32. *See also* alignment

Center Tab marker, 37

certificates, creating, 186–87

Change option (Setup dialog box), 294

Change Text Direction button (Tables And Borders toolbar), 85

Change Text Direction button (Text Box toolbar), 270

chapters of documents, 132. *See also* sections of documents

characters. *See* fonts; symbols; *names of specific symbols*

Character Spacing tab (Font dialog box), 278

charts. *See also* data; organization charts
creating, 159, 168–69, 170
editing, 159, 169, 170
formatting data in, 159
Microsoft Excel worksheets as, 168–69, 170

Chart tab (in Microsoft Excel worksheets), 169

Chart toolbar, 169

check boxes, adding to online forms, 291. *See also names of specific check boxes*

Check Box Form Field button (Forms toolbar), 291

Check Errors button (Mail Merge toolbar), 178

Choose Template option (Compose menu), *221*

clip art. *See also* graphics images
adding, 90
behavior of, *90*
downloading, 298

Clip Art tab (Clip Gallery dialog box), 90

Clipboard, text stored on, 14–15, 17

Clip Gallery. *See also* sound clips; video clips
described, 90
installing, *90*
online, 298
sound clips, 238
video clips in, 236

Clip Gallery dialog box, 90

Clip Gallery Live, 298

Close button (document window), 9

Close button (Picture toolbar), *92*

closing
documents, 9
drop-down lists, *23*
Picture toolbar, *92*
programs before running Setup, *294*

code, secret, *145*

colon (:) in cell references, *163*

colors. *See also* shading
background of text on Web pages, 245. *See also* backgrounds
of borders, 233
fill color in shapes, *251*
of text
Automatic setting, *233*
changing, 24, 233
default, *233*
for edits, *215*
for highlighting, 214
WordArt, 269

Columns command (Format menu), 261

Columns dialog box, 261

columns in documents
adding, 25
formatting, 261

columns in tables. *See also* AutoSum button (Tables And Borders toolbar)
adding, 88–89
borders, 76
creating, 76
deleting, 89
selecting, *87*, 88
size, 77, 80, 81, *87*
summing, 160, *161*
tabs compared with, *37*

combining graphics images, 251. *See also* grouping

combo box, *23*

comma (,) in cell references, *163*

commands. *See also* macros; *names of specific commands*
creating new, 98
in menus, 100, 101

Commands tab (Customize dialog box)
Categories, 110
Modify Selection button, 111
picture of, 100, 102, 110, 111

comments
adding to documents, 213
browsing through documents by, 120
location in document, *207*
reviewing, 207
sound clips as, 213

components of Word, 294, *296*. *See also* accessory programs; *names of specific components*

Compose menu, *221*

condensed text spacing, 278

Connect To Web For Additional Clips button (Clip Gallery dialog box), 298

Contemporary Fax cover sheet, 52

Continuous option (Page Setup dialog box), *131*

Continuous section breaks, *131, 157*

Control button (Picture toolbar), 275

Control Panel. *See* Windows Control Panel

converters
downloading, *296*
installing, *172*

converting
documents into templates, 60–61
documents into Web pages, 244–45
documents into Word 97 format, 172, 293, *296*
text into hyperlinks, 230–31

Convert wizard, 293

Copy button, 14, 17

copying
button on toolbar, 14, 17, *103*
data from Microsoft Excel, 166, 167
PowerPoint presentation slides, *226*
template items, 66
text, 14, 17, 25. *See also* text, moving
text formatting, 29, 38

Create AutoText dialog box, 96

Create button (Mail Merge Helper dialog box)
Catalog, 187
Envelopes, 182
Form Letters, 176
Mailing Labels, 180

Create From File tab (Object dialog box), *236*

Create Hyperlink Here command (Windows Explorer shortcut menu), 227

Create Labels dialog box, 180, 181
Create New tab (Object dialog box)
  Microsoft Equation Editor, 164
  Microsoft Organization Chart, 171
  Object Type options, 235
  picture of, 235
Create Subdocument button (Outline view), 138
Create Text Box Link button (Text Box toolbar), 265, 266
creating
  awards, 186–87
  backgrounds, 234
  callouts, 256–57
  captions, 153, 258
  chapters or sections, 132
  charts, 159
  commands, 98–99
  cross-references, 154
  data sources, 188–89
  documents, 8–9
  double-sided documents, 114
  drawings, 250–51
  drop caps, 259
  endnotes, 151
  envelopes, 70–71, 182–84
  fax cover sheets, 52–53, 223
  footnotes, 148
  form letters, 176–77
  hyperlinks, 224–29
  indexes, 174
  inline headings, 271
  letterheads, 68
  letters, 48–49
  lists, 40–41
  mailing labels, 69

creating, *continued*
  margin notes, 262–63
  memos, 50–51
  numbered headings, 155
  numbered lines, 156–157
  numbered outlines, 158
  online forms, 290–91
  organization charts, 171
  pull quotes, 260
  running heads, 115, 116–17
  side-by-side paragraphs, 264
  styles, 72–73
  style sequences, 64
  summaries, 136
  table columns, 76
  table rows, 77
  tables of contents, 133
  tables of figures, 152
  tab stops, 37
  templates, 58–59, 60–61
  watermarks, 274–75
  Web pages, 242–43
  WordArt, 268–69
Crop button (Picture toolbar), 93
Cross-Reference command (Insert menu), 154
Cross-Reference dialog box, 154
cross-references
  in indexes, 174
  to topics in documents, 154
Ctrl key
  +0, 36
  +1, 36
  +2, 36
  +5, 36
  +A, *36*
  +click, 16, *66*
  +End, *229*
  +Enter, 109, 261
  +F9, *291*
  +F9+Shift, 158, *289*

Ctrl key, *continued*
  +Home, 116
  +Hyphen (-), 277
  +Q, 32
  +Shift, 158, 261
  +Shift+F9, *289*
  +Shift+Hyphen (-), 277
  +Shift+Spacebar, 277
  +Spacebar, 271
  +Tab, *77*
  converting text fields to normal text, *289*
  copying text, 17
  copying toolbar buttons, *103*
  creating column breaks, 261
  creating page breaks, 109
  double spacing, *36*
  inserting text fields, *291*
  moving to beginning of document, 116
  moving to end of document, *229*
  removing formatting, 32, 271
  selecting items in lists, *66*
  selecting text, 16, *36*
custom dictionaries, 283, 284
Custom Dictionaries dialog box, 283, 284
Customize command (Tools menu), 100
Customize dialog box, 100
Customize Keyboard dialog box, 111, 147
customizing
  dictionaries, 283, 284
  editing, *13*
  grammar checking, *19*
  Letter Wizard, *67*
  menus, 100–101
  Office Assistant, 3
  paragraphs, 32–33
  spelling checking, *19*

customizing, *continued*
  table layout, 79
  templates, *56*, 58–59
  toolbars, 102–3, 110–11
custom menus, virus-protection feature, *57*. See also menus
Cut button, 15, 17. See also deleting

D

data. *See also* charts; Microsoft Excel, worksheets in Word
  copying from Microsoft Excel, 166
  fields, 185
  linking to Microsoft Excel worksheets, 167, 170
  records, 185, 190
Data Form dialog box, 190
data sources
  accessory programs, *190*
  creating, 188–89
  described, 175
  editing, 190, 191
  fields in
    adding new, 188
    defining, 188
    deleting, 188
    described, 185
    entering data, 189
    hiding and displaying, 191
  finding records in, 190
  of form letters, 176
  inserting fields into form letters, *177*
  merging data, 175, 194–95
  Microsoft Access databases as, 193, *194*
  Microsoft Excel worksheets as, 192

data sources, *continued*
    opening as documents, *189*
    opening as tables, *189,* 191
    records in, 190, 194–95
dates and times in footers, *117*
Decimal Tab marker, 37
Decrease Indent button, 34.
        See also paragraph
        formatting, indenting
default
    alignment of tables, 86
    colors of text, *233*
    tab stops, 37
Delete key, 12
deleting
    blank lines, 36
    borders, 43, 272
    button on toolbar, 15, 17
    drop caps, *259*
    fields in data sources, 188
    footnotes, *150*
    formatting, 32, 45, 271
    table cell boundaries, *76*
    text, 12, 25
Delivery Point Barcode check
        box (Envelope Options
        dialog box), 71
desktop publishing using Word,
        105–41, 247–78. *See also*
        specific topics
dialog boxes. *See also* names
        of specific dialog boxes
    buttons compared with, *33*
    creating, 198
dictionaries
    customizing, 283, 284
    non-English, *285*
Dictionaries button (Options
        dialog box), 283, 284
Different First Page [Headers
        And Footers] check box
        (Page Setup dialog box),
        68, 116

Different Odd And Even
        [Headers And Footers]
        check box (Page Setup
        dialog box), 116
direction keys. *See* arrow keys
Display Properties dialog
        box, *233*
distortion of shapes while
        resizing, 250
Distribute Columns Evenly
        button (Tables And
        Borders toolbar), 80
Distribute Rows Evenly button
        (Tables And Borders
        toolbar), 80
division operator (/)
    in formulas, 162
docked toolbars, 26. *See also*
        toolbars
Document Map. *See also* outlines
        of documents
    described, 121
    hiding and displaying, 25
    online documents, 217
    resizing, *121*
Document Properties option
        (Options dialog box), *287*
documents. *See also specific types*
        of documents
    adding text to, 10
    closing, 9
    creating, 8–9
    information about, 288–89.
        See also information
        about documents
    listed on File menu, *10*
    moving to beginning of, 116
    moving to end of, *229*
    naming, 9
    opening, 10
    printing, 20
    proofreading, 18–19
    saving, 9. *See also* saving

documents in workgroups
    comments to, 206–7, 213
    Document Map, 217
    editing
        limited access for, 216
        marking schemes, 215
        protecting for, 208, *209*
        routing for, 208–9,
            212, 215
    e-mailing, 210
    protecting
        against unauthorized
            access, 216
        for comments, 206
        for editing, *204,* 208,
            209, 240
        for tracked changes, *215*
    reviewing
        comments to, 207
        edits, 209
        routed documents,
            211, 212
    routed documents
        adding comments to, 213
        adding sounds to, 213
        reviewing, 211, 212
    routing
        for comments, 206–7
        for editing, 208–9,
            212, 215
    summaries, 218
    templates in, 204–5
    through e-mail, 210–11
document window
        elements, 6–7
dots around text, 232
double-sided documents
    formatting for, 114
    page numbers in, *129*
    printing, *262*
double spacing, 36. *See also*
        spacing
Down arrow key, 77

downloading
    clip art, 298
    from Microsoft Word and
        Office Web sites, *298*
    software, *296*
Down option (Find And Replace
        dialog box), 125
drafts of documents, *36*
dragging and dropping
    copying paragraph
        formatting, 38
    drawing AutoShapes in
        documents, 250
    moving
        Borders menu, 43
        boxes in organization
            charts, 171
        callouts, 257
        footnotes, 150
        tab stops, 37
        text, 13, 17
        topics in documents,
            122, 123
    resizing
        graphics images, 92
        video playback
            windows, 237
    +Shift key, 250
Draw button (Drawing toolbar)
    Align Or Distribute
        submenu, 252,
            254, 255
    Grid, 254, 255
    Group, 251
    Nudge, 255
drawings. *See* graphics images
Drawing toolbar
    formatting tools, 257
    hiding and displaying, 25
    picture of, 7, 250, 258
Draw Table button (Tables And
        Borders toolbar), 76,
            77, 83

Draw Table pencil, *83*
Drop Cap command (Format menu), 259
Drop Cap dialog box, 259
drop caps, 259
Drop-Down Form Field button (Forms toolbar), 290
drop-down lists. *See also* names *of specific lists*
   adding to online forms, 290
   using, 23

Edit Data Source button (Mail Merge toolbar), 190, 191
editing
   customizing editing settings, *13*
   data in charts, 159, 165, 169, 170
   data in data sources, *164*, 165, 190
   documents in workgroups, 208–9, 215
   equations, *164*
   footnotes, 150
   formulas, *160*, 161
   limited document access for, *141*, 208, *209*, 216
   linked text, 226
   marking schemes, 215
   pictures, 93
   routed documents, 212, 215
   running heads, *115, 117*
   subdocuments, 141
   summaries of documents, 137
   summed table cells, 161
   text, 12–13
   Web pages, 243
   WordArt, 269

Edit tab (Options dialog box), *12, 13*
Elegant Fax cover sheet, 52
e-mail
   fonts in, *220*
   formatting in, *221*
   sending documents, 200, 210
   sending sound clips, *213*
   signatures, 220
   software used for, *221*
   templates for, *221*
E-Mail tab (Options dialog box), 220
embossed text, 232
emphasizing text, 232–33, 259
End key, *229*
Endnote option (Footnote And Endnote dialog box), 151
endnotes. *See also* Footnote And Endnote dialog box; footnotes
   browsing through documents by, 120
   compared with footnotes, *151*
   creating, 151
end-of-document marker, 6
end-of-row marker (in tables)
   picture of, 78
   viewing, 89
engraved text, 232
Enter key
   +Ctrl key, 109
   +Shift, 277
   +Shift+Ctrl, 261
   inserting column breaks, 261
   inserting line breaks, 277
   inserting page breaks, 109
   using in tables, 77
Envelope Address dialog box, 182
Envelope Options dialog box, 71

envelopes. *See also* mailing labels
   addressing, 70–71, 182–84
   deleting return address from, 184
   printing, *182*, 184
Envelopes And Labels command (Tools menu), 69, 70
Envelopes And Labels dialog box, 69. *See also* mailing labels
Envelopes tab (Envelopes And Labels dialog box), 70
equal sign (=) in formulas, 162
Equation Editor. *See* Microsoft Equation Editor
equations
   captions for, 153
   creating, 164
   using in Word, 94
   using Microsoft Equation Editor for, 164
Eraser button (Tables And Borders toolbar), 79
Erasing. *See* deleting
errors. *See also* editing
   correcting, 18–19
   spelling, 18, 281
   "ZIP code not valid" message, *181*
Esc key
   canceling moving text, *13*
   closing drop-down lists, *23*
Even Page option (Break dialog box), 132
Excel. *See* Microsoft Excel
Exceptions button (AutoCorrect dialog box), 281
Exchange. *See* Microsoft Exchange
Expand Subdocuments button (Master Document toolbar), 141

Explorer shortcut menu. *See* Windows Explorer shortcut menu

F2 key, 17
F9 key
   +Alt, *62*
   +Ctrl, *291*
   +Ctrl+Shift, 158, *289*
   converting fields to normal text, 158, *289*
   hiding and displaying field codes, *62*
   inserting text fields, *291*
   updating calculations in table cells, 161
Facing Identification Mark (FIM-A code), 71
fancy first letter. *See* drop cap
Favorites button (in Internet Explorer), 241
faxes. *See also* Letters & Faxes tab (New dialog box); Microsoft Fax
   addressing, 222
   cover sheets, 52–53, 223
   documents as, *187*, 201
   Mail Merge toolbar, *222*
   programs for sending, *223*
   reviewing, 223
   samples of, 52, 53
   sending, 52, 222–23
   templates for, 52
   text in, 223
Fax Software step in Fax Wizard, *223*
Fax Wizard, 52–53, 222, *223*
Fax Wizard dialog box, 222

field codes
    described, 185
    hiding and displaying, *62*
    printing, *289*
Field Codes options (Options
        dialog box), 289
Field command (Insert
        menu), 288
Field dialog box, 288
Field Options dialog box, 288
fields
    browsing through
            documents by, 120
    freezing to prevent
            updating, *289*
    hiding and displaying, *62*
    information in, 288
    inserted by wizards, *49*
    text fields
        converting to normal
            text, 158, *289*
        in online forms, 290, *291*
    types of, 185
    updated information in, *289*
Field Shading list box (Options
        dialog box), *177*, 289
field shortcut menus, *288, 289*
figures. See objects; *names of
    specific objects*
File command (Insert
        menu), 118
File Locations tab (Options
        dialog box), *61, 62*
File menu, documents listed
        in, *10*
File Name box, 9
filenames, limitations in, 9
Files Of Type list (Insert Picture
        dialog box), *91*
Files Of Type list (Link To File
        dialog box), *241*
Files Of Type list (Open dialog
        box), 293

file types
    for graphics images formats,
        91, 93
    for routed documents,
        210, 211
    list
        in Insert Picture dialog
            box, *91*
        in Link To File dialog
            box, *241*
        in Open dialog box, 293
    opening non-Word format
            files, 172
    saving documents
        as different file types, 172,
            173, *210, 211*
        in HTML format,
            242, 244
        as Read Only, *204, 240*
        as Text Only, *173*
Fill Color button (Drawing
        toolbar), *251*
Fill Effects dialog box, 234
Fill-In field (Insert Word Field
        button), 198, *199*
Filter Records tab (Query
        Options dialog box), 194,
        195, 200
FIM-A code, 71
Find All Word Forms check box
        (Find And Replace dialog
        box), 124, *125*
Find And Replace dialog box,
        124–25. See also replacing
Find button (Data Form dialog
        box), 190
Find command (Edit
        menu), 124
finding. See also browsing;
        replacing
    highlighted text, 214
    objects in documents, 120
    records in data sources, 190

finding, *continued*
    Templates folder, 59
    text in documents, 124–25
    topics in documents, 121
Find Next button (Find And
        Replace dialog box), 124
Find What dialog box, *125*
Find Whole Words Only option
        (Find And Replace dialog
        box), 125
First-Line Indent marker, 35.
        See also paragraph
        formatting, indenting
floating
    images in tables, *264*
    text, 247
    toolbars, 26, 27. *See also*
        toolbars
Float Over Text option (Picture
        dialog box), *90*
flowing text, 247
folders, hyperlinks to, 227. *See
        also names of specific
        folders*
Font Color button (Standard
        toolbar), 233
Font command (Format menu),
        232, 278
Font dialog box, 72
Font drop-down list, 30
fonts. *See also* symbols; text
    changing, 24, *28*, 30, *33*
    in e-mail, 220
    emphasizing, 24, 28–29, *107*,
        232–33, *259*
    italics
        adding, 28
        applying to selected text
            only, *107*
        buttons on toolbar, 24, 28
    kerning, 278
    listing, 24, 30, *145*
    scaled, 278

fonts, *continued*
    size, 24, 30
    spacing, 278
    styles, 72, 271
    supported by Word, *145*
    Unicode, *145*
    WordArt, 268–69
Font Size drop-down list, 30
Font tab (Font dialog box), 232
footers. See also headers
    creating, 115
    formatting, *117*
    hiding and displaying, 115
    inserting information in,
        117, 135
    variable, 116
Footnote And Endnote dialog
        box, 148
Footnote command (Insert
        menu), 148, 151
footnotes. See also endnotes
    browsing through
            documents by, 120
    creating, 148
    deleting, *150*
    editing, 150
    endnotes compared
            with, 151
    formatting, 148
    hiding and displaying,
        149, *150*
    marks
        adding, 148
        moving, 150
    numbering, 148, 149, *151*
    placement on page, 149
    styles of, 149
    Zoom Control
            (magnification), *149*
Footnotes command (View
        menu), 149
foreign-format (non-Word) files,
        opening , 172

Format button (Find And Replace dialog box), 127
Format button (Format menu, Style command), 262, 276
Format button (Page Numbers dialog box), 129
Format menu, 234
Format Object button (Picture toolbar), 253
Format Painter button (Standard toolbar), 29, 38
Format Picture button (Picture toolbar), 253
Format Picture dialog box, 253
formatting. *See also* styles
  callouts, 257
  documents
    automatically, *230*
    parts of, *230*
    styles, 127, 128, 285
  in e-mail, *221*
  footers, *117*
  footnotes, 148
  headers, *117*
  line numbering, *157*
  margins, *262, 263*
  numbering, 156–57
  paragraphs, 32–33
  text wrapping, 8, 248–49
Formatting toolbar
  buttons on, 24
  hiding and displaying, 22
  moved to side of window, 7
  picture of, *6, 7, 24*
Form Field Options button (Forms toolbar), 290
form letters. *See also* merged documents
  creating, 176–77
  personalizing, 197, 198–99
forms, online, 290–92
Forms toolbar, 290

Formula command (Table menu), 161
Formula dialog box, 162, 163
formulas. *See also names of specific operators*
  automatically summarized, *160*, 161
  functions and operators in, 162
Frame dialog box, 262
FTP (File Transfer Protocol), through Word, 239
functions in formulas, 162

General tab (Options dialog box)
  Macro Virus Protection check box, *57*
  units of measure on, *253*
Get Data button (Mail Merge Helper dialog box)
  Open Data Source, 192
  options, 176, 187
  Use Address Book command, *181*
Gradient tab (Fill Effects dialog box), *234*
grammar checking. *See also* AutoCorrect feature; Spelling & Grammar tab (Options dialog box)
  customizing, *19*, 282, 285
  examples of, 46
  green squiggly lines under text, 18, *19*
  ignoring some text, 285
  starting, 18
  turning on and off, *19*
Grammar dialog box, 18

graphics images. *See also* AutoShapes; WordArt
  adding to documents, 274
  as borders, 273
  browsing through documents by, 120
  callouts, 256–57
  captions for
    creating, 153, 256
    grouping with images, 258
    in tables of contents, *152*
    text in, *153*
  clip art
    adding, 90
    behavior of, *90*
    downloading, 298
  cropping, 93
  downloading, 298
  drawings, 250–51, 252
  editing, 93
  resizing, 250
  in tables of contents, *152*
  in tables, *264*
  types of, *91, 93*
  as watermarks, *93*, 274–75
  on Web pages, 244, *245*
graphs, 94, 95. *See also* Microsoft Graph
grayscale images, *93*
greater-than sign (>)
  as bullets in lists, *40*
  enclosing hyperlink location names in, 230, 231
  in filenames, 9
  in Replace text, *146*
green squiggly lines under text from grammar checking, 18, *19*
gridlines. *See* Snap To Grid feature

grouping
  callouts with objects, 257
  captions with objects, 258
  graphics images, 251
  operations in formulas, 162
grouping operations sign { } in formulas, 162
gutters on pages, 113

hanging indents, 35. *See also* paragraph formatting, indenting
Header And Footer command (View menu), 115
Header And Footer toolbar, 68
headers. *See also* footers; running heads
  creating, 115
  first-page, 68
  formatting, *117*
  hiding and displaying, 115
  inserting information in, *117*, 135
  variable, 116
headings
  browsing through documents by, 120
  cross-references to, *154*
  inline, 271
  numbering, 155
  run-in, 271
  styles
    applying, 39
    assigned, *107*
    defining, 107
    hierarchies, 106
Headings command (Table menu), 87
help, online, 296–97
Help menu, 295, 296

Highlight button, 214
highlighting text, 214
Highlight Key Points option
    (AutoSummarize dialog
    box), 218
Home key
    +Ctrl key, 116
    moving to beginning of
        document, 116
    unselecting paragraph
        marks, 32
horizontal lines. *See also* lines
    creating columns, 76
    on Web pages, 244
HTML (Hypertext Markup
    Language). *See also* Web
    pages
    converting Word documents
        into, 244–45
    described, *243*
    limitations on styles, *244*
    saving documents in,
        242, 244
    storing documents, *245*
Hyperlink command (Internet
    Explorer's Insert
    menu), 241
hyperlinks
    adding automatically, 231
    converting text to, 230–31
    creating, 224
    cross-references as, 154
    distributing documents
        with, *225*
    editing linked text, 226
    to files, *225*
    to folders, 227
    inserted by Word, *229*
    location names, 230, 231
    from online Word
        documents, 241
    to parts of same document,
        226, 228–29

hyperlinks, *continued*
    in subdocuments, *141*
    using, 224–25
    to Web sites, 241, 244
Hypertext Markup Language
    (HTML). *See* HTML
    (Hypertext Markup
    Language)
hyphenation (automatic), *277*
hyphens (-)
    as bullets in lists, *40*
    at line breaks, 277

Image Control button (Picture
    toolbar), 93
images. *See* graphics images
Increase Indent button, 34
indenting. *See also* Decrease
    Indent button; Increase
    Indent button
    paragraphs, 24, 34–35
    tables on page, 86
indent markers, 34
Index And Tables command
    (Insert menu), 133
Index And Tables dialog
    box, 133
indexes
    creating, 174
    text boxes excluded
        from, *258*
    viewing entries, *174*
information about documents
    adding in headers and
        footers, 135
    adding to documents,
        288–89
    hiding or displaying,
        287, 289

information about documents,
continued
    printing, 135, 287
    updating in fields, *289*
    User Information tab
        (Options dialog box),
        70, 287
    version information, 134–35
information about your
    system, 295
inline headings, 271. *See also*
    headings
Insert AutoText button (Header
    And Footer dialog box),
    117, 135
Insert Columns button
    (Standard toolbar), 88, 89
Insert Comment button
    (Reviewing toolbar), 213
Insert File dialog box, 118
Insert Hyperlink button
    (Standard toolbar),
    224, 229
Insert Hyperlink dialog box, 224
Insert Hyperlink dialog box
    (Internet Explorer), 241
inserting text. *See* text, adding
insertion point for text, 6, 10
Insert Merge Field button
    (Create Labels dialog
    box), 180
Insert Merge Field button
    (Envelope Address dialog
    box), 182
Insert Merge Field button
    (Merge toolbar), 177
Insert Microsoft Excel
    Worksheet button
    (Standard toolbar), 165
Insert Picture dialog box, 91
Insert Postal Bar Code button
    (Create Labels dialog
    box), 181

Insert Postal Bar Code dialog
    box, 182
Insert Rows button (Standard
    toolbar), 88
Insert Sound Object button
    (Reviewing toolbar), 213
Insert Subdocument button
    (Master Document
    toolbar), 140
Insert Table command (Table
    menu), 87
Insert Table dialog box, 87
Insert Word Field button (Merge
    toolbar), 197, 198, *199*
installing
    Clip Gallery, *90*
    converters, *172*
    Microsoft Equation
        Editor, *164*
    Microsoft Excel, *165*
    Microsoft Office
        components, 294
    Organization Chart, *171*
    Web Page Wizard, *242*
    WordMail, *220*
Install/Uninstall tab
    (Add/Remove Programs
    dialog box), 294
integer values of results in
    functions, 162
Internet. *See also* online
    documents
    FTP (File Transfer Protocol)
        through Word, 239
    Web pages, 241, 242–45
Internet And Network Paths
    With Hyperlinks option
    (AutoFormat dialog
    box), 230
Internet Explorer, 241. *See also*
    Web pages
italic button, 24, 28

italics. *See also* emphasizing text; fonts
  adding, 28
  applying to selected text only, *107*
  button on toolbar, 24, 28

jumps. *See* hyperlinks
justified alignment of paragraphs, 24, 31, 32. *See also* paragraph formatting

kerning characters, 278
Keyboard button (Customize dialog box), 111
keyboard shortcuts
  assigning, 101, 111, 147
  assigning macros to, *99*
  deleting, *111*
  for adding symbols, 146–47
  for adding text, 97
  for adjusting spacing, 36
  mouse actions compared with, 98
  printing lists of, 108
  replacing, *111*

Label Options dialog box, 69, 180
labels. *See* mailing labels
Labels tab (Envelopes And Labels dialog box), 69
Landscape orientation, 44, 130, *131*. *See also* page formatting, orientation

Language submenu (Tools menu), *277, 286*
Las Vegas lights around text, 232
layers, 247
layouts. *See also* Online Layout view
  checking, 19
  selecting, 130–31
  of tables, 78, 79
Layout tab (Page Setup dialog box)
  Different First Page option, 68
  Headers And Footers option, 116
  Line Numbers button, 156
  picture of, 116, 131
  Section Start options, *131*
left alignment of paragraphs, 31, 32
left angle bracket (<)
  enclosing hyperlink location names in, 230, 231
  in filenames, 9
  in Replace text, *146*
Left Indent marker, 34
Left Tab marker, 37
less-than sign (<)
  enclosing hyperlink location names in, 230, 231
  in filenames, 9
  in Replace text, *146*
letterheads, 67–68
letters
  creating, 48–49
  form letters
    creating, 176–77
    personalizing, 197–99
  templates for, *49, 67*
Letters & Faxes tab (New dialog box), 52. *See also* faxes
letter spacing, 278

Letter Wizard
  customizing, *67*
  using, 48
Letter Wizard command (Tools menu), 48
Line And Page Breaks tab (Paragraph dialog box)
  options, 109
  Suppress Line Numbers check box, 157
  Widow/Orphan Control option, 276
Line Numbers button (Page Setup dialog box), 156
Line Numbers dialog box, 156
lines (drawing)
  as borders around pages, 272
  horizontal and vertical, 76
lines of text. *See also* text
  blank, 36
  breaking, 277. *See also* pages, breaking
  numbering, 156–57
  selecting, 16
  spacing, 36
linking to data in Microsoft Excel, 167
links. *See* hyperlinks
Link To File check box (Insert File dialog box), 118
Link To File dialog box (Internet Explorer), 241
list boxes on toolbars, 103. *See also names of specific list boxes*
lists. *See also* Bullets And Numbering dialog box; tables
  AutoFormat, creating, *40*
  bulleted
    bullet types, *40*
    creating, 40, 41
    on Web pages, 244

lists, *continued*
  buttons on toolbar, 24
  creating, 40, 41
  numbered, 40, 41
  selecting items in, *66*
Lock Anchor option (Format Picture dialog box), 253
Lock Document button (Master Document toolbar), *141*
locking documents. *See* protecting documents
logical operators, *195*

Macro command (Tools menu), 98
macros
  adding to menus, 101
  copying between templates, 66
  creating, 98–99
  enhancing fields in online forms, *291*
  storing, 98
Macro Virus Protection check box (Options dialog box), *57*
magnification. *See* Zoom Control (magnification)
mailing labels, 69, 180–81
Mail Merge command (Tools menu), 176
mail merge feature
  addressing envelopes, 182–83
  addressing mailing labels, 180–81
  creating awards, 186–87
  creating form letters, 175–76
Mail Merge Helper dialog box, 176. *See also* Merge dialog box

Mail Merge toolbar, *22. See also* Merge toolbar
Maintenance program, running, 294
MAPI (Messaging Application Programming Interface), *200*, 210
marching ants around text, 232
margins. *See also* page formatting
    changing, 44, 131
    for double-sided pages, 114
    formatting, *262, 263*
    letterhead fitting into, 67
    text in, 262–63
Margins tab (Page Setup dialog box)
    Apply To, 131
    Gutter, 113
    Mirror Margins check box, 114
    options, 44
    picture of, *113, 114*
Mark Entry button (Index And Tables dialog box), 174
Mark Index Entry dialog box, 174
marking schemes for editing documents, 215
master documents (in multiple-author documents)
    creating, 139, 140
    deleting section marks from, *141*
    described, 138
Master Document toolbar, 140, *141*
Master Document View button (Outline view), 138
Master Document command (View menu), 140

Match Case check box (Find And Replace dialog box), 125
mathematical equations
    captions for, 153
    creating, 164
    in tables, *160*
    using in Word, 94
    using Microsoft Equation Editor for, 164
Media Player, 237, *238*
memos, creating, 50–51
Memos tab (New dialog box), 50
Memo Wizard, 50–51
Menu Bar
    displaying toolbars from, 22
    picture of, *6, 7, 22*
menus. *See also names of specific menus*
    adding commands to, 100, 101
    adding macros to, *99*, 101
    changing automatically, *245*
    custom, *57*
    moving, *23*
    renaming items on, 101
    virus-protection feature, *57*
merged documents. *See also* form letters
    changing inserted text, 197
    conditional merging, 197
    creating
        awards, 186–87
        data sources, 188–89
        envelopes, 182–83
        form letters, 175–76
        mailing labels, 180–81
        using Microsoft Access databases, 193, *194*
        using Microsoft Excel worksheets, 192
        using Microsoft Outlook addresses, *181*

merged documents, *continued*
    described, 175
    e-mailing, 200
    envelopes, 182–83
    faxing, 201
    fields in, 185, 198, *199*
    personalizing, 197, 198–99
    records in
        filtering, 200
        merging in order, 196
        selected for merging, 194–95
        sorting, 196
    reviewing, 178–79
    settings for, *179*
    testing merge, 178–79
Merge dialog box, 177. *See also* Mail Merge Helper dialog box
Merge toolbar, 178
message bar. *See* status bar
Messaging Application Programming Interface (MAPI), *200*, 210
Messaging Service. *See* Windows Messaging Service, sending e-mail using
Microsoft Access
    as data source, 193, *194*
    installing, 294
Microsoft Equation Editor, 164
Microsoft Excel. *See also* data
    Chart Wizard, 168, 170
    installing, *165*
    worksheets in Word
        as data source, 192
        editing in Word, 165, 170
        inserting as charts, 168–69
        inserting as data, 166
        keeping formatting in Word, *166*
        linking to data in, 167, 170

Microsoft Exchange, *221*
Microsoft Fax, *223*
Microsoft Graph, 159
Microsoft Office
    Maintenance program, 294
    Personal Web Server in, *243*
    starting Word from, 8
    Templates folder location in, *61*
    Web site for support, *298*
Microsoft Office Assistant, 3
Microsoft On The Web command (Help menu), 296, *298*
Microsoft Outlook. *See also* WordMail (in Outlook)
    described, 219
    installing, 294
    merging with Word documents, *181*
    messages in, 221
Microsoft Outlook Address Book dialog box, *181*
Microsoft PowerPoint
    copying slides into Word, *226*
    installing, 294
Microsoft Support (on the Internet), 296–97
Microsoft System Information dialog box, 295
Microsoft Word. *See also specific topics*
    adding components to, 294
    document window elements, 6–7
    as e-mail editor, *221*
    newsgroups for Microsoft Word, 297
    scrolling window while text is selected, *13*
    starting, 8
    Web site for support, *298*

MIDI (Musical Instrument
    Digital Interface)
    sequences, 238. *See also*
    sound clips
Mirror Margins check box
    (Page Setup dialog box),
    114, *262*
mistakes, undoing, 11. *See also*
    Redo button; Undo
    button (Standard toolbar)
Modify button (Style dialog
    box), 64, 276
Modify Selection button
    (Customize dialog
    box), 111
Modify Style dialog box, 64
modular arithmetic in
    functions, 162
More button (Find And Replace
    dialog box), 124
mouse actions compared with
    keyboard actions, 98. *See
    also* keyboard shortcuts
mouse pointer, changing to
    resizing pointer, 81. *See
    also* resizing
Move Object With Text option
    (Format Picture dialog
    box), 253
moving
    anchors on objects, *253*
    to beginning of
        document, 116
    boxes in organization
        charts, 171
    buttons on toolbars, 103
    callouts, 257
    cross-references to topics in
        documents, 154
    to end of document, *229*
    footnotes, 150
    list boxes on toolbars,
        23, 103

moving, *continued*
    margin notes, *263*
    menus, *23, 43*
    object anchors to different
        objects, *253*
    in table cells, 77
    tables, 86
    text, 13, 15, 17. *See also* text,
        copying
    toolbars, 26, 27, 112
    topics in documents,
        112, 122
MSNews.Microsoft.com, *297*
multimedia. *See* Media Player;
    sound clips; video clips
multiple-author documents,
    138–41
Multiple Pages button (Print
    Preview window), 19
multiplication operator (*)
    in formulas, 162
multiplying numbers in
    functions, 162
music. *See* sound clips
Musical Instrument Digital
    Interface (MIDI)
    sequences, 238. *See also*
    sound clips

names of paragraph styles,
    displaying, *61*
naming
    AutoText entries, 96
    documents, 9
    items on menus, 101
    macros, 98, *101*
    subdocuments, *139*
    tables, 163
    templates, *205*
    toolbars, 102

nesting paragraphs, 34
New button (Custom
    Dictionaries dialog
    box), 284
New button (Customize dialog
    box), 110
New button (Style dialog box),
    262, 285
New command (File menu), 50
New dialog box, 50
New Label button (Caption
    dialog box), 153
New Label dialog box, 153
newsgroups for Microsoft
    Word, 297
New Style dialog box, 72
Next Change button (Reviewing
    toolbar), 209
Next Comment button
    (Reviewing toolbar), 207
Next Record button (Mail Merge
    toolbar), 178
Next Routing Recipient button
    (Reviewing toolbar), 212
non-English spelling
    checking, *285*
nonprinting symbols, 25, 32
Normal style, *60. See also*
    paragraph styles
Normal View button, 6
Note Options dialog box
    (Footnote And Endnote
    dialog box), 149, 151
Nudge command (Draw
    button), 255
numbered lists, creating, 40, 41.
    See also lists
numbering. *See also* Bullets And
    Numbering dialog box
    button on toolbar, 24, 41
    captions, 153
    footnotes, 148, 149, *151*
    formatting, 156–57

numbering, *continued*
    headings, 155, 158
    hiding and displaying, *156*
    lines, 156–57
    lists, 40, 41
    outlines, 158
    pages. *See* pages, numbering
    paragraphs, 156–57
    on Web pages, 244
Numbering button, 24, 41. *See
    also* lists, numbered
numbers in functions, 162

object anchors, 252, *253*
Object Anchors check box
    (Options dialog box), *253*
Object command (Format
    menu), 248
Object command (Insert
    menu), 235
Object dialog box, 235
objects. *See also* graphics images;
    names of specific objects
    aligning, 252, 254–55
    anchored, 252
    captions for
        compared with
            callouts, 256
        creating, 153
        grouping with
            objects, 258
        in tables of contents, *152*
        text in, *153*
    grouping, 251
    on layers, 247
    positioning on page, 252–53
    snapping to grid, *252*
    stacking, 251
    wrapping text around,
        248–49

objects alien to Word, 94
object shortcut menus, 251
Odd Page option (Break dialog box), 132
Office. *See* Microsoft Office
online documents. *See also* Internet
    creating, 240
    hiding and displaying, 217
    hyperlinks to Web sites, 241
online forms, 290–92
online help, 296–97
Online Layout view
    backgrounds in, *234*
    button on toolbar, 6, 217
    setting up, 217
    using, 240
Online Layout View button, 6, 217
Open button (Standard toolbar), 10
Open command (File menu), 60
Open Data Source dialog box, 192
Open dialog box, 172
opening
    data sources as documents, *189*
    documents
        non-Word types, 172
        from standard toolbar, 10
    templates, 58
operators, logical, *195*
operators in formulas, 162
Options button (Envelopes And Labels dialog box), 69, 71
Options button (Field dialog box), 288
Options button (Footnote And Endnote dialog box), 149
Options button (Index And Tables dialog box), 133
Options dialog box, 215

Options dialog box (Media Player), 237
order of objects, changing, 251
Organization Chart, *171*
organization charts, 95, 171. *See also* charts
Organizer button (Templates And Add-Ins dialog box), 66
Organizer dialog box, 66
orientation of pages. *See also* page formatting
    changing one page only, 130
    Continuous, *131*
    Landscape, 44, 130, *131*
    pictures of, 130
    Portrait, 44, 130
Or (logical operator), *195*
orphan lines, 276
Outline Numbered tab (Bullets And Numbering dialog box), 155
outlines of documents. *See also* Document Map; tables of contents
    creating new documents from, 158
    hiding and displaying, 122
    numbering headings in, 155, 158
Outline view
    button on toolbar, 6
    buttons in, 122, 138
    limitations of, *123*
    of multiple-author documents, 138
    numbering headings in, 155, 158
Outline View button, 6
outlined text, 232
Outlining toolbar, *22*
Outlook. *See* Microsoft Outlook

Page Border tab (Borders And Shading dialog box), 272, 273
page formatting
    borders, 272–73. *See also* borders
    double-sided, 114
    gutters, 113
    margins
        changing, 44, 131
        for double-sided pages, 114
        formatting, *262, 263*
        letterhead fitting into, 67
        text in, 262–63
    numbering
        double-sided documents, *129*
        in indexes, 174
        in tables of contents, 133, 158
    orientation, 44
        changing one page only, 130
        Continuous, *131*
        Landscape, 44, 130, *131*
        pictures of, 130
        Portrait, 44, 130
Page Layout View button, 6
Page Number Format dialog box, 129
Page Numbers command (Insert menu), 129
Page Numbers dialog box, 129
pages
    breaking, 109, 276, *277.* *See also* lines of text, breaking
    browsing through documents by, 120

pages, *continued*
    numbering, *117,* 129
    recto and verso, 114
Page Setup command (File menu), 44
Page Setup dialog box, 44
Paper Size tab (Page Setup dialog box), 44, 130
Paper Source tab (Page Setup dialog box), 67
Paragraph command (Format menu), 107
Paragraph dialog box, 73
paragraph formatting. *See also* AutoFormat dialog box; paragraph styles
    alignment, 31, 32
    applying
        automatically, 45
        to existing paragraphs, 33
        to multiple locations, 38
        to selected text only, *107*
        as you type, 32
    borders, 42–43
    breaks, 276, *277*
    copying, 38
    headings, 39. *See also* headings
    indenting, 34–35
    numbering, 156–57
    removing, 45
    saving, *38*
    tabs, 37
paragraph marks
    copying formatting using, 38
    hiding and displaying, 32
paragraphs
    breaking, 276, *277*
    combining, 33
    converting into lists, 41
    creating, 8, *9*
    customizing, 32–33
    hiding and displaying, 8

paragraphs, *continued*
  highlighting, 24
  margin notes anchored
    to, *263*
  nesting, 34
  outline levels, 106
  selecting, 16, 33
  side-by-side, 264
  starting new, 8
  Widow/Orphan Control
    option, 276
paragraph styles. *See also*
    paragraph formatting;
    styles
  applying, *64*
  assigning automatically, *107*
  creating, *35, 38,* 73
  editing, *60, 107*
  as heading styles, 106–7
  names of, *61*
  outline levels, 106
  printing lists of, 108
  replacing, 127
  saving, *38*
  sequence of, 64
  standard, 39
  standardized, 110–11
  Style list, 39
passwords for document access,
    206, 216
Paste As Hyperlink command
    (Edit menu), 226
Paste Bookmark list (Formula
    dialog box), 163
Paste button, 14, 15
Paste Function list (Formula
    dialog box), 162, 163
Paste Link button (Paste Special
    dialog box), 119, 167, 170
Paste Special command (Edit
    menu), 119
Paste Special dialog box, 119

pasting text, 15, 25
Pattern tab (Fill Effects dialog
    box), *234*
pencil pointer, 76
personal dictionaries, 283, 284
Personal Web Server (in
    Microsoft Office), *243*
Picture command (Insert
    menu), 90
picture converters in Word, 91
Picture dialog box, *90*
pictures. *See* clip art; graphics
    images
Picture tab (Fill Effects dialog
    box), *234*
Picture toolbar, 93
pipe sign (|) in filenames, 9
playback windows (video), 237
Portrait orientation of pages,
    44, 130. *See also* page
    formatting
positioning objects on page,
    252–53
Position option (Drop Cap
    dialog box), *259*
Position tab (Format Picture
    dialog box), 253
Position tab (Picture dialog
    box), *90*
postal bar codes
  on envelopes, *71*
  Insert Postal Bar Code dialog
    box, 182
  on labels, 69, 181
Postal Numeric Encoding
    Technique (POSTNET)
    bar code, *71*
PowerPoint. *See* Microsoft
    PowerPoint
Press New Shortcut Key box
    (Customize Keyboard
    dialog box), 147

previewing. *See also* reviewing
  line numbering, *156, 157*
  multiple pages, 19
  page breaks, *277*
  pictures, 59
  Print Preview, 19
  table borders, *83*
Print button (Envelopes And
    Labels dialog box), 71
Print button (Standard toolbar),
    20, 25
Print command (File menu), 20
Print dialog box, 20
printers, 20, *182*
printing
  current page only, 20
  documents, 20, 25
  double-sided documents,
    114, *262*
  envelopes, *182,* 184
  even-numbered pages
    only, 114
  information about
    documents, 135, 287
  lists of keyboard
    shortcuts, 108
  lists of paragraph styles, 108
  odd-numbered pages
    only, 114
  online forms, 292
  on preprinted forms, 292
  selected text with macros, 99
Printing Options tab (Envelope
    Options dialog box), 71
Print option (File menu), 20
Print Preview, 19. *See also*
    Previewing
Print Preview button (Standard
    toolbar), 19
Print tab (Options dialog box),
    287, 289
Print What list (Print dialog
    box), 108

Professional Fax cover sheet, 52
programs. *See also* accessory
    programs; components
    of Word; *names of specific
    programs*
  data as Word data
    source, *190*
  described, 94
  for playing videos, *237*
proofreading document layouts,
    19. *See also* grammar
    checking; spelling
    checking
Properties command (File
    menu), 59, 287
Properties dialog box, 59, 287
Protect Document command
    (Tools menu), 206
Protect Document dialog
    box, 206
protecting documents
  against unauthorized
    access, 216
  for comments, 206
  for editing, *204,* 208,
    209, 240
  for tracked changes, *215*
  online forms, 291
  sections of, *291*
  subdocuments, *141*
  templates, *204*
pull quotes, 260

Query Options button (Mail
    Merge Helper dialog
    box), 194
Query Options button (Merge
    dialog box), 196, 200
Query Options dialog box, 194

question mark (?)
    in filenames, 9
    as wildcard character, *124*
quotes extracted from text, 260

Read Only documents, saving
    files as, *204*, 240
Record button (in Sound
    Recorder), 235
Record Macro dialog box, 98
records (data), 185, 190
records in merged documents
    filtering, 200
    merging in order, 196
    selected for merging, *194*
    sorting, 196
recto pages, 114
Redo button, *11*, 25. *See also*
    Undo button
red squiggly lines under text
    from spelling checking,
    18, *19*
references to table cells, 163
removing
    blank lines, 36
    borders, 43, 272
    drop caps, *259*
    fields in data sources, 188
    formatting, 32, 45, 271
    table cell boundaries, *76*
Replace command (Edit
    menu), 127
Replace tab (Find And Replace
    dialog box), 126
Replace Text As You Type check
    box (AutoCorrect dialog
    box), 146
replacing. *See also* Find And
    Replace dialog box
    formatting styles, 127, 128

replacing, *continued*
    paragraph styles, 127
    text, 13, 126, *146*
    text styles, 127, 128, *146*
Reset button, *149*
Reset Picture button (Picture
    toolbar), *93*
Resize mouse pointer, 81
resizing
    AutoShapes, 250
      without distorting, 250
    Document Map, *121*
    graphics images, 92, 250
    table cells, 81
    tables, *131*
    toolbars, 27
    video playback windows, 237
resizing handles, 92
return addresses. *See* addresses
Return key. *See* Enter key
reviewing. *See also* previewing
    documents in workgroups
      comments to, 207
      edited, 209
      routed, 211, 212
    faxes, 223
    merged documents, 178–79
    page breaks, *277*
Reviewing toolbar, 209
right alignment of paragraphs,
    31, 32
right angle bracket (>)
    as bullets in lists, *40*
    enclosing hyperlink location
      names in, 230, 231
    in filenames, 9
    in Replace text, *146*
right-clicking. *See also* shortcut
    menus
    for displaying toolbars, 22
    for displaying wizard lists, *49*
    for grammar checking, 18
    for spelling checking, 18

Right Indent marker, 34
Right Tab marker, 37
rotating
    AutoShapes, *257*
    buttons for, 85
    callouts, *257*
    text, 85, 270
rounding numbers in
    functions, 162
routed documents
    adding comments to, 213
    adding sounds to, 213
    distributing, 210
    reviewing, 211, 212
Routing Slip dialog box, 210
Row tab (Cell Height And Width
    dialog box), 86
ruler, 6, 34
Run command, starting Word
    from, 8
run-in headings. *See* inline
    headings
running heads. *See also* footers;
    headers
    creating, 115, 116–17
    editing, *115, 117*, 132
    in memos, *50*
    in sections of document, 132
    variable, 116–17, *132*

Same As Previous button
    (Header And Footer dialog
    box), 132
Save As command (File
    menu), 173
Save As dialog box, 62
Save As HTML command (File
    menu), 244
Save As Type box (Save As dialog
    box), 59, 62

Save button (Standard toolbar),
    9, 25
Save Preview Picture check box
    (Properties dialog box), 59
Save tab (Options dialog
    box), 216
Save Version button (Reviewing
    toolbar), 215
saving
    AutoText entries, *267*
    documents
      described, 9
      as different file types,
        172, 173, *210, 211*
      drafts of, *36*
      for routing, 210
      from FTP sites, 239
      in HTML, 242, 244
      outlines of, 158
      Preview Picture, 59
      as Read Only, *204*, 240
      as templates, *59, 62*
      as Text Only, *173*
      versions of, 134
      as Web pages, 242, 244
    paragraph formatting, *38*
    templates, *59, 62, 204*
    text boxes, *267*
    toolbars, *111*
    watermarks in templates, *275*
Screen Tips check box (Options
    dialog box), *150*
Scroll bars, 7
Scrolling Text command (Insert
    menu), 245
Scrolling Text dialog box, 245
scrolling text on Web pages, 245
scrolling window while text is
    selected, *13*
searching for text. *See* finding
Search The Web button, *239*
secret code, creating, 145

sections of documents
  breaks
    adding, *157*
    invisible, *132*
    on odd-numbered
      pages, 132
  browsing through
    documents by, 120
  chapters, 132
  creating, *130,* 132
  orientation of, 130
  running heads in, 132
  section marks, *141*
Section Start options (Page
  Setup dialog box), *131*
Select All command (Edit
  menu), 16
Select Browse Object button
  (on vertical scroll bar),
  120, 150
selecting
  list items, *66*
  methods of, 16
  paragraphs, 16, 33
  printers, 20
  styles in Style list box, 39
  table cells, *87,* 88
  text, 12, 16, *36, 267*
  types of graphics images, *93*
Select Objects button (Drawing
  toolbar), *248,* 251, 258
Select Table command (Table
  menu), 161
Send To command (File menu),
  210, 222
separators between footnotes
  and text, 149
sequence of styles, 64
Settings button (Options dialog
  box), 282
Setup, running, *294*
Setup dialog box, 294
Setup Wizard, 2

shading. *See also* Borders
  And Shading dialog
  box; colors
  adding, 233
  merged data in form
    letters, *177*
  table cells, 78, 83
Shading Color button (Tables
  And Borders toolbar), 233
shadowed text, 232
shapes. *See* AutoShapes; graphics
  images
Shift key
  +Ctrl+Enter, 261
  +Ctrl+F9, 158, *289*
  +Ctrl+Hyphen (-), 277
  +Ctrl+Spacebar, 277
  +dragging and dropping, 250
  +Enter, 277
  +F2, 17
  +Tab, 77, 164
  converting fields to normal
    text, *289*
  copying text using, 17
  creating column breaks, 261
  field text converted to
    normal, 158
  line-break options, 277
  moving between table cells,
    77, 164
  resizing shapes without
    distortion, 250
  while opening the Style list
    box, 39
shimmering text, 232
shortcut bar (Microsoft Office),
  starting Word from, 8
Shortcut Key button (Symbol
  dialog box), 147
shortcut menus. *See also* right-
  clicking
  for AutoShapes, 260, 265
  for fields, *288, 289*

shortcut menus, *continued*
  for objects, 251
  for spelling, 18
  for tables, 89
  for toolbars, *92*
  for Windows Desktop, *233*
  for Windows Explorer, 227
shortcuts, keyboard
  assigning, 101, 111, 147
  assigning macros to, *99*
  deleting, *111*
  for adding symbols, 146–47
  for adding text, 97
  for adjusting spacing, 36
  mouse actions compared
    with, 98
  printing lists of, 108
  replacing, *111*
shortcuts, virus-protection
  feature, 57
Show Gridlines command
  (Table menu), 264
Show/Hide Paragraph button
  (Standard toolbar), 7
  viewing anchors on
    objects, *253*
Show Next button (Header
  And Footer dialog box),
  116, 117
Show Number On First Page
  check box (Page Numbers
  dialog box), 129
Show Page Numbers check box
  (Index And Tables dialog
  box), 158
sidebars, 266–67
side-by-side paragraphs, 264
sideways text, 270
signatures in e-mail, 220
sizing handles, 92, 93
slash, forward (/)
  as division operator, 162
  in filenames, 9

slide-show icon in Word
  documents, 95
Slide Sorter view in Microsoft
  PowerPoint, *226*
Snap To Grid dialog box, 254
Snap To Grid feature, *252,*
  254–55. *See also*
  alignment
software. *See* programs
Sort Records tab (Query Options
  dialog box), 196
sound clips. *See also* Clip
  Gallery
  adding to documents, 238
  Clip Gallery, 238
  comments as, 213
  downloading, 298
  hyperlinks to, 224
  picture of in Word
    document, 95
  playing, 235, *238*
  recording, 235
Sound Recorder, *235, 238*
Sounds Like check box (Find
  And Replace dialog box),
  124, *125*
Sounds tab (Clip Gallery dialog
  box), 238
source documents, 118, 119.
  See also documents
Spacebar
  +Ctrl, 271
  +Ctrl+Shift, 277
  line-break options, 277
  turning off character
    styles, 271
Space Before box (Paragraph
  dialog box), 67
spaces
  in filenames, 9
  hiding and displaying, 8
  in names of macros, 98
  in names of menu items, *101*

spacing
    adjusting character, 278
    line spacing, 36
sparkling text, 232
Special Characters tab (Symbol
        dialog box), 145
speech balloons, 247, 256–57
Spelling And Grammar Status
        icon, 6, *18*
spelling checking. *See also*
        AutoCorrect feature
    automatic
        customizing, 281
        examples of, 46
        red squiggly lines under
            text, 18, *19*
        turning on and off, *19*
    corrections proposed, 18, 281
    customizing, *19,* 283,
            284, 285
    errors list, 18, 281
    examples of, 46
    non-English text, *285*
Spelling dialog box, 18
Spelling & Grammar tab
        (Options dialog box)
    Dictionaries button,
            283, 284
    options, *19*
    picture of, 282
    Settings button, 282
spelling shortcut menus, 18
split bar, 137
square brackets ([ ]) in Replace
        text, *146*
stacking order of objects, 251
Standard toolbar. *See also*
        names of specific buttons
        and list boxes
    buttons on, 25
    hiding and displaying, 22
    moving, 26
    picture of, 6, 25, 26

Start menu, starting Word
        from, 8
Startup folder. *See* Windows
        Startup folder, starting
        Word from
status bar, 6
Stop button (in Sound
        Recorder), 235
storing
    HTML documents, *245*
    macros, 98
    text, 14–15
    toolbars, 112
    video clips, 236
    Web pages, *245*
Style Area Width box (Options
        dialog box), *61,* 106
Style command (Format
        menu), 64
Style dialog box, 64
Style Gallery command (Format
        menu), 65
Style Gallery dialog box, 65
Style list box (Standard toolbar),
        38, 39
styles
    automatic assignments, *107*
    character, 271
    copying between
            templates, 66
    creating, 72–73
    fonts, 72, 271
    footers, *117*
    footnotes, 149
    formatting, 127, 128, 285
    for templates, 72
    headers, *117*
    headings
        applying, 39
        defining, 107
        hierarchies, 106
    paragraph. *See* paragraph
            styles

styles, *continued*
    sequence of, 64
    tables of contents, *152*
    in templates, *65*
    text. *See* text styles
subdocuments. *See also*
        multiple-author
        documents
    adding to master documents,
            139, 140
    distributing, 139
    dividing documents into, 138
    editing, 141
    hyperlinks in, *141*
    naming, *139*
    protecting, *141*
subtraction operator (-) in
        formulas, 162
summaries of documents. *See
        also* AutoSummarize
        dialog box
    creating, 136
    editing, 137
    reviewing, 218
Summary tab (Properties dialog
        box), 59, 287
summing table cells, 160, 161.
        See also AutoSum button
support for Word, online,
        296–97
Suppress Line Numbers check
        box (Paragraph dialog
        box), 157
Switch Between Header And
        Footer button (Header
        And Footer dialog box),
        116, 117
Symbol command (Insert
        menu), 144, 147
Symbol dialog box, 144
symbols. *See also names of
        specific symbols*
    adding to text, 144–47

symbols, *continued*
    converting text into, *145*
    in filenames, 9
    in formulas, 162
    in macro names, 98
    nonprinting, 25, 32
    wildcard, 124, *125*
    Wingdings, 144
Symbols tab (Symbol dialog
        box), 144, 147

Tab key. *See also* tabs
    +Ctrl, *77*
    +Shift, *77,* 164
    creating new table rows, *77*
    described, 37
    using to move
        in Microsoft Equation
            Editor, 164
        between boxes in dialog
            boxes, 189
        between table cells, *77*
        between text fields, 291
Table AutoFormat dialog box, 77
Table AutoFormat feature, 82
table cells
    borders, 83
    boundaries, *76, 79, 83*
    cell markers, 78
    coloring, 78, 83
    columns
        adding, 88–89
        summing, 160
        tabs compared with, *37*
    creating, 76
    deleting, *83,* 89
    headings in, 78, 79, 87
    merging, 78, *160*
    moving between, *77*
    paragraphs in, 77, 78
    references to, 163

table cells, *continued*
rows
adding, 76, *77,* 88
summing, 161
selecting, *87,* 88
shading, 78, 83
size, 80, 81, *87*
Table Of Contents Options
dialog box, 133
tables
adding, 25, 86, 87
alignment on page, 86
borders, 78, 82–83
boundaries, *76, 83*
browsing through
documents by, 120
captions for, 153
creating, 76–77, 87, 264
editing, 84–85, 161
elements, 78
formatting, 77, 78, 79
formulas in, *160*
graphics images in, 78
gridlines, 78, *83*
indenting on page, 86
large, 87–89
layout, 77, 78, 79
moving between cells, 77
moving in documents, 86
naming, 163
pictures in, *264*
resizing, *131*
shading, 78, 83
text in
adding, 77
alignment of, 78, 85
direction of, 78, 85
editing, 84–85
formatting, 84
paragraphs in cells,
77, 264
rotating, *85*
tabs in, *77*

tables, *continued*
values in, 160–63
on Web pages, 244
zoom setting, *83*
Tables And Borders button, 76
Tables And Borders toolbar
buttons on, 85, 233
displaying, 76
hiding and displaying, 25
rotating text using, *85*
tables of contents. *See also*
outlines of documents
creating, 133
figures listed in, 152
formatting, 133, *152*
text boxes listed in, *258*
tables of figures, 152
tabs. *See also* Tab key; *names of*
specific tabs in dialog boxes
inserting in table cells, *77*
table columns compared
with, *37*
tab markers, 37
tab stops, 37
technical documents
captions for objects, *152,* 153
charts, 159, 168–69, *170*
cross-references in, 154
endnotes, 151
equations, 153, 164
footnotes, 148–50
indexes for, 174
numbering
captions, 153
formatting, 156–57
headings, 155, 158
hiding and
displaying, *156*
lines, 156–57
pages in indexes, 174
pages in tables of
contents, 133, 158

technical documents,
numbering, *continued*
paragraphs, 156–57
viewing, *156*
organization charts, 171
summing table cells,
160, 161
symbols, 144–47, 162.
See also names of
specific symbols
tables of contents
creating, 133
figures listed in, 152
formatting, 133, *152*
page numbers in,
133, 158
text boxes listed in, *258*
Template button (Options dialog
box), 220
templates
copying between, 66
creating, 58–59
creating documents from,
56–57, 65
customizing, *56,* 58–59
for letters, *49,* 67
macros, *57*
modifying, *56,* 58–59
naming, *205*
opening, 56, 58
protecting from changes, *204*
running heads in, *117*
saving
documents as, 60–61
as Read Only, *204*
styles, *72*
in Templates folder, *59*
watermarks in, *275*
shown in Style Gallery dialog
box, *65*
styles in, *65,* 72
using several for one
document, 65

templates, *continued*
virus-protection feature, *57*
wizards compared with, 47
in workgroups, 204–5
Templates And Add-Ins dialog
box, 66
Templates And Add-Ins (Tools
menu), 66
Templates folder, *59*
text. *See also* AutoText feature;
fonts; paragraphs
adding
to AutoShapes, 265
to documents, 8, 10
to sidebars, 267
as art, 268–69
in callouts, 256–57
in captions, *153*
converting fields into, *289*
converting to hyperlinks,
230–31
converting to symbols, *145*
copying, 14, 17, 25
deleting, 12, 25
editing, 12–13
extracted from text, 260
finding highlighted, 214
finding in documents,
124–25
kerning, 278
lines of
blank, 36
breaking, 277
numbering, 156–57
selecting, 16
in margins, 262–63
moving, 13, 15, 17
pasting
in footnotes, 148
using keyboard
shortcuts, 97
using toolbar buttons,
15, 25

text, *continued*
pull quotes, 260
replacing, 13, 126, *146. See
also* Find And Replace
dialog box
reusing, 14–15
scrolling on Web pages, 245
selecting, 12, 16, *267*
shortcuts for adding, 97
shortcuts for adding
symbols, *145, 146–47*
in sidebars, 266–67
spacing, 278
storing, 14–15
in tables. *See* tables, text in
as watermarks, *275*
Text Box command (Insert
menu), 266
text boxes
in callouts, *256*
described, 247
excluded from indexes,
174, 258
excluded from tables of
contents, *258*
linking, 265
rotating text in, 270
saving as AutoText
entries, *267*
selecting text in, *267*
Text Box toolbar, 266
text fields
converting to normal text,
158, *289*
in online forms, 290, *291*
text formatting. *See also*
formatting
aligning, 270
colors
changing, 24, 233, 269
default, *233*
for edits, *215*
for highlighting, 214

text formatting, *continued*
floating, 247
flowing
into AutoShapes, 265
described, 247
into sidebars, 266–67
kerning, 278
line spacing, 36
with outlining, 232
rotating, 85, *257,* 270
scaling, 278
scrolling text on Web
pages, 245
wrapping text, 8, 248–49
Text Form Field button (Forms
toolbar), 290
Text Form Field Options dialog
box, *291*
Text Only files, saving Word
files as, *173*
text styles
changing, 24
drop caps, 259
emphasizing, 28–29, 232–33,
268–69
hiding and displaying, 24
pull quotes, 260
replacing, 127, 128
WordArt, 268–69
Texture tab (Fill Effects dialog
box), 234
Text Wrapping button (Picture
toolbar)
Distance From Text, *248*
Edit Wrap Points, 249
None, *275*
options, 252
Wrap To, *248*
Thesaurus, 286
Thesaurus dialog box, 286
times and dates in footers, *117*
Toggle Field Codes option (field
shortcut menus), 289

toolbars. *See also names of
specific toolbars*
buttons. *See also names of
specific buttons*
dialog boxes compared
with, *33*
labeling, 111
moving, 103
pictures of, 6–7
using, 22
changing automatically, *245*
creating, 102, 110
customizing, 102–3, 110–11
adding items to, 102
assigning macros to, *99*
moving, 26, 27, 112
renaming, 102
resizing, 27
restoring to original
settings, 102
deleting, 102
described, 21
docked, 26
floating, *26*
hiding and displaying, *22*
list boxes, 103. *See also names
of specific list boxes*
managing, 26–27
pictures of, 6–7
saving, *111*
shortcut menus, *92*
stacking, 112
storing, 112
using, 21, 22–25
virus-protection feature, *57*
Toolbars tab (Customize dialog
box), 102, 110
Tooltips
picture of, 7, 22
using, *150*
topics in documents
finding, 121
moving, 122, 123

Track Changes button
(Reviewing toolbar), 215
Track Changes tab (Options
dialog box), 215
"Try This" exercises
Address Book, using as data
source, *181*
anchors, moving objects
with, *253*
AutoComplete entries,
testing, *97*
AutoCorrect entries,
testing, *281*
AutoFormat entries,
testing, *280*
AutoShapes, stacking and
grouping, *251*
bar codes, adding to
envelopes, *71*
borders, adding to tables, *83*
bulleted lists, creating, *40*
charts, creating, *169, 170*
color of text, changing, *233*
cross-references to headings,
creating, *154*
data-source document,
creating, *189*
documents, comparing
versions, *134*
editing options,
customizing, *13*
grammar checking,
customizing, *19*
headings, numbering in a
long document, *157*
hyperlink, creating, *229*
keyboard shortcuts, printing
listing of, *108*
lines, numbering in a long
document, *157*
mailing labels, creating, *69*
online forms, saving as
template, *291*

"Try This" exercises, *continued*
  paragraph style names,
    viewing in
    document, *61*
  PrintSelection macro,
    recording, *99*
  rows, adding to tables, *77*
  secret code, creating with
    symbols, *145*
  spelling checking,
    customizing, *19*
  styles, printing listing
    of, *108*
  symbols, converting text
    into, *145*
  table, resizing between
    margins, *131*
  templates, sharing in
    workgroups, *205*
  wildcards, using to find
    text, *125*
  WordArt, creating 3-D
    effects, *269*
  ZIP codes on envelopes,
    creating, *71*
two-headed arrow resizing
  pointer, 81
typefaces. *See* fonts
Typing Replaces Selection
  option (Options dialog
  box), *12*

Underline button, 24, 28
underlining, 28. *See also* fonts
Undo button (Standard toolbar).
  See also Redo button
  picture of, 11, 25
  Reset Picture button
    compared with, *93*
  using, 11, 45

undoing
  formatting, 45
  table boundaries, *76*
  table cells or rows, *83*
Unicode fonts, *145*
units of measure, specifying,
  44, 253
Up arrow key, 77
Update Field option (field
  shortcut menu), *288*
Update Fields option (Options
  dialog box), *289*
Up option (Find And Replace
  dialog box), 125
Use Address Book dialog
  box, *181*
Use Relative Path For Hyperlink
  option (Insert Hyperlink
  dialog box), *225*
user information, editing,
  70, 287
User Information tab (Options
  dialog box), *70, 287*
User Templates (Options dialog
  box), *61, 62*
Use Wildcards check box
  (Find And Replace dialog
  box), 124

values in tables
  AutoSum, 160–61
  calculating, 162, 163
  updating, 161
Version command (File
  menu), 134
Versions dialog box, 134
versions of documents, *134*
verso pages, 114

vertical alignment buttons
  (Tables and Borders
  toolbar), 85
vertical lines, 76
Video Clip Object command
  (Edit menu), 237
video clips. *See also* Clip Gallery
  adding to documents,
    236–37
  in Clip Gallery, 236
  downloading, 298
  hyperlinks to, 224
  picture of in Word
    document, 95
  playing, 237
  resizing, 237
  storing, 236
  on Web pages, 244, 245
Videos tab (Clip Gallery dialog
  box), 236
View Comments button
  (Versions dialog box), 134
View Merged Data button
  (Merge toolbar), 178, 223
views of documents
  Online Layout, *234,* 240
  Outline, 6, 122, *123,* 138,
    155, 158
  Page Layout, 6
  Print Preview, 19, 25, *83, 156,*
    157, 277
  Slide Sorter (PowerPoint), *226*
View Source button (Merge
  toolbar), 191
View tab (Options dialog
  box), 289
  Field Codes options, 289
  Field Shading list box,
    177, 289
  Object Anchors check
    box, *253*
  options, 217
  picture of, 106

View tab (Options dialog
  box), *continued*
  Picture Placeholder, 91
  Screen Tips check box, *150*
  Style Area Width box,
    61, 106
  Wrap To Window
    option, 106
virus-protection feature in
  templates, *57*
voice messages, recording, 235.
  See also sound clips

watermark images
  creating, 274–75
  saving images for, *93*
  text as, *275*
Wave Sounds, 235, 238
Web pages, 241, 242–45. *See also*
  HTML (Hypertext Markup
  Language); Internet;
  Internet Explorer
Web pages for Microsoft Word
  support, *298*
Web Pages tab (New dialog
  box), 242
Web Page Wizard
  creating Web pages without,
    244–45
  installing, *242*
  using, 242–43
Web Page Wizard dialog
  box, 242
Web servers installed with
  Microsoft Office, *243*
Web toolbar, 25, 225
widow lines, *276. See also*
  orphan lines

Widow/Orphan Control
    option (Paragraph dialog
    box), 276
wildcard characters, 124, *125*
windows, elements of, 6–7
Windows Briefcase, *139*
Windows Control Panel, 294
Windows Explorer shortcut
    menu, 227
Windows Messaging Service,
    sending e-mail using, *221*
Windows Startup folder, starting
    Word from, *8*

Wingdings, 144. *See also*
    symbols
Winword folder, starting Word
    from, 8
wizards, 47, *49. See also names
    of specific wizards*
Word. *See* Microsoft Word
WordArt, 268–69. *See also*
    graphics images
WordArt button (Drawing
    toolbar), 268
WordArt Gallery dialog box, 268

WordMail (in Outlook), 219,
    220. *See also* Microsoft
    Outlook
WordPad documents in Word
    documents, 95
words. *See* text
workgroups. *See* documents in
    workgroups
worksheets in Word
    documents, 95
Wrapping tab (Object dialog
    box), 248

wrapping text, 8, 248–49
Wrap To Window option
    (Options dialog box), 106

ZIP codes, *71*, 181
Zoom Control (magnification)
    button on toolbar, 25
    using, *250*
    viewing footnotes, *149*
    viewing table boundaries, *83*

Jerry Joyce has had a long-standing relationship with Microsoft: he was the technical editor on 23 books published by Microsoft Press, and he has written manuals, help files, and specifications for numerous Microsoft products. You might also find him prowling around online bulletin boards and news groups, answering questions about getting work done with various software products. Jerry's alter ego is that of a marine biologist; he has conducted research from the Arctic to the Antarctic and has published 18 scientific papers on marine-mammal and fisheries issues. In his spare time he enjoys traveling, birding, and disappearing into the mountains.

Marianne Moon has worked in the publishing world for many years as proofreader, editor, and writer—sometimes all three simultaneously. She has been editing and proofreading Microsoft Press books since 1984 and has written and edited documentation for Microsoft products such as Flight Simulator, Golf, Publisher, the Microsoft Mouse, and Greetings Workshop. In another life, she was chief cook and bottlewasher for her own catering service and wrote cooking columns for several newspapers. When she's not chained to her computer, she likes gardening, cooking, traveling, writing poetry, and knitting sweaters for tiny dogs.

Marianne and **Jerry** own and operate **Moon Joyce Resources,** a small consulting company. They've had a 15-year working relationship and have been married for the last 5 years.

The manuscript for this book was prepared and submitted to Microsoft Press in electronic form. Text files were prepared using Microsoft Word 7.0 for Windows. Pages were composed using QuarkXPress 3.32 for the Power Macintosh, with text in ITC Stone Serif and ITC Stone Sans and display type in ITC Stone Sans Semibold. Composed pages were delivered to the printer as electronic prepress files.

Cover Design and Illustration
Tim Girvin Design
Gregory Erickson

Interior Graphic Designers
designlab
Kim Eggleston

Interior Graphic Artist
WebFoot Productions

Interior Illustrator
s.bishop.design

Typographers
Kari Becker Design
Blue Fescue Typography & Design

Proofreader
Alice Copp Smith

Indexer
Bero-West Indexing Services

Things are looking up!

Here's the remarkable, *visual* way to quickly find answers about the powerfully integrated features of the Microsoft® Office 97 applications. Microsoft Press® *At a Glance* books let you focus on particular tasks and show you with clear, numbered steps the easiest way to get them done right now.

Microsoft® **Excel 97 At a Glance**
Perspection, Inc.
U.S.A. $16.95   ($22.95 Canada)
ISBN 1-57231-367-6

Microsoft® **Word 97 At a Glance**
Jerry Joyce and Marianne Moon
U.S.A. $16.95   ($22.95 Canada)
ISBN 1-57231-366-8

Microsoft® **PowerPoint® 97 At a Glance**
Perspection, Inc.
U.S.A. $16.95   ($22.95 Canada)
ISBN 1-57231-368-4

Microsoft® **Access 97 At a Glance**
Perspection, Inc.
U.S.A. $16.95   ($22.95 Canada)
ISBN 1-57231-369-2

Microsoft® **Office 97 At a Glance**
Perspection, Inc.
U.S.A. $16.95   ($22.95 Canada)
ISBN 1-57231-365-X

Microsoft® **Windows® 95 At a Glance**
Jerry Joyce and Marianne Moon
U.S.A. $16.95   ($22.95 Canada)
ISBN 1-57231-370-6

Microsoft Press® products are available worldwide wherever quality computer books are sold. For more information, contact your book retailer, computer reseller, or local Microsoft Sales Office.

To locate your nearest source for Microsoft Press products, reach us at www.microsoft.com/mspress/, or call 1-800-MSPRESS in the U.S. (in Canada: 1-800-667-1115 or 416-293-8464).

To order Microsoft Press products, call 1-800-MSPRESS in the U.S. (in Canada: 1-800-667-1115 or 416-293-8464).

Prices and availability dates are subject to change.

Microsoft®*Press*

Get
quick,
easy
answers—
anywhere!

Microsoft Press® Field Guides are a quick, accurate source of information about Microsoft® Office 97 applications. In no time, you'll have the lay of the land, identify toolbar buttons and commands, stay safely out of danger, and have all the tools you need for survival!

Microsoft® Excel 97 Field Guide
Stephen L. Nelson
U.S.A. **$9.95** ($12.95 Canada)
ISBN 1-57231-326-9

Microsoft® Word 97 Field Guide
Stephen L. Nelson
U.S.A. **$9.95** ($12.95 Canada)
ISBN 1-57231-325-0

Microsoft® PowerPoint® 97 Field Guide
Stephen L. Nelson
U.S.A. **$9.95** ($12.95 Canada)
ISBN 1-57231-327-7

Microsoft® Outlook™ 97 Field Guide
Stephen L. Nelson
U.S.A. **$9.99** ($12.99 Canada)
ISBN 1-57231-383-8

Microsoft® Access 97 Field Guide
Stephen L. Nelson
U.S.A. **$9.95** ($12.95 Canada)
ISBN 1-57231-328-5

Microsoft Press® products are available worldwide wherever quality computer books are sold. For more information, contact your book retailer, computer reseller, or local Microsoft Sales Office.

To locate your nearest source for Microsoft Press products, reach us at www.microsoft.com/mspress/, or call 1-800-MSPRESS in the U.S. (in Canada: 1-800-667-1115 or 416-293-8464).

To order Microsoft Press products, call 1-800-MSPRESS in the U.S. (in Canada: 1-800-667-1115 or 416-293-8464).

Prices and availability dates are subject to change.

Microsoft®*Press*

Keep things running smoothly around the Office.

These are *the* answer books for business users of Microsoft® Office 97 applications. They are packed with everything from quick, clear instructions for new users to comprehensive answers for power users. The Microsoft Press® *Running* series features authoritative handbooks you'll keep by your computer and use every day.

Running Microsoft® Excel 97
Mark Dodge, Chris Kinata, and Craig Stinson
U.S.A. $39.95   ($53.95 Canada)
ISBN 1-57231-321-8

Running Microsoft® Office 97
Michael Halvorson and Michael Young
U.S.A. $39.95   ($53.95 Canada)
ISBN 1-57231-322-6

Running Microsoft® Word 97
Russell Borland
U.S.A. $39.95   ($53.95 Canada)
ISBN 1-57231-320-X

Running Microsoft® PowerPoint® 97
Stephen W. Sagman
U.S.A. $29.95   ($39.95 Canada)
ISBN 1-57231-324-2

Running Microsoft® Access 97
John Viescas
U.S.A. $39.95   ($53.95 Canada)
ISBN 1-57231-323-4

Microsoft Press® products are available worldwide wherever quality computer books are sold. For more information, contact your book retailer, computer reseller, or local Microsoft Sales Office.

To locate your nearest source for Microsoft Press products, reach us at www.microsoft.com/mspress/, or call 1-800-MSPRESS in the U.S. (in Canada: 1-800-667-1115 or 416-293-8464).

To order Microsoft Press products, call 1-800-MSPRESS in the U.S. (in Canada: 1-800-667-1115 or 416-293-8464).

Prices and availability dates are subject to change.

Microsoft® *Press*

Register Today!

Return this
Microsoft® Word 97 At a Glance
registration card for
a Microsoft Press® catalog

U.S. and Canada addresses only. Fill in information below and mail postage-free. Please mail only the bottom half of this page.

1-57231-366-8A   ***MICROSOFT® WORD 97 AT A GLANCE***   *Owner Registration Card*

NAME

INSTITUTION OR COMPANY NAME

ADDRESS

CITY   STATE   ZIP

Microsoft® Press
Quality Computer Books

For a free catalog of
Microsoft Press® products, call
1-800-MSPRESS

BUSINESS REPLY MAIL
FIRST-CLASS MAIL   PERMIT NO. 53   BOTHELL, WA

POSTAGE WILL BE PAID BY ADDRESSEE

MICROSOFT PRESS REGISTRATION
MICROSOFT® WORD 97 AT A GLANCE
PO BOX 3019
BOTHELL WA   98041-9946